The 1950s'
Most Wanted

Other Selected Most Wanted books
from Potomac Books

The 1960s' Most Wanted: *The Top 10 Book of Hip Happenings, Swinging Sounds, and Out-of-Sight Oddities* by Stuart Shea

Rock & Roll's Most Wanted: *The Top 10 Book of Lame Lyrics, Egregious Egos, and Other Oddities* by Stuart Shea

Dogs' Most Wanted: *The Top 10 Book of Historic Hounds, Professional Pooches, and Canine Oddities* by Alexandra Powe Allred

Business's Most Wanted: *The Top 10 Book of Corporate Greed, Eccentric Entrepreneurs, and Management Oddities* by Jim Romeo

Broadway's Most Wanted: *The Top 10 Book of Dynamic Divas, Surefire Showstoppers, and Box-Office Busts* by Tom Shea

The World Series' Most Wanted: *The Top 10 Book of Championship Teams, Broken Dreams, and October Oddities* by John Snyder

Country Music's Most Wanted: *The Top 10 Book of Cheating Hearts, Honky Tonk Tragedies, and Music City Oddities* by Francesca Peppiatt

The 1950s' Most Wanted

The Top 10 Book of Rock & Roll Rebels, Cold War Crises, and All-American Oddities

Robert Rodriguez

Potomac Books
Washington, D.C.

Library of Congress Cataloging-in-Publication Data

Rodriguez, Robert, 1961–
    The 1950's most wanted : the top 10 book of rock & roll rebels, Cold War crises, and all-American oddities / Robert Rodriguez.—1st ed.
      p. cm.
    Includes bibliographical references and index.
    ISBN 1-57488-715-7 (alk. paper)
      1. United States—Civilization—1945—Miscellanea.
2. United States—History—1945–1953—Miscellanea.
3. United States—History—1953–1961—Miscellanea.
4. Nineteen fifties—Miscellanea.   5. Popular culture—United States—History—20th century—Miscellanea.
I. Title.
E169.12.R588   2004
973.921—dc22   2004013424

Printed in the United States of America on acid-free paper that meets the American National Standards Institute Z39–48 Standard.

Potomac Books, Inc.
22841 Quicksilver Drive
Dulles, Virginia 20166

First Edition

10 9 8 7 6 5 4 3 2 1

"You should have been there."
—Dr. Winston O'Boogie (aka John Lennon)

To Mom and Dad, who were *there!*

Contents

Illustrations

Acknowledgments

I f I've learned anything at all throughout this entire process, it's this: it takes many hands to shave the pony. My profound thanks to everyone at Potomac Books, but especially Don Jacobs and Kevin Cuddihy, who were willing to take on an untested writer and suffer through his learning curve. Scott Tambert at PDimages.com was an inexhaustibly generous source of support as well.

An unpayable debt of gratitude is owed to Stu Shea. In addition to being a great friend, he more than any single individual is responsible for the book in your hands. Besides being a fine writer in his own, uh, right, he has been a de facto agent, pulling others into the orbit of publishing. Lives have been changed thanks to this man—what can I say?

To everyone at Shimer College in Waukegan, Illinois, who wittingly or unwittingly contributed to the process, I am likewise indebted. Standards were raised, and for that I thank you all, but especially Kathleen, Eileen, Bill, Albert, and Jack. Craig Locaciato made several key suggestions. Despite them, I wrote the book anyway. I cannot let pass the opportunity to thank my family, who in many ways big and small shaped the path that led here.

Lastly, but not leastly, there's my wife, Kati. It is she who everyday manages to inspire far more effort from me than I would ever achieve on my own. She kept the whole train in motion while I was otherwise occupied, and for that and many other reasons, this book made the transition from vague possibility to tangible product. My thanks and my love!

Preface

I am often asked, with the release of both *Spy Kids 3-D: Game Over* <u>and</u> *Once Upon a Time in Mexico* in 2003; how did you ever find time to complete a book on the fifties? The short answer is: easy—I just stopped going to see movies. There were lots of other interesting-looking films I had to pass up this past year, but to be honest, *The 1950s' Most Wanted* was only part of the reason. (Zane Rodriguez, who turned one year old earlier this year, had a lot to do with appropriating my time.) But if I may be permitted a shout-out to the maker of the two aforementioned movies, let me just say: "Congratulations, dude. Love the name, too."

Truth be told, *I* was using it first, but only by a few years. (To my way of thinking, there can never be enough Rodriguezes walking the earth, and if a little reflected glory gets spread around, all the better.) As a child of the sixties growing up in the seventies, I got to experience a bit of the fifties revivalism that occurred, precipitated in part by the release of the George Lucas film *American Graffiti* in 1973. Within a year of that, Bill Haley's "Rock Around the Clock" was back on the charts, and of course, *Happy Days* had hit the airwaves. For people who weren't there, the original series gave audiences their first taste of what those years were like. I had always been a bit intrigued, seeing as how both of my older brothers had been born in that decade, which also marked

the epoch before my family moved from Chicago to the suburbs. In my mind, the two eras were as clearly demarcated
from each other as Kansas is from Oz—a sepia to Techni-
color transition.

The pursuit of useless knowledge is a beautiful thing;
being raised in house full of books gave me ample opportunity to satisfy my curiosity on nearly any topic that struck
my fancy. Much of that interest was satiated by a set of volumes we owned called *The Art Linkletter Encyclopedia for
Young People*, a lavishly illustrated collection that apparently
stopped about the time I was born. (In it, JFK was still President, and there was no listing for Vietnam.) At the time, I was
vaguely aware of who Art Linkletter was—a show he hosted
was still on in the afternoons, but no one in my household
ever watched it. The man simply could not compete with the
array of reruns currently shown, many of them of fifties origin: *Jeff's Collie*, *Father Knows Best*, *The Adventures of Superman*, and best of all, *Leave It to Beaver*. So it was that I
formed my young perceptions of a time I would never know
firsthand.

Coinciding with my television exposure was a burgeoning awareness of fifties music, specifically early rock & roll.
Besides the showcase afforded by the *American Graffiti*
soundtrack album, oldies radio was just starting to take off
around the time I was old enough to assume control of the
stereo (at least when no one else was around). For reasons I
still cannot fully fathom, my interests inevitably turned
toward the music of an earlier age rather than what was popular at the time. Maybe feeling too old for the white-bread,
bubblegum of Top 40 and too young for the extended FM
"heavy music" of the day made this so. In any event, as I
grew up, my innate arrogance led me to believe I had a pretty
good understanding of what was what during the Eisenhower
era.

Fast forward many years. It was finally time to put my
money where my mouth was, when I was called upon to put
that lamentable "know-it-all" disposition to better use than

the crushing of egos. A good friend steered an opportunity my way, and that led to this book. In researching what I expected to be a cakewalk, I learned many things, first among them: I know *far less* than I think I do. Researching *The 1950s' Most Wanted* gave me ample opportunity to delve in depth into topics of long interest—music, film, politics, TV, and so forth—but more important, it gave me a shot at learning much, validating some perceptions and discrediting others.

I have attempted to cover enough ground to give the reader a pretty good grasp of what the fifties experience would have been like for the average person as well as which events were set into motion with repercussions in the years to come. As much as possible, I've tried to steer clear of the typical deep history found in best-selling tomes, offering just enough to give a bit of background. Instead, I give you matters of life and death, crime, sexuality, scandal, disaster—the stuff that makes life worth living. The reader will note a concentration on show business matters—TV, film, and popular music first and foremost. Within our popular culture lies rich material for mining the flavor and values of this long-gone era. Certainly, there are plenty of stories to tell—I've tried not to repeat the most shopworn ones. Dual icons Elvis and Marilyn are given their due, I hope not to excess. I have also tried, as much as possible, to tie subjects from then to our present day, where applicable. Nothing like the relevancy of history to give current events perspective.

People have asked me along the way about the top 10 best (you name it). Doesn't the *Most Wanted* format thoroughly lend itself to a 10 Best Films list (or worst even)? My answer is, yeah, maybe, but what would be the point? First off—books with such lists are a dime a dozen. Second, *my* opinions are no more valid than yours—I think that any Top 10 Best lists I compile would look a lot like anyone else's. (television, for example, would *have* to include *The Honeymooners*, *The Twilight Zone*, *Leave It To Beaver*, *Your Show of Shows*, and so on.) Likewise, in a work so steeped in pop culture, why so light on sports? The answer, in part, is ignorance. Coming from a background of sports lore limited chiefly to one sport and team (and even *that* restricted to events of my lifetime), I frankly didn't even know where to begin to do the subject justice. But I do offer consolation: Potomac Books offers a fine line of *Most Wanted* sports books, each covering a single sport: baseball, basketball, tennis, football, even NASCAR. I highly recommend any or all.

What I do bring to the table is, I think, a handle on what the average reader will be interested in learning about. And I do mean "reader": you'll note this ain't a picture book. There are lots of different ways to cover a decade and most people with any sense would have realized how daunting a task this was at the outset. In my naïveté, I have tried, in some small measure, to present an array of subjects that excite me, in the hope that these things will pull you in as well. There are lots of reasons to pick up a book like this one, but I would like to think that the desire to learn a thing or two is first among them. For that reason, I suggest that you use *The 1950s Most Wanted* any way you like: don't even start at the beginning (unless you want to)—just find a topic of interest and dive in. Soon, other chapters may beckon you—you never know!

Robert A. Rodriguez (not *the* Rodriguez)

This Could Be the Start of Something Big

I t's easy to assume that certain familiar objects have *always* been around, depending on one's age. But if you go back to see where something came from or how it got started, you invariably find roots reaching even farther back, as any particular innovation arrives only at the end of a long process. Or something like that. Here are 10 items of interest, some still with us, some faded away, but they all left a huge imprint on our culture.

1. CANNED LAUGHTER (1950)

It all began with a comedy long ago forgotten. *The Hank McCune Show* was an NBC sitcom with no big stars to its credit and, apparently, not much in the way of comedy. The one memorable feature that cropped up in reviews at the time was its use of "a sound track [containing] audience laughter." By its third month, the series was off the air, which should have meant that even artificial yucks cannot save humorless farce. Yet the innovation was just beginning. Charlie Douglass, a technical director of live TV at the time, heard of its use on *McCune* and decided the idea needed some finessing. He engineered a device he called a "Laff Box"—an organ-like contraption that precursed the Mellotrons of the sixties. It contained tape banks of assorted laughter samples that were activated through a series of keys and foot pedals, controlling the type of laugh as well as its duration. Even comedies filmed before a live audience used the Laff Box for "sweetening," to simulate what the audience *really* would have sounded like had they gotten all the jokes.

The practice soon became standard, although how judiciously it was used varied considerably. When used sparingly, it added a lift of mirth to shows that needed just a little accenting. When abused, it rang out continually whether appropriate to the onscreen action or not. It was particularly convenient for shows produced by film studios, which being set-bound, tended to rule out the presence of a live audience altogether. Shows where the action took place out of doors some of the time, like *Leave It to Beaver*, particularly benefited. By the sixties, laugh track use in sitcoms was practically universal, but with a movement away from artifice, purists began to question the use of phony contrivances. Some shows, like *The Monkees* during its second season, dispensed with canned laughter altogether. This made for sometimes jarring, insecure viewing ("Was that really funny or what?"). Today, the laugh track is still with us, though probably used more artfully. Astute ears may detect, even today, contemporary shows (*Frasier*, for instance) that implement *vintage* laughs, recorded decades ago from gags long forgotten.

2. CREDIT CARDS (1950)

The bane of modern existence has its roots back as far back as 1914, with something called "metal money" issued by Western Union to preferred customers in lieu of up-front payment. But the first modern, multipurpose plastic was born of an incident recalled within the industry as the "First Supper." Frank McNamara was hosting a business dinner at Major's Cabin Grill in New York City. Having changed suits earlier in the day, he'd left his billfold behind. When the time came to pony up, he discovered his error and had to suffer the indignity of having his wife bring it to him. The embarrassment caused him to consider the practicality of carrying a simple card certifying that the bearer was good for the debt. This required businesses to accept a deferred payment, but upon recognizing that people were inclined to spend more freely if they didn't have to rely on what was in their pockets, they readily began accepting the innovation.

So it was that Diners Club, a card intended for business and travel, was born, giving its users 60 days to make payment. American Express issued its first card that same year. The card known today as Visa originated in California in 1958, when the Bank of America began issuing a consumer card to customers within the state. BankAmericard's users had the option of paying in full or in monthly increments with interest. In 1965, it went national. The following year, competition arose from what was first known as Interbank, becoming Master Charge in 1969 and MasterCard 10 years later. In 1977, BankAmericard formally became Visa. In retrospect, it is amazing that what was intended as an expediency for consumers soon turned into an albatross, and how banks, at first resistant to the concept, quickly discovered they had a golden goose on their hands. Little could anyone have foreseen the profound impact a little convenience would have on a nation's spending habits.

3. *PEANUTS* (1950)

An only child, Minnesota-born Charles "Sparky" Schulz was the product of a loving home. Being gifted with above-average intelligence, sensitivity, and creative impulses resulted in Charles's becoming a metaphoric punching bag. At an early age, he matter-of-factly *knew* that his calling would be to produce a daily comic strip. Though he possessed a flair for drawing, a chronic sense of unworthiness, coupled with unrequited validation from his peers, informed his school life and subsequent career. (Characteristically, he never got over the editors of his high school yearbook rejecting his drawings.)

Following overseas service in World War II, Schulz returned to St. Paul and found work with a panel cartoon he created for the Pioneer Press called *L'il Folks*. Considerable persistence paid off in 1950 when United Feature Syndicate took on his work, on the condition that he expand the strip from one panel to four. Mindful of rival cartoons *L'il Abner* and *Little Folks*, they retitled his work *Peanuts*, a name he detested. The inaugural strip ran on October 2nd and set the tone for entire run. The first three panels show Shermy referring to "good ol' Charlie Brown" before delivering the punch line in the fourth: "How I hate him!" In touch with his inner dysfunctional child, Schulz tapped into the rich vein of everyone's secret insecurities and issues. His genius enabled him, with a minimum of ink, to flesh out fully realized characters with wide ranges of emotions. The initial series consisted of Charlie, Patty, Shermy, and Snoopy. Lucy and Linus came along in 1952; Schroeder in 1953 (though the Beethoven fixation came 10 years later); Pigpen in 1954; and Linus's security blanket (a term Schulz coined, by the way) the year after that. A key to the strip's success and what set it apart from all that came before was the blending of childhood trappings with adult inner lives. Besides the defeatist Charlie Brown, we had nihilism from the chronically dissatisfied Lucy; Linus as resident theologian; and as fantasist, Snoopy. Though the cartoon would mellow over time, the first couple of decades showed an unapologetic mean-spiritedness and casual cruelty—just like real kids. This alone marked it as a different breed from the standard cutesy kiddie hijinks. The unwitting existential bent that permeated *Peanuts* made it a campus favorite in the fifties, but its popularity among the masses would explode in the sixties.

4. "ONE NATION UNDER GOD" (1954)

A political football that bounces around in public consciousness every so often can trace its origins back more than 100 years ago. Francis Bellamy was a Baptist minister by trade but a Christian Socialist by creed. His Utopian vision wherein children of God would share in a society founded on social, economic, and political equality succeeded in getting him bounced from his church in Boston. Daniel Ford, a leading supporter of what today would be called "leftist" causes, was the editor of *The Youth's Companion*, a hugely popular periodical of the late 19th century. An admirer of Bellamy's sermons, he hired the out-of-work clergyman for his magazine. In commemoration of the 400th anniversary of Columbus's "discovery" of America, Bellamy was commissioned in 1892 to write a piece for school celebrations throughout the country. As written, the pledge honored the country's finest secular sentiments as embodied by "my flag."

In the 1920s, this was changed to "the" flag over Bellamy's objections. He would not live to see the results of heavy lobbying by the Knights of Columbus that provoked Congress to add the words, "under God," in 1954. The reasoning at the time, with which President Dwight Eisenhower concurred, was that a belief in God was all that separated our nation from Soviet heathens. Apparently, this needed pointing out. The following year, "In God We Trust" was added to all paper monies minted by the federal government.

There are many who would like to think that the motto so perversely applied by Congress to, of all things, filthy lucre, has historic precedent as some kind of officially sanctioned national slogan. They're wrong. The Constitution was ratified in 1789 without a single mention of God anywhere. The 1837 directive that clarified the Constitution's position on currency likewise made no mention of any mottoes. What it *did* stress was "Liberty." This was not enough for a group of religiously minded Protestants who banded together as a lobbying arm of the church, calling themselves the National Reform Association (NRA). Their first order of business was petitioning Congress to approve a rewrite of the Constitution's preamble to codify America as a God-fearing nation. Needless to say, this died in committee. However, one of the NRA's members, ex-Pennsylvania governor James Pollock, managed to finagle an amendment onto a coinage bill giving authority to the director of the Mint to designate mottoes on coins. Thus, in 1865, with the country distracted by the Civil War, the first In God We Trust coins were minted. Ninety years later, with coin use falling, the law bringing paper currency into line was passed. Supporters of the addition can point out that, among other benefits since this passage, the United States has been world war–free.

5. COLOR TELEVISION (1954)

It is hard to imagine that as late as 1965, most network programming was still broadcast in glorious black and white, particularly since working color had been around for longer than a decade. One reason that networks were slow to change was the price—on both ends. It cost much more money to produce a show in color, but more important, color TV sets were an expensive item, and most households did not own one until the late sixties. Therefore, any color TV viewing until then was limited to those with a bit more disposable income. Though the technology existed as early as 1950 (with limited color broadcasts originating from CBS that summer), its advance was sidelined by war in Korea. Moreover, this early setup was unwieldy, requiring a spinning drum inside the set. Eventually, RCA developed a superior system without moving parts, which, with the Federal Communication Commission's blessing, became the industry standard. It also gave NBC a leg up in broadcasting, because its owner, RCA, controlled the technological game.

The real era of color broadcasting arrived on New Year's Day, 1954, with the annual Tournament of Roses parade. Through 21 stations nationally, a mere 200 experimental sets throughout the country were able to tune in. Color receivers became available to the public that April, with RCA marketing models priced at $1,000 in 1954 dollars, back when minimum wage was 75 cents an hour). Suffice to say, it took some time to catch fire. Projected sales of 75,000 fell short at considerably less than 5,000. The end of the decade would see sales figures exceed 100,000, but considering the number of households in America, that number is miniscule.

CBS and ABC, meanwhile, moved toward color at a glacial pace, not wishing to boost their rival's profit margin with shows that would compel anyone to go out and buy an RCA set. The first regularly scheduled, nonspecial color programming was a short-lived sitcom featuring real-life husband and wife Hume Cronyn and Jessica Tandy, *The Marriage*. This live production was spun off from their radio show, beginning on July 8, 1954. The first regular *filmed* color program was an obscure comedy called *Norby*; it proved equally fleeting. Somewhat more durable was the TV western that arrived in 1959, *Bonanza*. This became the first big color program hit, paving the way for the color conversion of the sixties.

6. 45 RPM RECORDS (1955)

Though on the market since 1949, 45 rpm records only surpassed 78s in sales for the first time in 1955. The new format came about as a result of the rivalry between record giants Columbia and RCA, which vied for supremacy by developing a format to replace what had been the industry standard almost since the beginning. When Edison patented the first phonograph in 1877, his preferred method for sound storage had been the cylinder. But 11 years later, Emil Berliner came up with the world's first flat disc record, which soon became consumers' preference. Records had a number of limitations, however; for most of their existence, 78s were made from a cumbersome shellac concoction that was brittle and unwieldy, making discs fragile. There were also storage issues. Last, with the relatively fast spin, a side of groove was exhausted fairly quickly, limiting recording time to about five minutes per side. This made them fine for pop songs, but extended jazz recordings needed to be split between the two sides. For classical musical lovers, forget it. ("Albums," commonly meaning a collection of tunes released as a single entity, came from the days of 78s: classical works were often sold in a binder of 78 rpm discs that looked very like a photo album.)

Columbia's innovation hit the street in 1948 with the first successful "long-playing" record, or LP. These discs, made from a lighter grade of material, spun at 33 1/3 rpm, and therefore could hold much more music between the two sides. In popular music, however, a singer's success was measured by how many hits he or she could string together over time. No pop artist was thinking about releasing an entire body of a dozen or so songs all at once. So RCA's successful marketing of the "single" (or 45) in 1949 became the pop standard. (The jukebox industry was similarly delighted to be rid of the bulky 78s.) Fulfilling consumer demand to enjoy a continuous listening experience, turntable makers created a stacking device that could hold several 45s at once, necessitating a larger center hole than that in the LP. (This did not carry over into the UK, for some reason.) Those not stacking could insert a little plastic adapter that converted the hole to spindle size. Largely forgotten today is the fact that the earliest fifties 45s were issued in several colors of vinyl to designate their musical grouping: red for classical; blue for light classics; green for country and western; yellow for children's recordings; orange for R&B; and black for pop. RCA abandoned this practice by 1952, however. Implementing a breakthrough technology naturally meant that it would take some time for manufacturers and consumers to make the switch (as later years would see the change from eight-track to cassette, or vinyl to CD) in both acceptance and equipment upgrade. For years to come, record players came with three speeds: 78, 33, and 45.

7. DISNEYLAND (1955)

On July 16, 1954, work began on clearing more than 180 acres of orange groves owned by Ron Dominguez of South Anaheim, California. To buy the site, Walt Disney sold his vacation home and borrowed against a life insurance policy. Additional funding for his dream park came largely from the fledgling ABC network, which also gave priceless promotion for the venture in the form of an hour-long series beginning on Wednesday nights in October 1954: *Disneyland*. (In two years, the park began to turn a profit, leading to ABC's eventual buyout by Disney.) Disney's concept of "the happiest place on earth" took root during the war years. Originally, he was thinking of something more along the lines of a private playground for employees and their families, but the disrupting effects of World War II and the Red Menace gave him time to think, with ever grander notions resulting.

Run-of-the-mill amusement parks just wouldn't do; having a Hollywood studio at his disposal gave him license to let his imagination run wild. In many ways, the end result would resemble something akin to a World's Fair coupled with the attractions of a Coney Island or Riverview. Not surprising, Disney's original budget skyrocketed, reaching $17 million by opening day. A hands-on kind of guy, Disney kept an apartment on the premises, just to keep an eye on his baby. Located above the fire station on Main Street, it could have doubled as a New Orleans brothel. Also establishing residence were scores of local felines inhabiting Cinderella's Castle, uninhabited for the park's first two years. Until the walk-through was built, the feral cats found the castle a palatial litter box. Had Disney gotten his wish, Adventureland would have been likewise stocked with real jungle animals. It was pointed out, however, that most exotic creatures are nocturnal and therefore in no mood to be shouted at by endless streams of visitors as they sleep.

Another idea rethought concerned the shooting gallery in Main Street USA's Penny Arcade. For the first year the park was open, it featured live .22 ammunition. The idea was dropped after a year, due in no small part to the apoplectic fits suffered by Disney liability lawyers upon their first visit. A planned preview was to be held on July 17 for some 5,000 invited guests. However, the tickets were easily duplicated, and another 23,000 gate-crashers showed up for what Walt would later call "Black Sunday." Only 18 attractions were up and running on that day of record-setting heat. The asphalt stayed wet in places, trapping women's shoes; some rides, like the Casey Jr. Train, refused to run; ditto the drinking fountains; and the unexpected influx made for excruciatingly long, hot waits. But the park was an immediate hit, and on September 8, it hosted its one millionth paying customer, validating Disney's knack for gauging public sentiment.

8. FAST-FOOD BURGER CHAINS (1955)

Ray Kroc's place in fast-food history is akin to Henry Ford's status with automobiles: neither man invented his field, but each revolutionized it by streamlining production and mass-marketing it to America. Kroc was nothing if not driven and ambitious, qualities he felt were lacking in Dick and Mac Mc-Donald of San Bernadino, California. As a salesman working for a milkshake outfit, Kroc decided one day in 1954 to check out personally the customers who had bought so many of his machines. What he saw astounded him: the two brothers were running a wildly popular burger joint with methods that had essentially trimmed the fat from the process. Each employee had only one or two duties; the menu was limited; and the burger making was standardized, rather than done by individual order. The resulting efficiency made for the heretofore unknown concept of "fast food."

Kroc offered the brothers a partnership in which he would improve upon their methods and market them to potential franchisees. They agreed, and the first result was opened in Des Plaines, Illinois, on April 15. (A replica housing a McDonald's museum stands at the site today.) By the end of the decade, there were 228 franchises around the country. Kroc bought out the brothers in 1962 for $2.7 million; the original restaurant was not part of the deal, so he made them take their own name off it, while he opened a "McDonald's" of his own down the street. Meanwhile, back in 1954, James McLamore and David Edgerton opened a fast-food joint of their own in Miami, featuring a cartoon King sitting atop a burger bun. They called it InstaBurger King, drawing attention to their own method of fast mass production. In addition, they boasted of the better flavor of flame-broiled burgers. (The restaurants themselves were seatless, walk-up affairs.) In 1957, they added the "Whopper" to their menu and shortened their name. Four years later, their first franchise opened, triggering a rivalry with Ray Kroc's chain that continues today.

9. STEREO (1958)

In the days when record players and radios were voiced by a single speaker, binaural reproduction was not an issue. All sound came from one direction, and listeners were satisfied with this approximation of a live performance. As the technology improved, however, purists began to address the problem of creating a more true-to-life listening experience, separating the sonic mix into two components so listeners could hear a more accurate replication of what they could experience in a concert hall. Human hearing is binaural, as opposed to monaural. The left and right ears receive differing audio information, which the brain then processes. Back when ascertaining what direction a particular noise was coming from meant the difference between life and death, this innovation was an essential survival tool. Nowadays, it is the means through which artificial reproductions of authentic sounds sustain listener interest. Stereo separation, in fits and starts, was used in Hollywood for certain films beginning in the thirties, but 1954's *The Robe* was the first film of the modern age to get traction. By 1957, the necessary technology for a stereo stylus had been perfected, and the first stereo records reached the public the following summer. (Interestingly, stereo recordings had already been available to audiophiles a few years earlier, on *tape*.) CBS Classical released the first stereo album, a perfect conceptual fit. But applying the new gimmickry to popular music, especially rock & roll, was more problematic. To begin with, stereo records cost more. Teens could not be counted on to spring for both the extra cost of records *and* record players. Second, for most people, listener exposure to hit records for potential purchase came through radio, which was AM mono. FM stereo wouldn't begin until the early 1960s, and even then it was the domain of classical and jazz aficionados until more than halfway through the decade. Therefore, a stereo rock & roll single was of very little value to anyone, save perhaps the jukebox industry. Still, that first summer of enthusiastic hype brought a slew of stereo rock & roll recordings before interest waned. The first to chart was Roy Hamilton's "Don't Let Go." It would take another 10 years and a shift in the market from singles to albums for stereo to be embraced fully by the public. (As late as the early 1980s, record companies still issued mono/stereo promo singles to radio stations.)

10. LINCOLN MEMORIAL PENNY (1959)

In 1909, the U.S. mint honored the centennial year of our 16th President's birth by replacing the image of an Indian on pennies with that of Lincoln's profile. This marked the first time in American history that a real person appeared on a U.S. coin; earlier images were typically mythic "Liberty" figures. It was also the first time the slogan "In God We Trust" was used on a penny. On the obverse was an austere rendering of a pair of wheat heads framing the standard one-cent piece information. This somewhat generic design existed for 50 years, until the decision was made to update it for Lincoln's 150th birth anniversary. This time, an image of the Lincoln Memorial was used, making it the only American coin to have the same man on *both* sides of the same coin. (Look very closely where the statue of the seated Lincoln should be. *There* he is!) Of course, a penny back then, composed of 95 percent copper and 5 percent tin, was worth something. Nowadays, the compositional ratio is something like 3 percent copper and 97% zinc, validating the public's view of a penny as essentially worthless.

Take Me to Your Leader

Though recalled as the Eisenhower Era, the 1950s actually began midway through Harry Truman's last term. Back when getting the most votes meant victory in this country, new leaders began directing our national destiny. Around the globe, transition was likewise rampant, with dynasties beginning or ending in Great Britain, China, the Soviet Union—and Chicago. Here's a rundown of the top-tier personas whose stories defined the era.

1. HARRY S. TRUMAN

A charismatic, larger-than-life leader would be a hard act for anyone to follow in the middle of a world war, even more so if you are a man more overlooked than looked over. But such was Harry Truman's lot when tapped to be Franklin Delano Roosevelt's final running mate. While outwardly the very embodiment of ordinary, Truman saw his stock rise when he proved to be decisive and courageous. A come from behind victory in 1948, when much of the country had written him off, cemented his place in political folklore.

The last inhabitant of the White House without a college diploma, Truman prided himself on his down-to-earth common sense. Though publicly committed to upholding the dignity and decorum of the presidency, he possessed one of the saltiest vocabularies of any Oval Office occupant. This repertoire saw regular use, as its owner could also claim one of the shortest of fuses. A rare public glimpse of this side of the President occurred when his daughter, Margaret, an aspiring singer, received a savage review at the hands of a Washington, D.C., critic. Certain the bile was directed at him, Truman was outraged. Setting his retort to paper, he gleefully depicted in colorful terms the bodily harm he intended to inflict upon the writer should the two ever meet face to face. The public was not amused and Margaret was mortified, but the President felt he was acting as any father would.

First Lady Bess Truman hated the role thrust upon her and spent as much time as possible shunning the limelight. Indeed, her frequent absences from Washington found the president feeling out of sorts until her return. One particularly enthusiastic welcome home found Bess the next day abashedly requiring of the White House's head usher some assistance in repairing the couple's bed, which had been, shall we say, put through its paces and found wanting.

2. DWIGHT EISENHOWER

Nineteen hundred fifty-two found the country suffering from New Deal fatigue. The Red Scare, war in Korea, crippling strikes, all served to whet appetites for change at the top. The Republican Party, seeing its best chance to recapture the White House in a generation, tapped Dwight D. Eisenhower, the Supreme Allied Commander during World War II, as its standard-bearer. Though so apolitical as to have never voted before, much less have a party affiliation, Eisenhower happily seized the moment, eager to take on the stalemate in Korea and the Cold War.

His grandfatherly charm and easy grin were eminently marketable, as was the fortuitous nickname, "Ike," which suffixed nicely to "I Like. . . ." Without any baggage to speak of or a whiff of scandal about him, Eisenhower coasted to any easy win over his opponent, the reluctant Democratic nominee, Illinois Governor Adlai Stevenson. Urbane, witty, and intellectual, Stevenson would have been a hard sell at

President and Mrs. Eisenhower (center and right) tune in with an unidentified friend to check up on the vice president.

any time in history, but his being a divorced man in a time when cozy domesticity was the norm couldn't have helped. Interesting, then, to speculate the "what ifs" had the public known all there was to know about the man who ended up in the win column.

While overseas as leader of the Allies, Ike had entered into a love affair with his driver, a 24-year-old Englishwoman named Kay Summersby. That the liaison went unconsummated was revealed in memoirs published after her death in 1975. She describes two attempts, but, even though as Supreme Commander Ike could summon thousands of troops at will, his own privates remained stubbornly at ease. Nevertheless, he attempted to force the issue, writing to President Truman of his wish to be relieved of his command, so he could return stateside and divorce Mamie. Truman could ill afford to let his commander be swayed by a moment of foxhole lust and rebuked him accordingly. An appeal to Ike's sense of duty was apparently enough to let the episode fade out.

3. KING GEORGE VI

It is said that history often hinges on accidents. An encounter between heir to the British throne Edward VIII (then Prince of Wales) and American divorcée Wallis Simpson paved the way for this reluctant sovereign's ascent to the throne. Edward's enthrallment with the divorced, American commoner precluded his becoming King upon the death of his father, George V, in 1936. Instead of giving Wallace up, he sidestepped the role he'd been groomed for all his life and made his younger brother, Albert ("Bertie" to friends), the new king. Unlike his socially superior brother, George was introverted and awkward. Afflicted with a stutter and knock-kneed, the new role threatened to overwhelm him. Yet when history thrust duty upon him in a highly responsible role, the "accidental king" rose to the challenge. The constitutional crisis precipitated by the Simpson affair was followed quickly by the rising clouds of war, and George led his people through the ordeal.

His responsibilities took their toll, however, and his health suffered. George developed circulatory ailments and, later, cancer. Though surgery seemed to have arrested the latter, his weakened condition precluded a full recovery. He died in his sleep from a coronary thrombosis on February 6, 1952, at the age of 56. His widow, beloved by the public as the "Queen Mum," would survive him by 50 years, dying in 2002 at the age of 101.

4. QUEEN ELIZABETH II

Upon her father's death, 26-year-old Elizabeth became the first female ruler of Great Britain since Victoria a half-century before. Intelligent and dignified, Elizabeth II became a ubiquitous presence in the sunset of the British Empire, her image gracing stamps and currency the world over. The decorum for which she is duly noted was only enhanced by the lack thereof possessed by nearly everyone close to her. Sister Margaret, for example, was a reliable attention-getter. Following her doomed romance with Group Captain Peter Townsend, she was known primarily for her extravagant partying, acting less like royalty than a bored debutante. The "Swinging Sixties" found her on top of every fashion and fancy of the moment, in contrast to her trend-immune sister.

Philip Mountbatten, wed to Elizabeth on November 20, 1947, became known chiefly for his habit of saying exactly the wrong thing in the wrong place at the wrong time, often while on goodwill visits to other countries. Knowing life required him to stay three steps behind his bride forever, it is doubtful that he expected to see that day so soon. Elizabeth herself, though quite capable of dealing with the duties required of her role, would have preferred a quieter life, indulging in her passion for horses and country living. One can speculate how different her children's lives might have turned out had she been given more time to raise them before attaining the Crown. Had her father lived longer, or if her uncle hadn't become so bewitched as to abandon his kingly duties, we might all have been spared the tabloid fodder embodied by Di, Fergie, and Camilla.

5. JOSEF STALIN

The original "cult of personality" began with this man, for whom myth and fact are sometimes hard to distinguish. Beginning with the name he gave himself (Russian for "man of steel"), Iosif Vissarionovich Dzhugashvili was born into conflict. Torn between his father's demands that he follow in his footsteps as a cobbler and his devout mother's wishes that he study for the priesthood, young Soso became a revolutionary instead. It was in a seminary that the future dictator's conversion from theology to Marxism-Leninism came about. Stung by his teacher's punishments for reading banned Western writers, young Iosif turned away from his mother's faith, substituting one dogma for another. Though standing only five feet five inches with a pockmarked face and a left arm disabled in a carriage accident, the robust young man was a natural leader, who soon became a rising star among the Bolsheviks under Lenin. By the time of Lenin's death in 1924, Stalin had positioned himself as unquestioned successor, fighting off all rivals for sole leadership of the Soviet Republic. History records brutality and oppression carried out on his orders, rivaled in the 20th century only by that of the Nazis, the Chinese Communists, and the Khmer Rouge. It is believed that upwards of five million peasants were deliberately starved to death, and twice that number were sent to labor camps. Within the Red Army, the "disloyal" met a similar fate, decimating its ranks. These terrors only strengthened the absolute grip of the "man of steel" on his people.

Much of this repression remained unknown to the Western world. The waning days of World War II saw Allied leaders still cultivating Soviet support against Japan. Stalin would meet with Roosevelt, as well as his successor, Harry Truman, who judged the dictator a regular Joe. His skill at appearing benign and warm, quick-witted and shrewd demonstrated a talent for deception as keen as any conjurer's. The fifties found the effects of hard drinking and possible mental imbalance catching up with him. His final months found him plotting a final solution of his own for the remaining Jewish population of his empire before death claimed him at 73 on March 5th, 1953. Following precedent, his body was preserved and displayed alongside Lenin's in Red Square, until a wave of revisionism under his successor spurred its removal in 1961.

6. NIKITA KHRUSHCHEV

Whereas Stalin was seen as iconic and impenetrable, Khrushchev was perceived as all too human: capricious, short-fused, comical at times, and full of bluster. He was the first Soviet leader to actually travel to America, speaking at the United Nations and seeing much of the country (though, alas, not Disneyland, as he had wished). Americans were thrown by their preconceptions of what a dictator ought to be, and what disquieted them most about Khrushchev was his unpredictability. He was, Westerners thought, too much the peasant to be a nation's leader.

He may have proved that point when, demanding to be heard at the United Nations, he removed one shoe and pounded it loudly on the desk. "We will bury you!" he warned the West. Though U.S. intelligence was aware of the Soviets' arms deficiency, America could not help but be concerned by the spectacular success of the Soviet space program. Such public display of superiority—launching the first satellite, the first living creature, and, eventually, the first man—wounded American pride and forced our hand prematurely. A series of all too public American launch failures made the humiliation complete.

Khrushchev showed himself to be an autocrat of a different kind, first by condemning his predecessor before the party, and second by agreeing to work toward better relations with the West, something Eisenhower hoped would be his legacy. In a speech to the Politburo in February 1956, Khrushchev detailed the excesses of the Stalin era, freely revealing the mass murders that took place. Stalin was no Leninist, he declared. Thus did the dismantling of the Stalin cult begin. But such loose talk worried the hard-liners on the right, who would keep a close eye on their party leader.

7. MAO ZEDONG

Beatle lyrics notwithstanding, millions could and did "make it" with those carrying pictures of their country's leader, as a booming population attested. Mao became the first party chairman of what was called Red China in the West. The decades-long struggle for supremacy between the Communist insurgency that Mao led and the Nationalists under Chiang Kai-shek ended with the latter fleeing to Taiwan and the mainland falling to Communist rule in 1949. Though Mao was in power for years, most Americans had little insight into his persona until copies of his "Little Red Book" started appearing on college campuses in the sixties. The tome, more properly referred to as *The Quotations and Sayings of Chairman Mao,* was a compendium of such bon mots as "Political power grows out of the barrel of a gun," invaluable wisdom for would-be radicals everywhere.

Bred in Hunan Province, Mao never completely lost the habits of his peasant background. He eschewed such "modern" practices as brushing his teeth, insisting on rinsing his mouth with tea and eating the leaves afterward, leaving his teeth stained green until they eventually rotted and fell out. Both bathing and sleeping he saw as wastes of time. As long as his health permitted, he swam in Chinese rivers regularly, demanding those around him to do the same. Any protests that the waters were thick with human excrement left him unmoved. He did manage to get some use from his bed— despite any physical revulsion his person might have generated, he enjoyed a steady stream of young women proffering themselves to the Chairman, who espoused that the greater the numbers, the longer he would live. Severe insomnia led to a dependency on sodium seconal, while years of living outdoors made him forever restless and claustrophobic when inside.

Westerners tend to view all Communist nations as monolithic in solidarity, but in fact they could be as fractious as any democracies. Though the two would meet and host each other on occasion, Mao maintained a healthy disdain for his Soviet counterpart, Nikita Khrushchev, loudly criticizing him at every opportunity. While the root of his distaste lay in Khrushchev's denunciation of Stalin in 1956, Mao had no great love for the latter either. When seeking Soviet support back in the 1930s, Stalin had been dismissive of the upstart he saw as little more than a rural pretender. He called him a turnip, meaning red on the outside and white on the inside. Mao never forgot the insult.

8. RICHARD J. DALEY

As Franklin Delano Roosevelt was to the generation of kids raised in prewar America, so was Mayor Daley to hundreds of thousands of Chicagoans growing up in the baby boomer years—the only leader they had ever known. First elected Mayor in April 1955, Daley would continue serving until he died in office on December 20th, 1976. He was the last big city absolute ruler in America, an urban Mussolini making the trains run on time while controlling enough votes and voters to swing elections. Daley presided over the so-called Democratic Machine in Chicago, with armies of precinct captains at his command and free-flowing political patronage the engine that made the machine run.

Odd to realize that a man so thoroughly identified with the Democratic Party actually got his start as a *Republican!* Two weeks before the 1936 election, the incumbent GOP candidate for the Illinois General Assembly died, leaving Daley an opening as a write-in candidate. For one morning only, he was obliged to sit on the *opposite* side of the aisle. Twenty years later, when he took the office that would define him, Hizzoner, as he was known to the press, carried himself with the self-assured air of one who knows that life has placed him in the role for which he was born. Generally congenial, his temper would flair on occasion—face reddening, jowls quivering. His ongoing war with the English language rivaled that of Yogi Berra. (Through a quirk of genetics run amok, this trait would be passed on to the son who followed in his footsteps.) One better-known example came during the tense days of sixties unrest when put on the defensive after issuing his infamous "shoot to kill" order. "Let's make one thing clear," he told the press. "The policeman isn't there to create disorder. The policeman is there to preserve disorder."

Daley was nothing if not an enthusiastic booster of his causes, political and otherwise. In September of 1959, when his beloved White Sox clinched the American League pennant over the Cleveland Indians, a spontaneous celebration seemed in order. Fire Commissioner Robert Quinn, with Daley's blessing, blasted the city's numerous air-raid sirens for five minutes, thereby sending much of the populace into cardiac arrest (as well as their bomb shelters). Much political folklore would be spun the following year with charges that his precinct workers found just enough voters—living and dead—to carry Illinois and deliver the presidency to John Kennedy. Prizing recognition as a national kingmaker, Daley did little to dispel the rumors.

9. RICHARD M. nixon

With his thick brow, heavy beard, and dour demeanor, central casting could not have chosen a better candidate to be the GOP nominee for *Vice* President. By the time of his first run for national office, Nixon had already been branded with the sobriquet that would stick to him throughout his political life—"Tricky Dick." While Ike could remain statesman-like, above petty party politics, his second-in-command could beat the partisan drum and serve as attack dog as required. It's not surprising that the two men had a healthy distrust of and disdain for each other, with Ike attempting to drop Nixon from the ticket in both campaigns.

Most of the distaste that dogged Nixon stemmed from the rank opportunism he embodied and his no-holds-barred style of campaigning. Both in his 1946 House race and his Senate run four years later, Nixon earned his reputation as a dirty campaigner for whom red-baiting and smear tactics were all in a day's work. Typifying his style was hiring out-of-work actors during his first political outing to hand out his *opponent's* campaign literature (stolen from his office) while speaking in heavy Russian accents. He worked similar magic against incumbent Helen Gahagan Douglas in 1950, branding her "the Pink Lady" while suggesting she was a Kremlin dupe.

Both campaigns resulted in landslide victories, helped along by sizable contributions from the powerful, including former Ambassador Joseph Kennedy, the father of his future nemesis. Despite the Checkers scare, Nixon played the role of vice president well, twice being called upon to take provisional charge: following Ike's heart attack in 1955 and after his stroke in 1957. Never before had such a thankless office been fraught with such drama as when, on a goodwill visit to South America, Nixon's motorcade was besieged by rock and egg throwers. Nixon would turn this and other such episodes into a bestseller, *Six Crises*, the gist of which was, no matter how bad the circumstance, he *always* kept his cool. Despite all Nixon's efforts at self-promotion, Ike had the last word. When pressed by reporters to name an example of a major decision in which Nixon played a role, Eisenhower replied, "Give me a week and I might think of one."

10. JOHN F. KENNEDY

One could not imagine a more complete opposite as Nixon's rival. Charismatic, rich, and handsome, this decorated war hero was at ease with himself and popular with the ladies—everything Nixon was not. Jack seemed destined for a career in journalism until his older brother was killed in the war. Joe Jr. had been groomed by their father since birth to be the first Roman Catholic president of the United States. With him gone, the hapless second-born son was pegged to fulfill Joe Sr.'s fantasy. The reluctant candidate first won a seat in Congress in 1946, advancing to the Senate in 1952. Though his record was unblemished by any meaningful positions or major legislation, his path to the White House was never far from anyone's mind. To that end, a spouse would prove a sound investment. Debutante Jacqueline Bouvier, 24, wed the famously commitment-phobic junior Senator from Massachusetts on September 13th, 1953. Though the public now sees JFK as one half of the most glamorous couple outside of Hollywood, marriage represented a mere speed bump in Jack's continuing bachelorhood, as his private pursuit of female companionship barely slowed.

JFK's well documented drive for conquest garnered much press, not all of it favorable. Some writers have attributed his "habit" and sometimes reckless behavior to a deeply ingrained awareness of his own mortality. Sickly and frail as a child, he lived nearly every day of his life in severe pain caused by a chronically bad back. This condition, now understood to have been congenital, was aggravated further during his wartime misadventures with *PT-109* in the South Pacific. He acquitted himself ably, however, and returned stateside a hero. A prolonged recovery from "malaria" proved to be a masquerade for the then-deadly malady Addison's disease, an affliction of the adrenal glands. Considered terminal until breakthrough treatment arrived in the forties, the disease was nonetheless kept secret throughout JFK's lifetime, for obvious career reasons. Daily cortisone injections helped to erase the symptoms and keep the illness at bay. One side effect, however, was the "jowliness" JFK experienced on his otherwise lean frame. Another was an increased libido.

His back problems remained grave, however. By the fall of 1954, severe pain in JFK's deteriorating vertebrae required the use of crutches to get around. His doctors, who knew of his *other* condition, were loath to perform the necessary surgery to save his life for fear the trauma would kill him. This it nearly did, as last rites of the Catholic Church were given to him for the second time in his life. But he pulled through this and the follow-up surgery, though a long recuperative period resulted in his prolonged absence from the Senate. Recovery also meant wearing a surgical back brace, something like a corset, every day of his life. Ironically, this had the effect of keeping him erect continually. (In fact, the very brace meant to improve the quality of his life may actually have helped end it. Its rigidity was designed to keep him constantly upright. Until the final volley in Dallas destroyed all neuromuscular function, he literally could not duck to save his life.) The silver lining in all of this was the opportunity to write during his recuperation. *Profiles in Courage*, a bestseller of its day, placed the senator, little-known outside of New England, on the road to national recognition.

Done Got Hip to Your Jive

Every era and generation spawns its own popular jargon. Some words may even acquire identification with a specific time frame, once their period of heavy use subsides. For instance, it's impossible to hear the word, "groovy," without immediately thinking sixties or early seventies. (The fact that it was in use in the *fifties* is beside the point.) Here is a list of 10 words or terms that were commonly used during the Eisenhower era but have largely fallen into disuse—in most cases, understandably so.

1. LIKE

A word used to buy time to collect one's thoughts, much the same way "I mean" prefaces sentences today. Example: "Like, she's so bitchin'."

2. DDT

All-purpose insult denoting "drop dead twice." Fifties kids were a cruel bunch.

3. UNGOWA

All-purpose word of assent used in place of "yes" or "okay." Those not in the know assumed it was Japanese.

4. THE MOST

Used as a superlative for the highest or best form of whatever. Example: "That Donnie from *Happy Days* sure is the most."

5. FLAKED OUT

Exhausted. Used the way we might use "wiped" as an adjective today.

6. FLIP

Respond in an enthusiastic, positive way. Example: "My boyfriend flipped when my monthly visitor finally arrived."

7. GINCHIEST

An entire list could be compiled from the lingo spouted by TV actor Edd Byrnes on the hit show *77 Sunset Strip*. Beginning in the fall of 1958, Byrnes, playing a secondary character called Kookie, caught the public's fancy with his distinctive "hipster" language. Ordinarily, such contrived words would not be considered "real," but since the public adopted his coined language, it warrants inclusion here. The word in question signifies "the ultimate," in a good way.

8. BOSS

Another term for "great" or "cool." A rare use of irony from that decade, since not many of us are familiar with a "boss" who is "cool."

9. CUBE

To be square in an era of socially enforced conformity was pretty bad. To be a cube was to be square to the third power—*really* dull.

10. —VILLE

Applied as a suffix to any descriptive situation or place. Examples: "Squaresville," "Dullsville," "Coolsville," "Doody-ville."

Put Your Glad Rags On

O ne cannot take the authenticity of *Happy Days* at face value. At some point during the show's run, the producers simply stopped caring about sustaining audience belief with period accuracy, which explains why Scott Baio was running around with a 1976 haircut in (ostensibly) 1957. (Take that back—nothing explains Scott Baio.) It is in the spirit of clearing up audience confusion that the following list of '50s' fashion trends is offered.

1. POODLE SKIRTS

Ah, yes—no cliché says fifties femininity quite like a good old-fashioned poodle skirt. In truth, girls actually did wear them, usually when they dressed up for some less than formal but more than casual fun. Typically, swing skirts of ankle length were customized. Although the appliqué could be anything, the poodle seems to have lasted in public memory (maybe due to the popularity of the "poodle cut"—a coif best known on Lucille Ball.) For dressier situations, pleated skirts were required, with hemlines at or below the knee. Only in the most casual of circumstance, like hayrides and yard chores, did young girls wear jeans (called "dungarees" then—see below). The rest of the time, they wore pencil skirts. More form-fitting and with a narrower cut, such dress was considered "practical."

2. GIRDLES

While the girdle was considerable improvement over whole-bone corsets of an earlier era, no one wore one for pleasure, yet every woman was expected to. As you might have guessed, their purpose was to flatten the tummy, making clothing lie better on the wearer. Comfort was beside the point: to make this bitter pill easier to swallow, advertisers would play up the supposed glamour and sophistication that would come your way by wearing the fashions you could enjoy once you succumbed to the girdle's will. Though in use since the second decade of the 1900s, girdles reached their zenith before the sixties rebellion against restriction would see them die a death by 1970. Their progeny live on as "control briefs" today.

3. SADDLE SHOES/WHITE BUCKS

Those familiar black and white shoes everyone views so nostalgically actually date back to the thirties, but they experienced a decided resurgence in the fifties with youth, mostly female. Their name derives from the "saddle" or instep being cut from a different color of leather, usually black on white. While worn in just about any situation short of formal, these shoes were not worn for comfort. Style, yes, but their tendency to make the wearer clumsier than usual with their stiffness and bulkiness made them somewhat impractical. White bucks were also casual shoes. They would receive their greatest boost as a sort of trademark of singer/super-Caucasoid Pat Boone. With strictly adherence to the mandate that white shoes were being worn from Memorial Day to Labor Day, some would maintain their whiteness by applying a powder made for that purpose. Others wore them dirty, which was perfectly acceptable. Loafers were another shoe of the day that covered the same ground, so to speak: informal. And, yes, people did insert pennies into the front slot—exactly *why* (other than peer pressure) remains unknown. Sneakers (e.g., Keds, PF Flyers, Chuck Taylors) were, of course, for gym class or sporting events. A young boy could get away with them for play or on weekends but just barely.

4. DUNGAREES

Sounds Australian, doesn't it? Actually, this was the commonly used term for jeans in the 1950s. (The word "jean" actually refers to a type of fabric. What we call "jeans" were originally made out of "denim," which is distinctly different. Somewhere along the way, the word use got confused; for the record, "denim" was originally not made from cotton, but "jeans" are. Got it?) For most of this style's existence, this style of pants was worn by laborers. Beginning in the thirties and forties, these pants slowly began to lose their association with "work clothes." For guys, dungarees were matter-of-fact, everyday attire worn at any age, though generally limited to outdoor activities. To wear them to school or to church was to court social disaster. As for black jeans, forget it—only biker gangs and delinquents wore them. If you were female, your opportunities for denim wearing were much more limited (unless you lived on a ranch, but even then . . .). If you did wear them, you typically had the legs rolled up in wide cuffs, ever so sweetly, and white socks beneath. This was a time when formality and style ruled; even going to the movies meant dressing up, for that was an *event*. Anything less was considered trashy or socially inept, and you were ostracized accordingly. No boot cut, flares, acid-wash, or hip-huggers existed in the fifties. But you *could* buy them in "husky" sizes.

5. BLACK LEOTARDS

For those young women of a more nonconformist bent, these were a must. Certainly, for females in the so-called Beat movement, nothing coordinated better with a black beret and heavy black sunglasses. Obviously, this particular look could be found mostly in college towns and isolated urban pockets. Further setting off the black motif was the heavy use of black eye shadow. The beats were certainly ahead of the fashion curve in this respect, as the general female population would not embrace the raccoon look wholeheartedly until the sixties, when they also added false eyelashes, lest anyone miss the point.

6. BULLET BRAS

"You'll put your eye out!" This useful warning about Red Rider BB guns was equally applicable to these iconic fifties relics. This was an era whose dominant aesthetic seemed consciously modeled after the contours of World War II bombers: bold, spherical, jutting curves. (Just try to find a popular vehicle of the era that didn't sport some sort of prominent conical protrusion. As men liked their cars, so, too, did they want their women.) Curves were back with a vengeance, so any sense of function was thrown out the window as garment manufacturers met the challenge of emphasizing curvature. Lingerie was now worn to create a particular effect. In these pre-breast-augmentation years, the choice of undergarment was critical. (A man named Frederick Mellinger designed one for the underendowed that could be *inflated* like a beach ball. He would go on to found the Frederick's of Hollywood chain of lingerie shops.)

As it happened, the most practical solution was the creation of the conical-cupped brassiere. Fondly as these are recalled in hindsight, they were no great joy back in the day. Most women weren't too fond of the concentric design that squeezed their bodies so unnaturally. As for guys, you were overzealous at your own risk. Ease of access was not specifically built into the bra's design, and in subdued lighting, initiative was seized at one's own risk. Watching television or films from the time depicting women wearing these devices elicits mostly wonder today, but for very different reasons, depending on one's gender.

7. HAWAIIAN SHIRTS

For American males, the prevailing mindset didn't allow for much frivolity unless it came in the context of manly activities. Being colorful was acceptable for guys in the fifties only if it originated from some exotic culture. Therefore, the wearing of flower-print attire could be tolerated when it was universally recognized as being of foreign origin. The movement in the fifties toward Hawaiian statehood made wearing the possession's native shirt practically patriotic. The influx of Pacific Island influence in this country, starting with returning World War II servicemen (as well as the popularity of the musical *South Pacific*), paved the way for the Hawaiian shirt boom of the late fifties. For men to go around sporting such peacock colors would have been unthinkable any earlier.

The origin of these comfortable, easy-to-wear shirts began in the 20th century with the heavy Japanese migration to Hawaii. Earliest versions were made from kimono fabric. In the early thirties, an entrepreneur named Ellery Chun began marketing "Aloha shirts." With island tourism increasing over time, the shirts became extremely popular. As the demand grew, the design shifted naturally away from Asian styling to a more homegrown one: palm trees, hula girls, pineapples. By the time the postwar tourist boom began in earnest, the shirt that we know today came into its own.

8. CAT'S EYE GLASSES

What else would the well-bred myopic be wearing? Though first seen in the late forties, this particular style of frame was ubiquitous in the fifties. It came in a wide range of styles, from the plain-Jane black plastic to deluxe "high-fashion," rhinestone-studded with marble inlays, but most wearers fell somewhere in between. For males, youth favored the bold black frames made famous by Buddy Holly. Clearly, options were far more limited than now. Contact lenses of the day were still "hard"—plastic, cumbersome things that didn't allow the eye to breathe, were usually painful to wear, and over time actually harmed the corneal surface. Soft lenses as we know them—that is, gas-permeable—weren't developed successfully until 1960 and weren't marketed in the United States until 1971.

9. BOWLING SHIRTS

This could be the male equivalent of the poodle skirt in terms of conveying fifties kitsch to later audiences. Nothing promoted male bonding, sportsmanship, competition, and the flow of beer better than bowling, especially in the fifties. It provided a convenient escape from the dreariness of middle-class existence as well as socialization in a typically all-male environment. Though team shirts emblazoned with a logo or sponsor's name on the back and the player's name on the front had been around at least since the thirties, it was in the fifties that the style and flamboyance we associate with such attire came into its own. These shirts were built for comfort, not speed—usually fitting loosely over a gut and best left untucked. Any compliance with good taste was purely accidental.

10. THE D.A.

Somehow, someone who studied the matter must have concluded that this fifties-paradigm hairstyle for men really did resemble a duck's back end. (How the individual arrived at this particular comparison will make for fascinating study some time, but not here.) Nothing screamed "trouble" more than a youth sporting this 'do, in an era where conformity was king and the male masses largely adhered to butch cuts. When a D.A. was present, hubcaps were at risk. *Grease* notwithstanding, this hairstyle wasn't particularly common. For one thing, it was high maintenance. Combing the requisite hair into the desired shape took time and effort to get it just so. Creating the vertical part required one of those rattail combs. Then there was the emollient necessary to hold its shape. Though this was the heyday of Brylcreem, a "little dab" was laughably insufficient. Either you went broke maintaining a supply, or you resorted to the far less expensive

Vaseline (which was good enough for Grampa the sheik back in the twenties). Styling gels and mousse did not exist, and hairspray was out of the question. It's no wonder that only those with extra time on their hands were seen sporting one of these.

Better Led than Red

No generation is immune to them, and we all think everyone else's were ridiculous. What are we talking about? Those fancies of the moment that, by the time everyone was on to them, had already become passé, to be relegated to the closet or discarded entirely. The shelf life of your average trend is all too brief, but while it's in full swing, the attendant urgency will put any thought of the money you're throwing away right out of your head. You've just got to have it and now! Here are 10 examples of mass delusion that at one point or another throughout the decade made someone somewhere a boatload of money.

1. DAVY CROCKETT

The mother of all fifties fads was the unprecedented boom in all things Davy that began in 1954. Considerable Disney muscle helped to jump-start the craze that autumn with the premier of *Disneyland,* Walt's first foray into television. The series was designed to showcase his soon-to-open amusement park, with each segment geared toward a particular aspect, be it Fantasyland, Tomorrowland, or Adventureland. Davy Crockett, as depicted by the studio, was to anchor Frontierland. The show presented a trilogy of Crockett stories, spread out over three months. In a show of shortsightedness, the final installment killed him off just as Crockettmania began to explode. Backpedaling quickly, some hastily contrived vignettes from Davy's earlier life kept the ball rolling.

No small part of Crockett's success stemmed from the seemingly endless airplay of his theme song, constructed by a couple of Disney employees (and not some rediscovered folk chestnut, as many believed). From March to mid-June of 1955, Bill Hayes's recording of the "Ballad of Davy Crockett" was in the national Top 10. For five weeks of that stint it was at number one; most amazing, nine solid weeks of that run found it sharing the Top 10 with *two competing recordings* of the same song! One came from country singer Tennessee Ernie Ford, another from actor Fess Parker. The latter, a six-foot five-inch journeyman actor, was spotted in the sci-fi flick *Them!* before Disney signed him to play the Texas legend. His other credits would include *Old Yeller* and TV's *Daniel Boone*.

If an entire fad could be encapsulated by a single item, it was the trademark coonskin cap. These were churned out by the millions, along with every other conceivable piece of merchandise. In a rare instance where Disney did not have a lock on a property, a court ruled that as a historical figure, Crockett was not copyrightable; therefore, anyone could market Crockett merchandise—and they did. But by early 1956, the boom was over. Once the supply of vintage 1920s raccoon coats to turn into hats was depleted, public interest fell off, leaving the phenomenon just a pleasant boomer memory.

2. "BRIDEY MURPHY"

In 1952, amateur hypnotist Morey Bernstein tapped a Pueblo, Colorado, housewife named Virginia Tighe as his subject. While Virginia was in a trance, Morey asked her to think back to her childhood, and then go back further still, to a different time and place. She responded with an Irish brogue, describing herself as a little girl, scraping paint off of her metal bed frame. When asked who she was, she re-

Naturally—
the **best** lemonade
comes from
Sunkist

Can't you almost taste it?

These thirsty days there's nothing quite so *cooling* as a big glass of lemonade. And when it's Sunkist Frozen Lemonade you know it's the very finest.

The Sunkist growers make it up themselves. They use their own juicy California lemons and control the processing every step of the way in their own new plant out in lemon country.

The result is *delicious*—a tangy, refreshing flavor that cools you off and perks you up! Plus all the wholesome goodness of a *natural* fruit drink with vitamin C. It's so good—and so good for you! Sunkist Quick-Frozen Lemonade —naturally the *best!*

Sunkist
Quick-Frozen
Lemonade

*The most
refreshing drink of all!*

This fifties child reflects the current fashion

sponded, "Bridey Murphy." Further details followed: her parents, her husband, where she lived, descriptions of 19th-century life in County Cork, Ireland, how she died. The colorful narrative was turned into a bestselling book, *The Search for Bridey Murphy*, in 1956. Part of what made the story so compelling was that it didn't center on some vainglorious past life as Joan of Arc or Cleopatra—it was an ordinary woman describing an ordinary existence. A film treatment starring Teresa Wright hit the screen (somehow, Shirley MacLaine missed the role of a lifetime[s]). The reincarnation phenomenon, heretofore little discussed in America, was suddenly on everyone's lips. "Come as You Were" parties were held, and theologians scrambled for an explanation.

Then the *Chicago American* newspaper sent a reporter to Ireland to check out the details. What followed was a stinging indictment of the case as essentially reconstructed from details of Tighe's childhood. While there were some things that seemingly checked out in Ireland, such as descriptions of the grocer and local landmarks, it was also uncovered that as a little girl, Tighe took Irish dancing lessons, sometimes spoke with a feigned accent, and, most damning, lived across the street from one Bridey Murphy Corkell, a neighbor who often told tales of her native Ireland. This effectively burst the bubble on Bridey-mania. Serious inquiry evaporated, and the seemingly disreputable Bernstein faded away. But in due time, he was back, armed with a set of counter-facts that seemingly discredited the discreditors. The rise of a John Edwards today confirms that the fascination with lives beyond our own remains undiminished since the fifties.

3. THINK PINK!

Somewhere in the midst of the monochromatic mind-set that seemed to dominate the national zeitgeist, the color pink—formerly associated with all things feminine—suddenly became not only fashionable, but hip—for *everyone*, guys included, and everything. Think about things commonly associated with the decade: pink Cadillacs (you couldn't get much more cutting edge than Elvis); pink flamingos; pale pink lipstick; pink poodles; "tan shoes with pink shoelaces," as the song went; even pink aluminum Christmas trees. Businessmen could be seen sporting pink shirts beneath charcoal gray suits or even pink ties. People who may have lacked any other fashion sense knew that, for one brief shining moment, you couldn't go wrong with pink.

4. MAMBO

A musical styling that could be traced to West Africa found its way into America via a pre-Castro Cuba in the early fifties, setting off a dance craze among grown-ups that rivaled anything the kids were up to. This being the last gasp of big bands as popular club entertainment, the postwar extension of what began in the forties as the Carmen Miranda phenomenon was embodied by puffy-sleeved percussionists wielding claves. For most Americans, the Tropicana scenes in *I Love Lucy* were their first exposure to an exotic musical world. But beginning in New York, a musical scene that included Perez Prado (the "King of Mambo") and Tito Puente soon fanned out across the rest of the country. The entry was eased initially by mambo rhythms being applied to pop standards, but in time this situation reversed: pop singers were releasing their takes on mambo, being sure to include the word in the title, lest anyone miss the point. Hits of the day included "Mambo Italiano" (a contradiction if there ever was) from Rosemary Clooney and "Papa Loves Mambo" from Perry Como. Soon, housewives were signing up for dance lessons, and accessorizing one's living room with a conga drum was not unknown. Like so much else, the phenomenon ran its course, with rock & roll burying it for the remainder of the decade. The odd resurgence arises periodically but with nowhere near the same intensity.

5. LOUNGE MUSIC

The rise of the hi-fi and subsequent introduction of stereo led directly to a style of music that was completely studio-oriented, without any real prospect of live performance. It was the precursor of what one day would be called "ambient" music, meant to provoke an atmosphere rather than to dance to or whistle along with. The atmosphere in question included martinis, animal print furniture, tiki artifacts—in short, a bachelor pad. Lounge albums were meant to be listened to in their entirety—you could even stack several on your turntable's spindle and let the music play for hours. Musically, the genre covers a lot of ground, including unfamiliar scales and sounds imported from exotic locales. It's simpler to describe by saying what it isn't: definitely not rock, being far more complex and requiring a longer attention span. It wasn't jazz, where virtuosity is a virtue. It was too nebulous to be considered good pop—really, lounge is a listener-friendly castoff of many styles, somewhat experimental in nature. The advent of stereo led to much speaker-to-speaker panning of sounds and effects in what was sometimes called "space-age pop." Among the style's best known practitioners was Esquivel! (yes, often spelled with that punctuation). He recorded a string of albums for RCA in the late fifties that defined "lounge," with their heavy use of musically colorful instrumentation and wild stereo mixing. The music experienced a revival in the early nineties with a slew of reissues on CD, embodying the fine line between cool and kitsch.

6. PHONE BOOTH CRAMMING

Gather 'round children, and hear now the story of something that used to be found on every street corner, once upon a time. A glass enclosure, roughly three feet square and seven feet tall, equipped with a fold-in door, a directory on a chain, and a coin-operated dial telephone used to be a common sight. This contraption's brand of public privacy made possible the transformation of Clark Kent into something super, but it couldn't last. First the glass booths went, then one by one the telephones—by now reduced to mountings beneath metal enclosures—vanished from the scene. But speak to anyone who came of age during the fifties, and you might hear about a popular sport that enjoyed a brief heyday.

The pursuit, known as "phone booth cramming," enjoyed enormous popularity on college campuses, starting around 1959. It began innocently enough, when word got around that in South Africa, a group of 25 managed to squeeze into a booth. Of course, *they* were at an advantage, what with the utter lack of McDonald's restaurants at the time. But Americans rose to the challenge, though they could never beat that record. Once things got competitive, rules were laid down to govern the pursuit. Should the door be closed or open? Must the booth be upright? What about English phone booths (which were bigger)? The closest anyone came was when some students at St. Mary's College in Moraga, California, applied their formidable skills to the task. Giving the matter careful consideration, they came up with a well-thought-out plan of arrangement, instead of just having everyone stuff themselves in every which way. Also, they wisely picked students who were on the small side. Still, in the end, the best they could manage was 22.

7. DRIVE-INS

As the demographic dubbed "teenager" came into focus in the fifties, businesses of every kind sat up and took notice, tailoring their wares to this select group. Teenagers' unprecedented economic power was something to cherish. Here were people—not quite adults, not quite children—who were more affluent than ever before. Many held part-time jobs, and, most important, many owned their own cars. So it was that drive-in movie theaters, in existence since the late 1930s, really began to take off.

There were several important reasons why this was so: in the competition for teenage dollars, Hollywood became aware of the windfall to be made by cranking out cheaply made sci-fi or horror movies that drew in the kids. Acting, story, and production values were nearly irrelevant—what mattered was providing the cheap thrills to be had when your date got startled. In addition, when you took a girl to a movie in your car, if things went badly, you could always watch the film. The same could not be said for parking at some secluded make-out spot. (It was also a less obvious means of signaling your intent.) Finally, the facilitation for social interaction was so compelling. Drive-ins were excellent meeting places for hanging out, showing off your wheels, or just gathering en masse in a friendly environment. For these and many other reasons, the number of drive-ins in America increased from 820 in 1948 to 4,063 10 years later. By the nineties, most of these were replaced, literally and figuratively, by malls.

8.   3-D MOVIES

In an era rife with experimentation in movie-making technology, one more gimmick could be added to the pile of incentives implemented to lure TV viewers back into theaters. Although in concept the idea of 3-D cinema had been around since the silent era, a truly practical method of viewing such films was elusive until the development of the Polaroid system developed by Edwin Land. This system made for much more natural movie viewing, eliminating the need for those red-and-blue lensed glasses. The first vehicle for the new process was radio mystery maven Arch Oboler's telling of the Tsavo lion man-eater story, *Bwana Devil*, in 1953. (The same incident was recounted in 1997's *The Ghost and the Darkness*). A routine jungle adventure flick starring Robert Stack, this film only rated a second thought because it was made in 3-D. "A lion in your lap," the film's posters promised. To be sure, the material did lend itself to the 3-D treatment, but better films would follow.

Possibly the best was the 1953 Vincent Price flick *House of Wax*. Another notable effort was *Dial M for Murder*, a rare instance of Alfred Hitchcock following a trend. Despite some quality releases, 3-D never fully clicked with audiences. One reason was that not everyone took to watching a film through glasses. Another was that theaters weren't too thrilled with the need to run a film through two projectors, with a certain amount of precision required to make the effect work. It was ultimately too expensive and too much trouble. Finally, the audiences themselves seemingly were easily satiated. Having seen a film this way once was plenty; repeated viewings revealed the process for what it was—an expensive, unnatural gimmick.

9. CHLOROPHYLL

Social pressures demanded that certain personal grooming standards be met throughout the fifties. In case anyone missed the point (despite all those short films young people were subjected to in school), Madison Avenue was there to remind you that you were in danger of being judged at every turn. To this end, products whose purpose was to eradicate every last vestige of humanity were marketed, from breath mints to deodorants to even items whose job was to eliminate "personal odors." What did all of these products have in common? Chlorophyll—the stuff that green plants are made of. The belief that chlorophyll was to odor what kryptonite was to Superman was driven home by a slew of goods, all containing the new wonder ingredient and usually featuring a reminder of that fact in its name.

Probably the best known and longest-surviving relic of the time was Clorets gum. For such an item to cleanse the breath—even only momentarily—is no great achievement. But what about breath, BO, feet, and, um, personal odors? For that, you had Ennds Chlorophyll Tablets. Just one pill rendered you inoffensive within minutes. Other items with the magic stuff included mouthwash, cough drops, cigarettes, shoe insoles, dog food, and toilet paper. Perhaps what would prove to be the final nail in this particular craze's coffin was the observation that cows and goats do nothing but ingest chlorophyll and they *still* smell. By the time the sixties arrived, science had moved on to other, more pressing matters, like ring around the collar.

10. UFOS

We examine here not the existence of extraterrestrials, but the impact of public awareness of the phenomenon on fifties culture. The prospect of visitors from other planets arriving at a particularly troubled time for this world, with the possibility of nuclear apocalypse looming, seemed to be almost cathartic. Rather than heightening paranoia, turning aliens into a form of entertainment seemed to lighten Cold War tensions. UFOmania largely appeared in two forms: movies and music. By the time rock & roll had established itself, the public was prepared to laugh at would-be space invaders with songs like "Flying Saucer Rock and Roll" by Billy Lee Riley, "Flying Saucer" by Buchanan & Goodman; and the deathless "Purple People Eater" by Sheb Wooley.

There are far too many space invader movies to list here, so we'll just mention the best ones. *The Day the Earth Stood Still* (1951) without a doubt has held up the best among the plethora of cinematic junk films. It plays like an extended *Twilight Zone* episode, showing the folly of nuclear war. Also up there is *The Thing from Another World* (1951), which featured a pre-*Gunsmoke* James Arness in the title role. John Carpenter would recast it as a post-*Alien* gross-out flick in 1982. *Earth vs. the Flying Saucers* (1956) featured a cast of nobodies, but excellent Ray Harryhausen special effects depicting the destruction of Washington, D.C., landmarks. No list would be complete without mention of the original 1956 *Invasion of the Body Snatchers*, a chilling exercise in fifties paranoia. Finally, *It Came from Outer Space* (1953), based on a Ray Bradbury story, depicts an *accidental* UFO invasion. Some ETs are forced to crash-land, then interact with humans as they try to repair their ship.

Oh Baby, That's What I Like!

Although microwave ovens did exist in the fifties, junk food gorging in those days generally took longer than it does now, thus postponing obesity for many. (Huh?) To put it another way, convenience foods were just coming into their own, and with them, the eating habits of a nation would be forever changed. Looking over this list of dining landmarks points inevitably toward one conclusion—people wanted their meals quicker and with less effort. Maybe moms joining the postwar workforce in greater numbers than ever before had something to do with it. But one could make the case that a change in what had been the norm, that is, the entire family sitting down together for a home-cooked dinner, was but a stepping-stone on the road to the erosion of the family unit. Or not. Here are the culprits.

1. POTPIES (1951)

In one form or another, the concept of a potpie had been around in Europe since at least the 18th century. The term gained use in the colonies in the pre-Revolutionary era, but the notion of a premade potpie that you simply had to bake came along when an Omaha poultry distributor decided to test the market. When Swanson frozen chicken potpies hit the stores, they were an immediate hit. What was intended as a convenience became a comfort food, a childhood staple for the baby boomers whose mothers had had all they could stand. Turkey, beef, and even tuna soon joined forces with the trailblazing chicken in supermarkets' frozen food section.

2. MRS. PAUL'S FISH STICKS (1952)

Ed Piszek was a Philadelphia entrepreneur who sold crab cakes in the late 1940s. Business was good, but he'd reached a plateau. Casting about for a way to expand his business, he discovered a way to freeze fish successfully and market it in an easy-to-use way. So it was that Mrs. Paul, his seafood distributorship, became the country's largest marketer of scrod. But Piszek's real story doesn't end there. Following his tremendous success, he began to investigate his Polish ancestry in the early 1960s. Taking a trip to the land of his grandparents opened his eyes to the hardships the country faced under the Communists. Using his fish stick fortune, Ed bought a supply of medical supplies and equipment, worked his way through government red tape, and almost single-handedly eliminated the scourge of tuberculosis from the motherland. Not a bad legacy.

3. TV DINNERS (1954)

CA Swanson & Sons had a problem in December 1953. A surplus of unsold turkeys left over from Thanksgiving—10 full refrigerated boxcars' worth—vexed the company. The frozen poultry and pot pie company needed a creative way to market them, and from such distress great ideas are born. Inspired by the aluminum-tray meals served on airplanes, one Gerry Thomas hit upon the idea of creating an entire dinner built around the turkey, complete with sides and dessert. For Swanson, already well established with frozen convenience foods, the next step was marketing genius. The product would be called "TV dinner." The appellation was purely a matter of hitching the company's wagon to the rising star of the moment—a few years on, it might have been called "rocket dinner" or "space dinner." But in so doing, Swanson tacitly blessed the growing habit of eating meals in front of the one-eyed monster. Would the coupling of this with Zenith's unholy new invention, the TV remote control, make Swanson the father of the couch potato? Let he who is without sin cast the first Tater Tot!

4. KENTUCKY FRIED CHICKEN (1952)

Harlan Sanders was only six years old when he lost his father. When his mother went to work, young Harlan was left to cook and care for his two younger siblings and, by the age of seven, was quite an accomplished hand in the kitchen. This talent stayed with him, as he pursued one interest after another, including the military, studying law, working on the railroad, and selling tires. By midlife, he owned a service station in Corbin, Kentucky that offered meals to hungry travelers. When its reputation as a quality diner began to bring in more income than the station's auto services, Harlan saw the writing on the wall and moved to a bigger site across the street.

By 1935, Harlan had been named a Kentucky colonel on the strength of his culinary skills. By the early fifties, the highway that brought him so much business was slated to be moved, so he liquidated his assets, and with nothing but his Social Security check, hit the road. Such was the demand for his particular recipe of "11 herbs and spices" that he decided to spend his "retirement" traveling about the country, personally selling franchises to locals on a handshake basis. Twelve years and 600 stores later, he sold his interest in the country's biggest fast-food chicken outlet for $2 million, though he stayed on as spokesman until his death in 1980.

5. JIF PEANUT BUTTER (1956)

When this brand came along, choosy mothers were given a choice at last. The first product resembling what we recognize as peanut butter came about as a physician worked in the 1890s to develop a nutritious meat substitute for them who lacked the choppers. By the second decade of the 20th century, there were several commercially available peanut butters on the market, but they tended to be gritty and lacked a shelf life.

Joseph Rosefield developed the process to overcome these limitations and, by 1928, Peter Pan was on the market. Skippy followed in the 1930s, adding crunchy style in 1935. "Jif" was coined for its memorability and simple spelling. Also, it connotes "jiffy," which suggests "quick" as well as aurally resembling "Skippy"—the perfect name. The creamy version of Jif came out two years later, and extra crunchy was introduced in 1974.

6. FROZEN PIZZA (1957)

The origin of pizza is such a touchy subject among historians, with hairsplitting over what constitutes an authentic pizza (as opposed to any other dish prepared on a flat round piece of dough), that we won't even address it. Let's begin with the first recognized pizza restaurant in America, opened by one Gennaro Lombardi in New York in 1905. Beyond dispute is the creation of deep-dish, Chicago-style pizza, which originated at Pizzeria Uno in 1943. GIs returning from the Mediterranean brought a taste for pizza home with them, and as the fifties got underway, pizza became big business in America. Considering the natural evolution of food, a "convenience pizza" was inevitable. In Newark, the Celentano brothers opened an Italian specialty shop in 1947. Their product line included every imaginable meat and cheese, freshly made, for Italian cooking. In 1957, the brothers applied their expertise to pizza, making a frozen version available for home cooking. This begat a giant component of the frozen food industry, with countless brands and styles available today. (Some sources credit Rose Totino with inventing frozen pizza; however, her product didn't hit the market until 1962. So there.) A would-be inventor in Bensonhurst, New York, conceived the idea for lo-cal pizza during the mid-fifties, but met with failure.

7.   TANG (1957)

Though deeply associated in the public mind with the U.S. space program, this granulated breakfast drink actually began as the next logical step after instant coffee and instant milk. The trick was to create a breakfast drink that didn't need refrigeration, yet tasted good and was nutritionally valid content. Science met the challenge, and General Mills introduced the concoction in 1957, going national two years later. The name was derived from "tangy," simultaneously evoking tangerine as well. The product really took off (so to speak) when Gemini astronauts in the sixties began bringing it aboard flights. This boosted its appeal as not only good for you, but cutting-edge as well. Currently, it's available in 30 flavors around the world but, alas, only three at home.

8.   RICE-A-RONI (1958)

It's hard to believe that there was ever a time that San Francisco was lacking a treat, but its arrival was surely cause for rejoicing. In 1934, Gragnano Products, purveyors of pasta products, changed its name to Golden Grain after seeing the phrase in a tobacco ad. An Armenian rice dish that a neighbor often prepared provided the inspiration to the DeDomenico family, the company's owners. One of the brothers concocted a mixture of rice, noodles, and chicken broth and dubbed it Rice-A-Roni. It was easy to make, yet somewhat exotic, adding a bit of local flavor to the dinner table. What really pushed it over the top was capitalizing on the DeDomenicos' home town of San Francisco and its sunny ambience. Dubbing the product, "the San Francisco treat," gave people around the country an appetite for some of that dolce vita. The TV ads, with their memorable jingle and cable car imagery, made the product an instant smash.

9.   JIFFY-POP (1959)

Perhaps the oldest snack food around was enjoyed in Mexico more than 5,000 years ago. Other cultures throughout the

Americas enjoyed their own variation of popped corn, including some tribes who contrived a way to cook oiled corn *on the cob*! Colonizing Europeans took to it and aped the indigenous peoples' custom of stringing it together for decorative purposes. The invention of Cracker Jack boosted popped corn's viability by the turn of the century. Commercially available popcorn, more or less as we know it, hit the market by the 1920s. During the Depression and World War II, it was one of the few guilt-free snacks allowable, because it was cheap and didn't require sugar. TV and popcorn were a natural fit, and riding the wave toward ease of use was an Indiana fellow named Fred Mennen. It took him five years to perfect a strain of hull-less yellow corn, then conceive the familiar aluminum foil-topped pan. As much for the fun in watching it cook as anything else, Jiffy-Pop caught on in a big way, its portability making it a favorite of campers. A new, improved version is available today, along a Jiffy kettle corn!

10. METRECAL (1959)

For those inclined to overindulge in fifties convenience foods, Mead Johnson, which introduced Pablum to the world in the thirties, came to the rescue with the forerunner of Slim-Fast. According to some sources, the product was developed to help its users *put on* weight, when used to supplement meals. However, its purpose flip-flopped when buyers began to use it *in place* of meals. Available in liquid or wafer form, Metrecal was intended to supply full nutritional requirements without causing malnutrition on the part of the people who subsisted on it. Like many fad diets, it was a popular craze for a time before dying out in the late sixties. By then, Mead Johnson had introduced Nutrament, essentially the same stuff, but with its weight-building aspect amplified. Soon enough, other weight-loss products like Dexatrim and the unfortunately named Ayds candies supplanted Mead Johnson's wares, leaving Metrecal a long-forgotten artifact.

Who Wrote the Book?

This was a fertile time for literary innovation, when any number of classics found an audience, and an assortment of newsstand mainstays came into being. Profound social change was underway, reflected in the popular reading material of the day. Disaffected youth found its voice, a new literary movement (the Beats) caught fire, and with newfound leisure time, the public was eager to explore new avenues of thought that read like science fiction—when not perusing the tube. Here are 10 immortals of the era.

1. *DIANETICS: THE MODERN SCIENCE OF MENTAL HEALTH* BY L. RON HUBBARD (MAY 1950)

Never was the notion that one man's church is another man's cult made more explicit than with the publication of this book and all it begat. Hubbard was a purveyor of pulp science fiction throughout the thirties and forties, a low-level peddler of fantasy to the socially impaired. Accounts of his heroics during World War II were propagated by his organization, but the release of his service records under the Freedom of Information Act revealed his extreme exaggerations, not to mention a series of disciplinary actions. (What else might one expect from a creature of fiction?) In addition, his personal life was colored by bigamy, a highly publicized kidnapping charge (of his own child) in 1951, and charges of breaking into the Internal Revenue Service and stealing 30,000 documents relating to his organization, resulting in convictions for Hubbard's wife and nine others. In other words, unexceptional malfeasance by organized religion standards.

The original seed for Dianetics appeared, appropriately enough, in a publication called *Astounding Science Fiction*. This was fleshed out into a book-length tome, quickly emulating the success usually accorded fad diet books. Indeed, its slim credentials coupled with obese claims of curing every manner of mental illness made it catnip to the weak-minded and a lightning rod to anyone demanding a little proof. It is not without reason that Hubbard parlayed his pseudoscience into a religion (Scientology) in 1953, removing it from the strenuous demands of empirical proof that true science demands. As an organized religion, the group not only enjoyed a tax break but was also able to steer its adherents into accepting its teachings on faith. What critics point out as its potential harm is the methodology that resembles nothing so much as psychoanalysis, with its emphasis on the purging of "engrams" (traumatic memories) through "auditing" (therapy). The goal is to move from being a "preclear" (neurotic) to a "clear" (a penniless but enlightened soul). All in all, not something for amateurs. The deep pockets necessary to fully master Hubbard's program has made his brand of wisdom a favorite among a certain show biz stratum (resulting in a *Battlefield Earth* to traumatize an unsuspecting public). Seems like a match made in heaven—or somewhere.

2. *THE CATCHER IN THE RYE* BY J.D. SALINGER (JULY 1951)

Required reading for disaffected youth and celebrity stalkers alike, *Catcher in the Rye* remains Salinger's only published novel. Despite occasional lapses into slang, the book holds up remarkably well today, prescient in its depiction of disillusioned youth in the rocky transition to adult awareness. The story itself defies easy description, being the classic whole that is greater than the sum of its parts. (Maybe the lack of a linear plot explains in part why it hasn't been filmed.) It's more a series of encounters in the life of Holden Caulfield, a 16-year-old student who suffers a nervous breakdown. The world, largely composed of "phonies," is seen through his eyes as he makes his way from the Pennsylvania prep school he has flunked out of to his home in New York at Christmas break. (The title comes from a misremembered Robert Burns poem; Caulfield aspires to be the savior of errant children who stumble blindly toward a "crazy cliff.")

Salinger's reputation was certainly elevated by his unheard of reclusivity. In a culture that celebrates and exploits achievers, his pathological shunning of the spotlight was itself novel (and inspired the Sean Connery character in the film *Finding Forrester*). His affluent background included prep schools, trips to Europe, and writing classes at Columbia University. For a time, he dated playwright Eugene O'Neill's daughter, Oona, and was reportedly crushed when the teenager went off with Charlie Chaplin. He served in the Army, witnessing war's horrors up close at Normandy, before beginning his writing career with a series of short stories in magazines.

When *Catcher in the Rye* was published, Salinger did little to promote it, going so far as to request that his likeness not be used. His only novel and the handful of short story collections that followed kept his name alive, despite his best efforts. Periodically, predicated on the political winds of the moment, outraged parents attempt to banish his book from school curriculums, largely on the basis of language (quaintly tame by current standards). Its reputation was likewise tainted by both John Lennon's killer and Ronald Reagan's would-be assassin, who armed themselves with copies of the book, along with guns, when they achieved their infamy.

3. THE DIARY OF ANNE FRANK (1952)

As the world struggled to put its horrific recent past behind it, a face and a voice unexpectedly emerged, personalizing victims of the Holocaust. The year 1952 saw the English translation of *Anne Frank: The Diary of a Young Girl* reach the masses. With it came insight into the futile struggle for survival endured by so many in attempting to stay a step ahead of the Third Reich. The Franks were German Jews who had settled in Amsterdam in 1934. Otto and Edith, along with daughters Margot and Anne, went into hiding in 1942 after Margot received orders to report to a work camp. Sharing the attic above a warehouse with them were five others, all sustained by the supplies and small comforts brought them by some of Otto's employees, who naturally were sworn to secrecy. Anne, a lively, precocious 13-year-old, wisely brought with her a diary to keep herself company, addressing many of the entries to her imaginary friend, Kitty. While indulging in normal adolescent musings, Anne possessed a fine eye for detail, capturing their surreal existence. Her poignant optimism in the face of suffering and her belief in the eventual triumph of good over evil could not save Anne's life.

In early August 1944, the Nazis, tipped off by an informer, raided the hiding place and dispatched its occupants to the death camps. One by one, they were murdered or felled by disease; Margot and Anne, at Bergen-Belsen, were stricken with typhus. Only three weeks before the camp was liberated, Anne, 15, followed her sister in death, believing herself to be an orphan. Unbeknownst to her, Otto, though deathly ill, survived. It would be several years before the Red Cross was able to provide confirmation that he'd lost his children. By that time, he'd been given Anne's extant writings, rescued by one of the family's caregivers. Knowing of his daughter's desire to make public their experiences, he edited the work and arranged for its first publication in 1947, with a limited run of 1,500. (Years later, pages that he had excised surfaced, detailing Anne's observations on her parents' marriage and unflattering comments about her mother.) The public recognized the compelling nature of the work as well as its rich dramatic potential; a hit Broadway play was staged in 1955, followed by a Hollywood treatment four years later (when Anne would have been 30). The unfortunate tendency by attention-deprived individuals to broadcast their beliefs that the diary was a hoax persists, belying Anne's belief that "people are truly good at heart."

4. *MAD* MAGAZINE (OCTOBER 1952)

William M. Gaines became publisher of EC's line of comic books upon his father's death in 1947. Prior to, EC had been known for its educational and religious stories, but all that soon changed. Gaines steered the company from mere survival to the top of the comic book world with a succession of new titles, such as *Tales from the Crypt*, *The Vault of Horror*, and *Weird Science*. In 1952, a young EC staffer named Harvey Kurtzman prevailed upon Gaines to add a satirical work to the company's line, one whose raison d'être was mocking other comic books. He called it *Mad*. The new comic set itself apart by the high quality of its writing and art. Though the humor was sometimes sophomoric, it was mostly quite intelligent. Gaines was willing to give the upstart time to find an audience, mostly because he loved it so much, and by the fourth issue it was selling out. Imitators confirmed its success, and things for EC might have rolled merrily along but for two reasons: first, congressional "morality" police were putting pressure on publishers of lurid, grisly wares to clean up their act. Some comics folded, and once an oversight authority was in place, EC didn't have a chance. By the time the smoke cleared, only *Mad* was left. The second event was the departure of Harvey Kurtzman, leaving the direction of *Mad* to Gaines and Al Feldstein. Kurtzman's leaving resulted in an expansion of input that gave *Mad* the flavor of its heyday. Characteristic staples of the magazine began appearing, including *Spy vs. Spy*; the fold-in; artist-writers like Don Martin, Al Jaffee, and Dave Berg; and, most important, its mascot and cover boy, Alfred E. Neuman. The image of the jug-eared, freckle-faced, gap-toothed figure with the inane grin actually appeared under a couple of different names, and his eventual moniker was applied to other characters as a running gag, until both were finally united in May 1956. *Mad*'s creative peak coincided with its greatest popularity. With its dead-on movie and TV parodies, prescient political commentary, and regular features by writers at the height of their powers, the golden era shone briefly in the seventies before its inevitable fade. Changing times, departing writers, and a slump in sales forced *Mad* to mutate into a shell of its former self. Gaines maintained control until his death in 1992; under new management, the current version is almost unrecognizable, with the addition of advertising and glossy color spreads. The potted plant, "Arthur"; "Portzebie"; the *Mad* Zeppelin; "furshlugginer"; and Roger Kaputnik—these and other artifacts from their glory days remain a fond memory for those who loved *Mad*. What, me worry? Too late now.

5. *TV GUIDE* MAGAZINE (APRIL 1953)

Walter Annenberg inherited a publishing interest from his father, a long-time Hearst associate. In 1944, Annenberg achieved his first success with *Seventeen* magazine. The roots of what became Annenberg's biggest publication began in 1948. In that year, three separate TV schedule entities began: one in Chicago, one in Philadelphia, and one in New York. The last one, started by Lee Wagner in June 1948, was called *Television Guide* and featured Gloria Swanson on the first cover. (In March 1950, the name was changed to *TV Guide*.) With only 300,000 sets in the whole country, small localized guides were enough to do the job. Annenberg saw the potential of locking up the television guide market by publishing a single, magazine-format guide, with local listing inserts for the appropriate markets. In 1952, he bought out *TV Guide* and Philadelphia's *TV Digest*, effectively taking control of the East. By spring of 1953, he was ready to launch his new enterprise in 10 cities from coast to coast. The first issue, published for the week beginning April 3, featured on its cover the best-known infant in America, Desi Arnaz, Jr. By summer, Annenberg had added five more cities, but his circulation was dropping quickly. Clearly, the public was unwilling to pay for they could get for free in their newspaper, a problem that persisted through the years. In September, he hit upon an idea to get viewers excited about network offerings: he published the first Fall Preview edition, detailing the upcoming shows for the 1953–54 season. (Photos of stars perusing the issue were contrived with dummy covers on blank contents.) This concept became the first gimmick to keep people interested through the years. Annenburg's fortunes turned around, and the ensuing years saw *TV Guide* virtually monopolizing the TV listing business. Annenberg sold out to Rupert Murdoch in 1988, precipitating a downward slide in content, epitomized nowadays by such cheap come-ons to suckers as multiple covers for the same issue. ("Collect 'em all!")

6. *CASINO ROYALE* BY IAN FLEMING (1953)

At the height of the Cold War, an English journalist about to end his bachelorhood at 43 undertook to write a spy thriller. Based somewhat on his experiences with British naval intelligence during the war, he took the name of an American ornithologist for his hero. At his home in Jamaica (which he called "Goldeneye"), he set to work, at last completing work on what he likely intended to be a one-time character: James Bond. No longer bound by the nonfiction demands of reporting, Fleming imbued his fantasy character with many of his own traits, which included a fondness for women, vodka martinis, fast cars, women, gambling, gadgets, travel, and, last but not least, women. The tremendous success of the book would lead to another 13 from Fleming (and even more from others after his death), and an entire series of big screen treatments beginning in 1962 with *Dr. No.*

His initial actor of choice was David Niven, but after seeing Sean Connery in *Dr. No* and then in *From Russia with Love*, he changed his mind. Niven ironically would be given the role in the film that typically has been disowned by Bond fans—*Casino Royale* (1967). As is usually the case, the novels and movies differ greatly in characterization. Bond of the books, especially the first one, is conspicuously lacking the sense of humor film fans are accustomed to. He comes off as much less of a superhero and more of a human being in print, with the audience being invited into his head to feel his desperation, self-doubt, and vulnerability. Before becoming the familiar franchise of the sixties and seventies with Sean Connery, this first Bond novel was adapted for the CBS television series *Climax!* in 1954. A live, one-hour weekly anthology, this early treatment is notable for, if nothing else, the decision to make Bond an *American* card-sharp. Barry Nelson has the distinction of playing Jimmie Bond, and badly too, by some accounts. (At least Peter Lorre did a commendable job as his nemesis.) Eon Productions took control of the remaining Fleming properties. Since the company did not own the rights to *Casino*, other producers became responsible for the film version, which was perverted into a parody because they felt they could never compete with Connery's characterization head-on. A new movie adaption of *Casino Royale* entered production in 2006.

7. *PLAYBOY* MAGAZINE (DECEMBER 1953)

Sometimes all a great idea needs to get off the ground is good timing. Surely the concept implemented to such great success by Mr. Hefner had been kicking around forever, at least since the invention of photography: what if we can get good-looking, attractively built women to *willingly* agree to take off their clothes? I mean women who in normal life wouldn't give us the time of day, much less a peek. Not *too* beautiful—nope, they have to at least appear approachable. Let us then get these pretty, naked girls to pose "artistically" (nyuk nyuk nyuk). Finally, let us get these pretty, naked, artistically posed women to allow us to *photograph* them— for mass publication, for all to see. And make them *like* it, even *compete* for the chance. Surely a fantasy held by every right-thinking heterosexual male in America, if not the world, no? So it was that fate destined a "repressed" (his word) young editor from Chicago to bring the fantasy to life, to make the girl next door "available" (for a small price), to bring beauty within reach. From time immemorial, awkward, hormone-driven adolescents had to watch in frustration from afar while their better-off, socially skilled peers got all the girls.

With the first issue of *Playboy* hitting the street in December 1953, relief was at hand. The ex-*Esquire* employee had been kicking around the idea of a "lifestyle" magazine for sometime, anticipating the needs of tuxedo-owning, martini-guzzling, hi-fi buffs to look at naked girls while feeling that their shallowness was intellectually defensible. Enter "Hef" with the "Playboy philosophy," his pseudoacademic clap-trap that at once elevated materialism while simultaneously slandering an entire gender. He firmly warned any women who might accidentally happen upon his wares to "please pass [*Playboy*] along to the man in your life and get back to your *Ladies' Home Companion*." (Ouch!) At least he had the good sense to change from his intended title, *Stag Party*, to a name and logo (the bunny) that sort of made sense, considering what rabbits are known for. (It also spared the wait-resses in Playboy clubs from the humiliation of sporting little antlers and enduring the clever come-on from drunks: "Are you horny, baby?")

Despite some rough times and attacks from the religious right and women's groups, the magazine has survived, if not thrived. Today in his dotage, the Viagra-popping, multimillionaire Hefner enjoys the effects that a fat wallet and a private grotto have on loosening the legs of nubile peroxided and surgically enhanced young women (at least those who've fantasized about jumping the creaky bones of an octogenarian). But to many males at least, he is regarded with reverence bordering on holy.

8. *HOWL!* BY ALLEN GINSBERG (OCTOBER 1955)

"I've seen the best minds of my generation destroyed by madness." With that deathless line begins the poem that for many, along with Kerouac's *On the Road*, defined Beat literature. Ginsberg was the son of a poet and a woman whose mental illness culminated in treatment by lobotomy. His college years found him in the company of Jack Kerouac, Neal Cassady, and William Burroughs, a counterculture Rat Pack of sorts. As a group, they experimented with a variety of intoxicants and illegal substances. Ginsberg turned them on to serious literature while they in turn freed him from his repression, pulling him out of the closet, as it were. Associating with various low-level criminals brought him arrest and a stint in an institution, leading to a last brief attempt at a straight life before succumbing to his own natural bent. Though Ginsberg had written reams of poetry by this time, his real breakthrough came when, encouraged by his friends to abandon "normal" meter and rhyme, he embraced free verse. Inspiration from Walt Whitman and William Blake fused with insights induced through illicit means resulted in a groundbreaking style.

In October 1955, Ginsberg premiered *Howl!* at a San Francisco art gallery, publishing it in book form early the following year. His readings, really performance art, were a sensation, and further attention was drawn when the piece with its frank accounts of his homosexuality, was declared obscene. Authorities seized the book's entire printing, while the ensuing courtroom comedy of errors made Ginsberg a legend. He used the publicity to champion Kerouac and Burroughs, resulting in contracts for *On the Road* (1957) and *Naked Lunch* (1959). Today, *Howl!* continues to be admired for its use of meter and rhythm, its expression of what society's artistic outcasts endured during the time, and Ginsberg's own commentary on the false idols of the day. Though he felt much of his subsequent work was superior, never again would Ginsberg garner so much national attention.

9. *PROFILES IN COURAGE* BY JOHN F. KENNEDY (1956)

This is one of those books that is more talked about than read. Unless you're a political junkie, you might find the prose decidedly wordy and arcane, and its subject matter, eight U.S. senators in history, not exactly page-turning material. That said, the concept is pretty solid: examining political showdowns that were potentially career-destroying, and how these men went against their own self-interests in the name of what was "right" (although contemporary readers can certainly quarrel with that definition). The book itself came about during a rare lull in skirt-chasing for the then-senator, having endured a couple of catastrophic back surgeries in late 1954 and early 1955. Restless in recovery, Kennedy alleviated his boredom (and insomnia) by devouring political biographies. His hyperactive intellect began conceptualizing a volume centering on character-defining incidents that bespoke greatness. (By inference, one can divine a subtle wish to include himself among such company.)

Assisting the bedridden patient was his right-hand man, speechwriter and alter ego Ted Sorenson. Their close working relationship would fuel a controversy that rages to this day, with Kennedy-bashers loudly denying JFK's authorship, while others assert that, regardless of how much physical work he actually did, it's still his book. It won the Pulitzer Prize in 1957, raising the senator's own profile in jockeying for a presidential run three years on. But there were some who could not accept his authorship at face value, among them, newspaper columnist Drew Pearson. In a program on ABC that same year, Pearson told interviewer Mike Wallace as much, touching off considerable aggravation for JFK and livid rage by his father, who was prepared to sue for damages. Ever pragmatic, the senator instead gathered his handwritten notes, manuscript pages, and all supporting documentation, and met with ABC execs (except for Mike Wallace, who absented himself). Witness statements attesting to his work on the book were produced, and when Pearson, over the phone, repeated his assertion that Sorenson had written *Profiles*, the latter testified under oath to ABC's lawyers, acquitting himself solidly in denying authorship. That he accepted $6,000 from Kennedy for his assistance was readily conceded, but hardly an admission of anything fishy. ABC duly issued a retraction to the story, though Mike Wallace privately felt he'd been had.

10. *ON THE ROAD* BY JACK KEROUAC (1957)

For those seeking greater understanding of the movement termed "Beat," look no further. "Beat generation" was coined in 1948 by this man, in conversation with writer John Clellon Holmes. Fashioned directly after Ernest Hemingway's label for the post-World War I crowd of artists he called the "Lost Generation," "Beat" as used by Kerouac had a double meaning: as short for "beaten," meaning he and his fellows who felt so defeated by society's demands and their inability to live up to them, and, second, implying "beatific"—the inner holiness of the common rabble. It took a mere 10 years from the time of Kerouac's epiphany for the term to become twisted into a pejorative, with "beatnik"—modeled after *Sputnik*—coined as a slam for those who were viewed as lazy, dissolute, unclean bums.

In time, Kerouac himself would have concurred. His success after years of rejection brought him little joy, and he turned bitter, cranky, and conservative, supporting the war in Vietnam and ridiculing various youth movements of the sixties. He would die a chronic alcoholic at 47 in 1969. *On the Road*, however, was his finest hour. Though he'd already published one novel by 1950, *The Town and the Country*, its conventional, sentimental prose was hardly attention-worthy. His cross-country trips with Neal Cassady would foment a new creative drive, one impatient with the demands of mainstream dictates. A straightforward plot description is futile; suffice it to say, it stands as an account of his travels, with all of his notable friends present, though their names were changed. The prevailing atmosphere is one of unplanned, carefree wandering, casual relationships, and an utter lack of materialism. Life experiences were to be savored as they unfolded, and following your dream, no matter how illogical it may have been, was what really mattered.

The resulting manuscript, completed in three weeks, was in apparent need of editing, but its very rawness was exactly the point—Kerouac called his style "spontaneous bop prosody," infused as it was with the energy of unplanned impulse. It was rejected by publishers until Ginsberg's success, when Kerouac suddenly found himself an unexpected celebrity, and *On the Road* a bestseller.

Let's Go for a Ride

A ny discussion of what the fifties were like would be re-
miss if it didn't address the impact on our national identity of the cars we drove. The first generation to fully embrace
car culture came of age in this decade, a fact that was celebrated in song and cinema. If an automobile can be said to
be iconic, the fifties had many to choose from, from the
'vette to the T-Bird to the '57 Chevy, and so on. The youthful
obsession with all things fast (as embodied by James Dean)
reached its full flower in the early sixties, especially with the
proliferation of hot rod/drag race tunes, but its roots lie here.
After all, Chuck Berry was motivatin' over the hill long before
Daddy took her T-bird away.

1. THE STUDEBAKER COMMANDER, 1950

The automobile industry, sidelined by World War II, took a
few years to regain its bearings. With rare exceptions (for
example, the Tucker), most postwar offerings were utilitarian, uninspired affairs. By 1949, the country was ready for
some of the bold styling that had typified the thirties. Studebaker, which had begun as a carriage maker in pre-Civil War
Indiana, was at the top of its game after years of mediocrity
and also-ran status. Its popular postwar products had proved
that the public was ready for style *and* power. For model
year 1950, the company revamped its popular Commander,

creating an often imitated look that set the tone for chrome-mania in fifties auto design. The design was meant to evoke the illusion of speed, even while the car was standing still. By later standards, the cars were tank-like, but one mustn't overlook the forward pitch to the contours, sculpted rear fenders, and "fastback" rear deck. Most arresting of all was the redesigned face. New for 1950 was the distinctive "spinner," the bullet-nose chrome third eye that sprang from the car's center, between the headlights. A resemblance to the late, lamented Tucker's third headlight did not go unremarked upon, but in fact it was all part of the bomber motif Studebaker aspired to. *Commanders*, priced around $2,000, came in a variety of models, the four-doors sporting "suicide" hinging. A convertible was available as well, for those going for all out sportiness.

2.   THE KAISER HENRY J, 1951

Henry J. Kaiser was a renowned industrialist who made a fortune during the war building ships. No sooner had the radiation settled over Japan when he and automaker Joe Frazer teamed up to create a new independent company, commandeering Ford's old bomber factory at Willow Run. The concept involved twin lines of production, the more upscale Frazers and the plebian Kaisers. (With the United States having beaten Germany decisively twice in two separate world wars, the name, "Kaiser," was no longer as taboo as it might have been in less forgiving times.) Henry Kaiser conceived of a mass-production model that would essentially update the Model T: a car everyone could afford, yet one that was dependable and slightly more stylish. "Built to better the best on the road" was its slogan. To spur buzz over his pending design, Kaiser held a nationwide contest to choose a name for what he solemnly called "the most important new car in America." In a competition distinctly reminiscent of the day Dick Cheney was called in to reveal the vice presidential candidate his exploratory committee had uncovered, Kaiser announced the car's winning name to be—the Henry J.

As the Frazer line had ceased production by the time this car hit the market, Kaiser was able to dedicate itself completely to the design and promotion of economy cars, before such a term existed. Maybe a more accurate word would be "austere." These vehicles were built for anyone who merely needed transportation and didn't want to be completely embarrassed if seen in public. To that end, the model's creature comforts were few. These four cylinder, two-door cars (about the size of a Ford Pinto) lacked an opening vent window, arm rests, and a glove compartment, for starters. But they were reliable, fuel efficient, and cheap, the American equivalent of a Volkswagen Beetle. A modified version made available in 1952 through Sears (that's right—the catalog people) was called the Allstate. But car buyers of the fifties were tired of deprivation, having suffered through a depression *and* a world war. Following production of the 1955 models, Kaiser packed up and moved its operation to South America, where going without was a way of life.

3. THE CHEVROLET CORVETTE, 1953

To put it into simple terms, a "muscle car" is a little bit of automobile built around a lot of engine. Though first applied to the Pontiac GTOs, which came into being in 1964, an American car aspiring to that rough criterion arrived 11 years earlier. Chevrolet's Corvette was billed as America's "only sports car"; if that characterization was questionable at the time, it was beyond doubt by the end of the fifties, when Chevy had finally gotten all the bugs worked out. (The first *real* rival would drop off the Ford assembly line more than a decade later—the Mustang.) Powered by the "Blue Flame Six," an in-line, three-carb, 150 horsepower engine, the two-seater could do 0–60 in 11 seconds, enhanced by the lightness of its fiberglass body. For that first year only, it came in "Polo White" with a black roof and red interior. Three hundred were hand-built, and the $3,500 sticker price could easily drive one to buy a Cadillac instead. Though the Corvette was recognized as a classic in the coming years, at the time folks wondered what Chevrolet's intent was: Since the car only came with automatic transmission and an engine that wasn't exactly setting the world on fire, what was the point? The potential only hinted at in 1953 was fully realized two years later when the 265ci OHV V-8 engine superceded the Blue Flame, kicking the horsepower up to 195 and shaving two seconds off the 0–60 time. At last, the Corvette lived up to its billing.

4.   THE FORD CRESTLINE SKYLINER, 1954

It was evident to anyone paying attention that as its 50th anniversary came and went, Ford was in need of something distinctive to set apart its product. The two-speed "Ford-o-matic" automatic transmission, introduced in 1952, was duly appreciated, but it wasn't sexy. Though sales had been consistently strong, Ford products simply didn't have the buzz their rivals did—it was as if it was selling to people accustomed to buying Fords out of habit, rather than excitement for something fresh. One "better idea" the designers came up with to tart up the line was inspired by the trend for more glass. Since one-piece, wraparound windshields had become common two years before, rival automakers (Studebaker in particular) had made a selling point of their dramatically increased sightlines. With the Crestline Skyliner, Ford boldly took the next step, making the 1954 model the first car to feature a hardtop roof with an inlay of tinted glass that extended *over the front seat*. That the effect in bright sunshine was to bake the passengers didn't seem to have occurred to its designers. Still, it was a handsome devil, sporting the new overhead valve Y-block V-8 and producing 110 horsepower. Nonetheless, the public was cool to this oven on wheels, and the concept was quietly shelved in 1956, in favor of the retractable hardtop. Today, it remains the most collectible of the early fifties Fords.

5.   THE FORD THUNDERBIRD, 1954

The debate continues to this day over whether the T-Bird was truly intended as Ford's answer to the Corvette. Though the car was a *sporty* two-seater, Ford seemed distinctly ambivalent about marketing it as a "sports car" per se. After using the term in a couple of early ads, it dropped that approach and switched to "personal car." What the T-Bird excelled in was style, features, and luxury—only in 1957 did the original two-seater reach a competitive level with the Corvette in performance. The following year saw the Thunderbird recast as a boxy four-seater, something unthinkable if intended to compete with the Chevy product. Though equipped with a powerful-enough engine (a Mercury 292ci V-8, delivering nearly 200 horsepower), its looks were its real selling point.

The car seems to have had a rocky gestation period, with up-to-the-last-minute battles going on between upper management and the car's designers, centering on, of all things, whether to apply Fairlane-like chrome side trim. The result was a series of confusing publicity pictures showing an ever-evolving design. Although the model was introduced to the public in February 1954, production did not start until September, with the first cars hitting showrooms in late October, three weeks before the *1955* line was due out. From such auspicious origins did a classic emerge. Sporting a wrap-around windshield, hooded headlights, a twin-bullet-tipped front bumper, and the famous porthole rear side windows, the first Thunderbirds lived up to their European aspirations. Strange for such a small-framed car, the T-bird sported the same 15-inch tires as other Ford products, making them appear to be oversized. The removeable hard-top was standard; the optional soft convertible roof cost almost $300 extra—Ford sold more of those models to people who wanted rain insurance for days when they left the hard top at home in the garage. A 5000 rpm tachometer was also standard, as was the three-speed transmission, though automatic was offered—for more money. With a base price of nearly $3,000, the first Thunderbird reached 16,155 in production, compared to 700 Corvettes sold that year. If this was competition, in 1955 Ford smoked 'em.

6. THE CHRYSLER C-300, 1955

While Ford and Chevy jockeyed for supremacy in the "sporty" car derby, Chrysler at last warmed to the twin issues of style and power. The company realized that goal with this 18-foot beast that would effectively shut down the dust-choked competition that traveled in its wake, at least until the GTO. Before we get under the hood, though, let's see how the monster was put together. Under the auspices of designer Virgil Exner, alumnus of the legendary Raymond Loewy, the car was a two-ton, two-door example of what was called the "Forward Look"—aerodynamic but with taste and restraint. The $4,100 price tag bought a lot of luxury, including a leather interior; power windows, antennae, and seats; and air conditioning. Outwardly, an Imperial-style grille graced the forward end. But the engine was the real selling point.

The series' name was derived from the horsepower it provided: even before the advent of "new math," it was clear that the goal of one horse per cubic inch had been met by the 331ci Hemi V-8. Though featuring twin four-barrel carburetors, solid valve lifters, and 8.5:1 compression, all this power didn't necessarily translate into quickness. The two-speed automatic transmission fired up the behemoth from 0–60 in 10 seconds, covering a quarter-mile in 17.6 seconds, but the true value was the top end speed. In 1955, a C-300 virtually right off the showroom floor was clocked at 127.58 mph at the flying mile in Daytona Beach, beating the record by seven miles per hour while scarcely breaking a sweat. Its dominance in NASCAR competition in 1955 and 1956 was inevitable, where it won most races and an overall championship. The "Beautiful Brute" secured Chrysler's place as a performance force to be reckoned with.

7. THE CHEVROLET BEL AIR, 1957

The Corvette notwithstanding, Chevrolets of the early 1950s were not usually associated with youth. Instead, they were thought of as "functional, reasonably tough, and as utilitarian as a spittoon." Though dominant in the market as a reliable family car, Chevy underwent a sea change with its 1955 models, representing a seismic shift in direction for the car company in a decade that would end with Nomads, Impalas, and El Caminos to their credit. But no model captured both the imagination *and* the flavor of the decade like the Bel Air of 1957. A fresh prince indeed, this model was the culmination of three years of "hot ones" unleashed to the public, each memorable in its own right. The Bel Air imprint, marketed since 1950, underwent a complete cosmetic overhaul in 1955, catapulting this Chevy line into the fifties at long last.

The key improvement would be the small block V-8, with horsepower ranging from 162 to 180 (depending on whether one chose the four-barrel carb option, which also came with twin pipes). Lowering the body a few inches gave the illusion of increased length; hooded headlights, a Ferrari-like grille, and the signature belt-line dip all suggested a car that was, dare we say it, sporty. All the incremental improvements reached the point of payoff in 1957. Having groomed its customer base to look to Chevrolet to set the stylistic trend, the company's offering that year put it all together. Tail fins only hinted at the last two years suddenly exploded from the rear deck. The preoccupation with aviation-inspired ornamentation reached full flower, with a perky pair of twin-bullet points jutting from the bumper (say, maybe airplanes aren't the most obvious comparison after all) and what resembled a pair of chrome rifle muzzles set on either side of center on the hood. Beneath that was a powerhouse available in options ranging from the standard 185 horsepower two-barrel to a 270 horsepower twin four-barrel all the way up to a Ramjet fuel-injected 283 horsepower with 10.5:1 pistons! The Corvette engine, perfected at last, was now available in a Bel Air. To a Chevy fan, could it ever get any better?

8. THE EDSEL FIASCO, 1957

Then as now, nothing screams punch line like Ford's lamented attempt at launching a mid-priced product line in the late fifties. Indeed, given the invaluable contributions to the company that its namesake gave, it seems a pity that his name has been maligned with the taint of failure. (It is an irony of history that Henry Ford, the century's most renowned Jew-baiter this side of Adolf Hitler, gave his only son a Hebrew name, which means "from the rich man's hall"—just one more fact the old man was ignorant of.)

The most beautiful thing that ever happened to horsepower

It steals the show wherever you go—the long, clean, powerful 1958 Edsel

PDImages.com

The failure to end all failures—the much-maligned Ford Edsel.

Edsel, the man, was known for the very qualities his father lacked: good taste, artistic flair, receptivity to new ideas. The Lincoln marquee was his baby, and he ran it with great success until his death in 1943. The Edsel, available in the Corsair, Ranger, Pacer, and Citation models, was intended to fill the market niche between Lincoln and Ford. Alas, the timing couldn't have been worse, a June 1957 market nosedive signaled a recession for 1958, sending every carmaker scrambling for Bromo Seltzer and Edsel's makers casting about for a graceful exit strategy. (Something that would elude top Ford bean counter Robert McNamara 10 years later in the Vietnam War that he had architected).

All hype aside, what about the car? Had everyone not been in such a frenzy to dump on Ford, people might have seen a stylish vehicle brimming with innovations. Some of these, like the remote trunk release, would become staples in later cars. Others, like the push-button controlled transmission, located in the steering wheel hub, would cause many an owner's headache. But the most notable and distinctive feature was undoubtedly the center grille design. At a time when automakers prided themselves on some signature design (for example, Buick's side-vent holes, Pontiac's chrome strips on the hood), the Edsel's singular feature backfired, drawing much ridicule. Kind folks likened it to a horse-collar; others, a toilet seat; still others, a part of the female anatomy. Another source of derision came from the extensive test-marketing to understand what car buyers *really* wanted. The apparent insecurity of the car's makers was typified in their decision to contract *poet* Marianne Moore to come up with a pleasing name (before they settled on Edsel, much to his heirs' distaste.) Moore's contributions included the Resilient Bullet, the Varsity Stroke (this one died in committee), and best of all, the Utopian Turtletop. By any other name, the Edsel was dead meat in 1959, living on in memory as Ford Motor Company's *Titanic*—a delayed comeuppance for the crimes of the father.

9.   THE BUICK LIMITED, 1958

If all the extravagances that fifties men denied themselves in personal dress were channeled into their cars, this one would be exhibit A as the greatest reach of suppressed ostentation. The Unholy Trio of car design in the fifties entailed bullet-pointed, spherical protuberances; tail fins; and lots of chrome. The 1958 Buick Limited embodies all of these sins, meant to appeal those who believed that too much was not enough. It represented Buick's incursion into Lincoln and Cadillac territory; in fact, a comparable Caddy went for $30 *less*. Still, starting with a $5,100 *base* price, a wondrous array of perks awaited: underseat heaters, a tissue dispenser, a "Speed-minder" (an alarm warning those with lead feet to lay off), a foot-controlled radio station tuner, Frigidaire air-conditioning, and power brakes, steering, antennae, doors, windows, and seats. Furthering the car's will to power was the 364ci V-8 with a Rochester four-barrel carb, generating 300 horsepower. At 5,000 pounds, this leviathan needed all the muscle it could get, cruising comfortably at 90 mph like it was 30 mph. The standard Flight Pitch automatic transmission, coupled with air ride suspension, ensured smooth-as-silk handling on rough roads. If all this weren't enough, there was the matter of the chrome. It is said that the Limited sported more than any other American car ever made, inside and out. (The grille alone, which even had a name—the "Fashion-air Dynastar"—comprised 160 shiny little squares.) Even if this fact is unverifiable, one thing is for certain: you approached one of these vehicles head-on on bright sunny days at your own risk—the sheer dazzle effect of so much shiny steel was certain to blind you.

10.   THE CADILLAC SEDAN DE VILLE, 1959

The unchecked excesses of the decade came to full bloom with this, the culmination of Cadillac's tail fin game of brinksmanship with every other automaker. Completely restyled for the fifties' close, the entire Cadillac line sported supersized fins that rose four inches above the 1958 editions. When this particular whim started with the 1948 models, it drew upon inspiration from bomber planes. Eleven years later, jet fighters and rockets were the role models, and it showed. In addition, the car sported an orgy of chrome throughout that looked as though it had been applied with a trowel. Of course, a big car needed lots of chrome just to cover the vast expanses of empty steel—there was even a faux grille of chrome at the car's *rear*, between the trunk and bumper. In the war of ostentation, Cadillac was taking no prisoners. While going all out with glitter, the company had a certain method to its madness. Designers of 1959 models were ordered from above that, no matter what else they came up with, it was imperative that the new design allow for interchangeable front doors with other GM C-body models. This meant that rather than retool for every individual model, Buick and Cadillac saved the company money by sharing the same door.

As a result of trimming production costs with tricks like these, the base price was actually *lowered* on the more prestigious Eldorado series by a hundred bucks from the year before. For all models, the list of standard features expanded, increasing the purchaser's buying power. For around $5,000, you got power steering and brakes, windshield washers with two-speed wipers, and a vanity mirror, for starters. Extras included air suspension, cruise control, radio with rear speaker *and* remote control, and *four* cigarette lighters—two front, two back. Naturally, the de Ville, which weighed in at about a dollar a pound, required megapower. This it got from a 390ci V-8, which delivered a respectable 325 horsepower. The 1959 models represented the zenith of unfettered, free-spirited automotive gluttony. Beginning in the next model year, all stylistic abandon was reined in, and by 1965, tail fins were just a memory.

Elvis Has Entered the Building

I n reexamining the events that befell Elvis throughout the decade, one has to marvel at how quickly he went from being a talented unknown to a full-blown phenomenon. Blessed with looks, talent, motivation, and—above all—good timing, the rise (and subsequent fall) of Presley reads in retrospect as no less than a Greek tragedy. The first act of our hero's adventures unfolded with uncanny ease, as if the world parted willingly to let the golden boy through. It went something like this.

1. ELVIS VISITS SUN STUDIOS FOR THE FIRST TIME, JULY 18, 1953

It makes for a sweet story, but contrary to legend, his first foray into professional recording was motivated more by vainglory than filial devotion. Having graduated from Hume High School the month before, the ambitious 18-year-old took his first tentative step toward a career as a singer. Harboring a vague drive for stardom, the future King of Rock & Roll yearned for discovery. As his kingdom did not yet exist, the role of pop crooner would have to do. Memphis Recording Service was just the place for the aspiring to test their mettle. Run by 31-year-old Sam Phillips, the former radiator shop also housed Sun Records, Phillips's imprint for releasing recordings of his beloved gospel and R&B acts.

On the day in question, Elvis left his job at the Parker Machinist Shop and headed to his date with destiny. Clutching the battered beginner's guitar he'd been gifted at age 11, he arrived to discover the owner absent and assistant Marion Keisker in charge. Seeing the fidgety figure before her—though obviously neither hillbilly nor black, Phillips's typical clientele—Keisker demanded, "So who *do* you sound like?" "I don't sound like nobody," came his assured reply. The two sides he recorded that day were throwbacks to another time: "My Happiness" and "That's When Your Heartaches Begin." Though the signature crooning of his later Sun recordings is evident, the unmistakable fingerprint of the Ink Spots' plaintive tenor can be heard as well, jarring in its creepiness.

Without being terribly forward about his intentions, Elvis plainly hoped the studios would be so knocked out by what they heard that they would immediately offer him a recording contract. It was not to be, although the foresighted Keisker did note her customer's unique styling. Jotting down (and misspelling) his name, she wrote: "Good ballad singer. Hold." Mortified at the sound of his own performance, a momentarily disheartened Elvis presented the disc to his mother as a birthday present (albeit three months late).

2. "THAT'S ALL RIGHT (MAMA)" RECORDED JULY 5, 1954

Once his ambition reasserted itself, and undeterred that the operators of Memphis Recording Service had failed to reach out to him, Elvis began haunting the building on Union Avenue, inquiring whether any bands were looking for a singer. In time, the tenacious youth, now driving a truck for Crown Electric, attracted the attention of Sam Phillips himself. Phillips was savvy enough to recognize that white audiences chilly to the idea of buying "race records" might warm to a similar sound coming from a white man. Unsure if Elvis fit that description, he called him in to try out a project song of his called "Without You." With guitarist Scotty Moore and bassist Bill Black in support, the trio strove mightily to nail the song but without success. Convinced he might have something despite all evidence to the contrary, Phillips patiently put the boys through their paces, ordering them to run through their entire repertoire.

During a break in the session, the musicians began clowning around on an Arthur Crudup tune, "That's All Right." What began in levity as a speeded-up hoot caught Phillips's ever alert ears. He made them begin the song again, while he rolled tape, and with each pass the performance grew in confidence and verve. Finally convinced they'd hit it, he had the song pressed, backed with "Blue Moon of Kentucky," a reworking of the Bill Monroe bluegrass chestnut. Forty-eight hours after it had been recorded, the song began getting airplay on *Red Hot and Blue*, a popular late-night radio show DJ'd by Dewey (no relation) Phillips. Audience response was overwhelming, prompting the host to summon the unknown singer to the station. (The interview subtly revealed Elvis's race.) The success of this record led to four more Sun single releases, followed by invitations to appear at the Grand Ole Opry (less than successful) and *Louisiana Hayride* (thereafter a Saturday night staple). The King was on his way.

3. ELVIS MEETS "COLONEL" TOM PARKER, APRIL 16, 1955

A steady gig at the aforementioned Shreveport-based radio show assured Elvis's close contact with many of country music's famous names. Sustained by Sun's follow-up releases, Elvis found his services in demand as a support act, solidifying his reputation as a dynamite entertainer. As if being a singular vocalist with unparalleled charisma weren't enough, his wild, sexually charged performances left scarcely a dry seat in the house. The trio toured steadily throughout the South, making only one foray into a big Northern city. The New York trip ended in disappointment when *Arthur Godfrey's Talent Scouts* turned Elvis down. Still, his successes pointed to bigger triumphs ahead. The same month Godfrey snubbed him, Elvis drew the attention of one of the circuit's heavyweights. Country star Hank Snow was in a management partnership with ex-carnival barker Tom Parker. (The "colonel" sobriquet existed only as a Southern honorific; the former shill had never shouldered a weapon for his country, as his true identity would reveal decades later. Andreas van Kuijk was born in the Netherlands in 1909. Having entered the country illegally, Parker had a lifelong paranoia about authority figures. The upshot of his secret was that, unlike his peers, Elvis would never be allowed to tour outside U.S. borders, despite his enormous worldwide popularity.)

Having managed, in addition to Snow, country singer Eddy Arnold, Parker was now ready to tap into the youth market. Young Presley was just the ticket. Only in hindsight did Parker's pattern of self-serving deals and critical missteps become obvious. His MO was to milk maximum dollars out of every act before its shelf life expired, then move on. Though Memphis DJ Bob Neal had been acting as Elvis's manager, a deal Elvis signed with Parker's promotion company in August assured his eventual takeover. Playing directly to Elvis's father (over his mother's strong objections), Parker shouldered Neal aside and began filling his young protégé with visions of the megadollars their partnership would generate. In the short term, he was correct, but at an enormous artistic cost. Elvis's deal with the devil had been struck.

4. "HEARTBREAK HOTEL" RECORDED, JANUARY 10, 1956

The first of Parker's schemes to bear fruit was extricating Elvis from his legal ties to Sun Records and Sam Phillips. Though history has not looked kindly upon Phillips's decision to let Elvis go, losing millions in the process, his thinking at the time was sound enough. Sun was a small, provincial label; despite its chart success, he simply did not have the means to distribute records on the grand, nationwide scale Elvis's success demanded. Instead he sold his interest in Elvis to RCA for $40,000, funds he then poured back into his business. Figuring he still had an ace in his hole, Phillips began promoting the talent he was convinced would eclipse his departing star: Carl Perkins. (Goes to show you how wrong you can be.)

On November 20, Elvis inked an unprecedented deal with RCA, winners of the bidding war. In addition to the multiyear recording deal, Elvis received a $5,000 signing bonus which he splurged on a pink Cadillac for his mother. After reissuing the Sun sides, RCA execs took stock. Mae Axton, mother of songwriter Hoyt, was moved to pen "Heartbreak Hotel" after reading a news account of a suicide. ("I walk a lonely street," the man's farewell note read). Two days after his 21st birthday, Elvis's first RCA session was held. Not wishing to stray *too* far from formula, the recording was drenched in echo in an attempt to ape the Sun sound. The added tinklings of ivory tickler Floyd Cramer boosted the project's prestige. Unlike anything ever released on the label, the song defied easy classification. A momentary loss of nerve and effort to scrub the launch went nowhere when execs realized that they needed *something* in the marketplace. They needn't have worried. Even before events reached critical mass, the record's merits drove it to a remarkable eight weeks at number one. The "Memphis Cat" was fast becoming a national phenomenon.

5. "HOUND DOG" ON THE *STEVE ALLEN SHOW*, JULY 1, 1956

Within weeks of his first RCA single release, Elvis was given a coast-to-coast platform on the Jackie Gleason-produced *Stage Show*, hosted by big band leaders Tommy and Jimmy Dorsey. A stint of six weekly appearances solidified his position as the country's top attraction. Elvis followed this with an electrifying performance of Big Mama Thornton's "Hound Dog" on the *Milton Berle Show*, complete with a lascivious bump-and-grind coda that sent millions of adult viewers scrambling for their nitroglycerin pills. As Elvismania grew by leaps and bounds, the rising star was increasingly caught in the crossfire between teen adulation and adult condemnation of equal hysteria. Politicians, clergy, and showbiz figures decried the "immoral" corrupting influence of rock & roll in general and Elvis in particular. No less an authority than Ed Sullivan, newspaper columnist and host of the popular *Toast of the Town* variety program declared that he, for one, would never hire such filth for *his* show.

Meanwhile, renowned arbiter of good taste and white-bread cool Steve Allen watched the tempest brew and it vexed him. He, too, wished to pull in the viewers Berle's show did, but didn't want to be seen as caving in to crudity by showcasing the singer. Having Elvis on would surely grab the teens, but at the risk of alienating Allen's core audience. Shrewdly, he decided to have it both ways. He booked the singer, but with a wink to his "grown-up" fans, he decided to have a little fun at the Presley's expense. With much fanfare, he introduced "the new Elvis," clad in white tie and tails amid a set design appropriate for Shakespearean recitations, and had him perform "Hound Dog" to a top-hatted basset. Get it?!? Hound *Dog?!?* Clever stuff. (No wonder they called the man a genius.) Elvis took the ribbing with good grace, though privately was said to have felt he'd been had. Allen's fans got a good laugh, and Steverino got his ratings. Now Sullivan was the odd man out. His two biggest competitors had outflanked him, and here he was on record, squarely in the anti-Elvis column. It was time to eat crow. His people contacted Colonel Parker, and $50,000 later, a three-show deal was inked, grabbing headlines and, for Sullivan, his share of the Presley pie.

6. HIS FIRST FILM, *LOVE ME TENDER,* OPENS, NOVEMBER 1, 1956

On April 1, between all manner of recording and performing commitments, Elvis screen-tested at Paramount Studios for a possible film project. It took another five days for a seven-year, multimillion dollar contract to be signed, giving the Colonel the cash cow he'd longed for (film plus soundtrack revenue) and his young charge the shot at Hollywood he'd always dreamed of. Elvis had been styling himself after his idol, Tony Curtis, since high school, eventually dying his natural chestnut hair black and growing out his sideburns. Now at long last, his day had arrived to add the silver screen to his conquests. A post-Civil War drama, *The Reno Brothers,* was to be the starring vehicle. Starring Richard Egan and Debra Paget, it was conventional big screen entertainment, now given an added boost by the singing star of the day.

The thin plot concerned the return from the war of a soldier believed dead (Egan), who now finds his girl romantically involved with his younger brother (Elvis). Times being what they were, someone had to die, and that someone was the newcomer. Elvis's on-camera death scene as originally shot was scrapped after it horrified his mother Gladys at an early screening. A substitute ending was quickly tacked on, showing the "dead" Elvis singing the title song (with an extra verse) superimposed over a view of his grave. Four tunes were recorded for the film, including 1860s warhorse, "Aura Lee," now retooled with updated lyrics as "Love Me Tender." Despite flat singing evident in parts, the song got the nod as the standout track, compelling the film's producers to retitle the picture. With the single providing excellent cross-promotion, *Love Me Tender* premiered in New York City with a 50-foot-tall cardboard likeness of Elvis adorning the theater. Third billing notwithstanding, everyone knew whom the teens were turning out to see. (Elvis, beating wildly on a stringless guitar!) The film finished second at the box office that year, just behind the late James Dean's *Giant* in gross dollars.

7. THE "MILLION DOLLAR QUARTET" SESSION, DECEMBER 4, 1956

For decades, rock and roll aficionados speculated on the existence of session tapes that were said to feature the four biggest past and future stars from the Sun stable: Elvis, Carl Perkins, Johnny Cash, and Jerry Lee Lewis, playing together in a one-off jam. That the four might actually have done a recording together was a tantalizing dream, a much-sought-after Holy Grail. Rock has a way of mythologizing its heroes, and not infrequently, recordings no one has actually heard take on a legendary status nearly impossible to live up to. Consider as examples the *Smile* recordings by Brian Wilson or the Beatles' unissued psychedelic track, "Carnival of Light." Each has been regarded as some sort of lost master-piece when in reality, they're all more properly assessed as curiosities that have little to add to what we already know about the artist(s).

So it was with the long-lost tapes recorded at Sun that cold December evening. What they reveal is what any rea-sonable person might expect: Carl Perkins and his band had booked a session with the intent of recording "Matchbox" as their next single. Elvis, back in Memphis for the holidays, decided to pay Perkins and Sam Phillips a visit, one year after his world conquest had commenced. Present at the stu-dio that night was the newly signed Jerry Lee Lewis, whose premier single, "Crazy Arms," was about to be released. Al-ready a married man, Lewis often hung around to pick up extra income as a session player. The fourth man was Johnny Cash, but his participation is questionable. That he was eventually present is not in doubt, as once Sam Phillips realized the priceless publicity gathered before him, he phoned the local paper and had them send a photographer over. What's less clear is that Cash performed, as the evi-dence on the tapes is scant. What can be heard is a stunning array of mostly gospel tunes, songs every Southern boy could be expected to know by heart. The mood is light and jokey—Jerry Lee manages to work his newly recorded single into the jam, while Elvis counters with "Don't Be Cruel." Chuck Berry's phantom presence is represented by "Too Much Monkey Business" and numerous stabs at "Brown-Eyed Handsome Man" (revisited each time someone recalls more of the words).

Elvis is shown as he was among friends, at ease with himself and comfortably cranking out songs at the piano, without a hint of competitiveness or superiority. (Although it must be said that Perkins was initially mildly irritated to have his session disrupted. However, apparently all was forgiven with Elvis for "stealing" "Blue Suede Shoes" from its writer).

8.   SHOWN FROM THE WAIST UP ON THE *ED SULLIVAN SHOW*, JANUARY 6TH, 1957

Having witnessed the ratings surge prompted by Elvis's appearances on *Stage Show, The Milton Berle Show,* and *The Steve Allen Show* (as well as Allen's subsequent plunge in ratings following the "Hound Dog" fiasco), Ed Sullivan wasted no time in securing the performer's services for his show (by now officially retitled *The Ed Sullivan Show).* Not wishing to blow the $50,000 wad all at once, Sullivan contracted Elvis's three appearances to be spread out over several weeks: September 9th, October 28th, and January 6th. Having all too publicly declared Elvis's act inappropriate for family viewing earlier in the year necessitated considerable backpedaling, but there was a karmic price as well. Contrary to most people's collective memory, Ed Sullivan did *not* introduce Elvis at his premiere appearance; Charles Laughton did. The rotund expatriate Englishman, star of such film classics as *Mutiny on the Bounty* and the sound remake of *Hunchback of Notre Dame* (as well as director of the classic, *Night of the Hunter,* the year before) filled in that night. Sullivan was in a New York hospital recovering from a near-fatal car wreck the month before. Brilliant though he was, Laughton introduced the singer to Sullivan's audience as *Elvin* Presley.

In retrospect, it seems odd that the famous censorship by camera of Elvis's act would occur nearly a full year after all the nationwide hullabaloo over his supposed indecency began. Maybe what weighed on Sullivan by the third scheduled appearance was the incident in Florida that had occurred during the past summer. Concerned over reports of lewdness in Elvis's stage show, a juvenile court judge ordered the singer to tone down his act. In protest, Elvis stood stock-still, except for his one, wriggling finger. In any event,

Sullivan decided to take no chances and issued his infamous edict: medium and closeup shots only, waist up. It is not known whether Elvis knew about the ploy in advance. What is known is that, unlike his two earlier shows where he performed his pop hits, Elvis decided to close the show with one of his beloved gospel tunes, "Peace in the Valley." *That* had to make his critics sit up and take notice. His performance was reverent, soothing, and pious, everything his critics said he wasn't. Moved by what he had just witnessed, Sullivan decided to issue a mea culpa for all the world to see. As if to atone for his earlier pronouncements, he bestowed his blessing on the star who would never return to his stage. Elvis is, he wanted the country to know, "a real decent, fine boy . . . He's thoroughly all right." Elvis's discomfort at the compliment is evident; he looked as though he'd just received a Judas kiss before being publicly neutered and declared to be safe as milk.

9.   INDUCTED INTO THE U.S. ARMY, MARCH 24, 1958

As if to further confound his critics throughout the land, Elvis continued to do the unexpected. By the time his draft notice came in December 1957, rather than set up some sort of arrangement wherein he could do his time by entertaining the troops overseas, as so many of his peers did, he elected to serve his hitch without complaint. Anticipating a two-year tour of duty, the foresighted Tom Parker, not knowing whether time away would erode his client's audience, stepped up the pace of production with RCA's blessing. An uninterrupted flow of releases continued throughout Elvis's absence. The draftee himself laid the groundwork for his future by purchasing Graceland in April 1957, on the outside chance that his earning capacity would dry up.

While Parker cracked the whip, Elvis worked harder than ever: in addition to live appearances, he released *two* LPs in 1957, plus a Christmas album; recorded many more tracks to be issued during his hitch; and along the way completed work on his second and third feature films, *Loving You* and

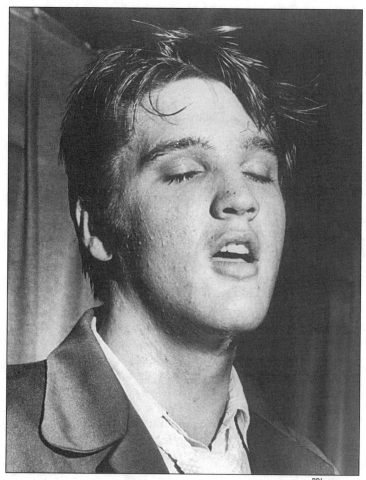

"A real decent, fine boy . . . He's thoroughly all right."

Jailhouse Rock. Never one to abandon bones when marrow might still be had, the Colonel got the U.S. Army to agree to a 60-day deferment to squeeze one more film out of the star—*King Creole*, completed on the eve of Elvis's induction. Never was a manager's 25 percent commission paid for more dearly. (This would rise to 50 percent during Elvis's last decade, a time that saw Parker's gambling addiction rival his client's pharmaceutical habit.)

Christmas saw the Presley family spend its last holiday together, newly ensconced at its Memphis digs. After performing a pair of shows in his hometown the following March, Elvis reported to his draft board. On March 25, the following day, the press followed the inductee to Arkansas, where they documented the army barber reducing his famous locks to a GI-issue flattop. The symbolic emasculation is striking. A few days later, Elvis arrived in Fort Hood, Texas, to receive basic training.

10. GLADYS PRESLEY DIES, AUGUST 14, 1958

Much has been written about the unusually close relationship between Elvis and his mother, often with the suggestion of something unhealthy afoot. Whatever the dynamic, each meant the world to the other. Elvis, sole survivor of a pair of twins delivered by Gladys, would reap the love and attention normally given *two* boys. Vernon Presley undoubtedly loved his son, too, but he wasn't exactly a role model, given his reputation as a drinker and womanizer. Chronically unemployed, he eventually did time for writing bad checks. Certainly he wished for his son to be successful, but probably not for the same reasons as his wife. Vernon was simply ill-equipped to instill in his son the boldness and initiative that the innately gifted need to succeed. It can be said that his son's success came in spite of rather than because of him.

Once Elvis settled into the routine of army life, his parents stayed close by, living near the base. But Gladys had not handled the induction of her only son well. Visions of his being called up for combat and killed on a battlefield plagued her. As always, Vernon was no help at all, spending his time making merry with the local talent. Despairing, depressed, and lonely, Gladys began to neglect her health, putting on weight, not sleeping, and doing some drinking of her own. Now that events had slowed down, it was as though she suffered a posttraumatic stress reaction to his success. She'd wanted him to succeed, but not so that he would be apart from her. The hysteria of the crowds frightened her, and with this latest change bringing the possibility of physical harm even closer, it was more than she could bear.

For months she had displayed symptoms of some vague malady: she was tired, her weight ballooned, her eyes were ringed with dark circles. Doctors diagnosed liver problems. Treatment at the hospital in Memphis was recommended, so she and Vernon left Texas in August. Once there, her condition worsened. She began speaking of a future for her son without her, insisting that Vernon find a strong woman to care for him and their son. Meanwhile, Elvis grew increasingly frantic. He hadn't wanted any undue privileges, yet he despaired of not getting emergency leave to see her. Finally, he told his superior that if leave wasn't granted in two hours, he would go AWOL. The leave came, and a special plane was chartered to bring him home. He got to spend two days with her, leaving only to sleep. Hours after Elvis's last visit, Vernon called with the sad news: "Son, she's gone." The grief that engulfed the singer could scarcely be exaggerated. His own exit at age 42, 19 years later, would mirror hers.

Music! Music! Music!

T here must be hundreds of charted songs from this decade that a high percentage of the current living population knows intimately, down to the last note. For most, their
familiarity comes from the endless exposure they are subjected to through films, TV, oldies radio, or satellite feeds.
Others may be the right age to have firsthand knowledge of
these recordings; still others may have sought them out
purely through academic interest. However you know them,
the following hits were new at one time. Before the staggering repetition of airplay squeezed every last bit of soul and
feeling from them, each had a story of how it came into
being. Here are 10 of them.

1. "GOODNIGHT IRENE" BY THE WEAVERS, 1950

It wouldn't be giving away too much to postulate that the
typical folkies of the day were somewhat left-leaning in their
politics, and the Weavers were no exception. Ultimately, it
was their outspoken attacks on injustice as they saw it that
got them blacklisted, despite their impressive hit-making
ability. Their first and biggest hit was a version of this Leadbelly song, a tune that despite its sunny harmonies and
catchy chorus ("goodnight, Irene—I'll see you in my
dreams") was deceptively dark with its allusion to suicidal
impulses.

Huddie Ledbetter's famous nickname alluded to his physical toughness, something of a necessity when so much of your life is lived behind bars. His story has been so embellished by legend that it's hard to know what's what, but the essential facts seem to be that he was sent up on a murder charge in Louisiana, but his sentence was commuted after seven years served. This "bad boy" aspect to his persona would serve him well after being "discovered" by musicologist Alan Lomax, who, when not recording Leadbelly, led him around like a trained bear among the East Coast aristocracy who were thrilled to be slumming with the talented outlaw. Though Leadbelly was quite gifted musically, it is not always clear which songs he authored and which he appropriated, but tunes associated with him included "The Midnight Special," "Rock Island Line," and "Cotton Fields." (In 1993, Kurt Cobain sang the Leadbelly song "In the Pines" retitled "Where Did You Sleep Last Night," in a sort of public self-exorcism at the close of Nirvana's *Unplugged.*) Six weeks after Ledbetter died in December 1949, "Goodnight Irene" had sold two million copies.

2. "HIGH noon" BY TEX RITTER, 1952

When it was first screened, the film *High Noon* failed to impress. The story of a go-it-alone sheriff abandoned by his allies in the face of adversity was a tough sell amid the herd mentality that dominated the public mind-set. Even worse, the man tapped to sing the film's title song balked at recording it properly for a record release. Tex Ritter (father of actor John) was a second-string Roy Rogers in the thirties and early forties. As his film career waned, he made the transition into radio and recording. Dimitri Tiomkin, the legendary Hollywood composer, scored *High Noon* and had high hopes for his title tune (known to many as "Do Not Forsake Me, Oh My Darlin'"). When Ritter turned down the composer's request to sing the song for commercial release, Tiomkin turned to singer Frankie Laine, who had enjoyed hits with "Mule Train" and "Jezebel." *His* version, released four months before the film, went on to become a million-seller, piquing interest in the movie, which would lead to its eventual success. Duly embarrassed, Ritter finally agreed to cut the song, but his version would forever be overshadowed by Laine's. Meanwhile, the tune Ritter didn't like went on to win an Oscar.

3. "UNCHAINED MELODY" BY LES BAXTER, 1955

Another song of Hollywood origin, most people associate this tune with the Righteous Brothers' version, renewed in popularity by its use in the film *Ghost* (1990). But their 1965 release was actually the *fifth* hit recording of this song and not even the most successful. Anyone at all familiar with the lyrics (karaoke, anyone?) might have wondered what the relevance of the title was to the song's content. It speaks of longing and waiting for reunion with a loved one after return from an undisclosed commitment. So where do the chains come in (besides ironic metaphor)? They come from the 1955 *prison* film, *Unchained.* Following *On the Waterfront* (1954) as one of those movie "inspired" by real-life events, the film, which featured no major stars, concerned the plight of prisoners in a California *minimum* security prison. It was scored by Alex North and used this melody as its theme. Singer Todd Duncan, who performed in the original *Porgy and Bess*, did the vocal honors. Band leader Les Baxter, taken with the haunting tune, recorded an instrumental version that immediately shot up to number one in April 1955. Holding down the number three spot the same week was a vocal version by Duke Ellington alumnus Al Hibbler. Still another performance by Roy Hamilton peaked at number six, two weeks later. (Yet a fourth version, sung by June Valli, charted two months after that.) All and all, an impressive achievement for a song spawned by a long forgotten film.

4. "AIN'T THAT A SHAME" BY FATS DOMINO, 1955

It's not often that the originator of a song and a watered-down cover of it compete on the charts. It is even less common when the song in question undergoes a name change while in release. Such is the story with what would become Pat Boone's first number one and Fats Domino's first national hit, despite the latter already having a string of gold records to his credit. July 1955 marked the showdown between the slim, white-bread crooner and the portly, earthy, piano-pounder. It also vividly demonstrated the demarcation in audience sensibilities: would record buyers opt for the smooth, polished, polite take or the spirited, rough-hewn original? Abetted by the heavy airplay and exposure allotted the pop singer, it was a foregone conclusion that Boone would best Domino in sales. However, even with an establishment artist going head-to-head with him, the Fat Man did astoundingly well, finally peaking at 16.

Little known is that the song everyone knows so well, in whatever incarnation, was renamed. As originally recorded by both men, the song was titled "Ain't *It* a Shame." Halfway through its chart ascent, the name was modified to the current title. *Why* this change occurred is unclear, but what is known is that even the revision stuck in Boone's throat—had it scanned nicely, he would have sung "*Isn't* it a shame . . . ," which rumor has it is how he introduced it onstage. There are many who lambaste Boone mercilessly for his perceived exploitation of black performers by "stealing" their hit material. Others hold that in drawing attention to these songs, white cover artists did the black originators a favor not only by introducing their work to a larger audience, but also by sending some royalties their way. In any event, Fats never complained, reliably churning out hits for the remainder of the decade. As for Boone, years later he would redeem himself among some critics by recording a tongue-in-cheek album of hard rock covers, *In a Metal Mood*, featuring on the cover the middle-aged singer in leather bondage gear—proof that not every mid-life crisis is disastrous.

5. "SIXTEEN TONS" BY TENNESSEE ERNIE FORD, 1955

Country legend Merle Travis was the son of a tobacco farmer turned coal miner. A mantra he grew accustomed to hearing his father intone daily—"another day older and deeper in debt"—would stick in his brain, eventually seeing use when the folk craze took off in the late forties. When approached by producer Lee Gillette to record a 78 rpm album of some of his "native" Kentucky folk tunes, Travis pointed out that he didn't know any. "Then write some," came the response. So Travis hunkered down, coming up with an eight-song collection entitled *Folk Songs from Our Hills*. It included one actual preexisting folk song ("Nine-Pound Hammer"), plus seven written to order by Travis, including "Dark as a Dungeon." Enter Tennessee Ernie Ford. For all his bumpkin posturing ("Bless your little pea-pickin' hearts" was his signature saying), Ford was a conservatory-educated singer and radio personality. In summer 1954, he took over hosting duties on *Kay Kyser's Kollege of Musical Knowledge*. The resulting TV exposure made him a star and led to a variety of demands on his time in addition to his TV, radio, and recording responsibilities. Lee Gillette, still in the employ of Capitol Records, Ford's label, suggested one of the Travis tunes for Ford, feeling it suited to his rich, deep voice. While running through the tune in the studio, Gillette noticed Ford's habit of snapping his fingers to keep time as he became familiar with the song. "Keep doing that," he ordered. The resulting recording of "Sixteen Tons," aided no doubt by Ford's television career, zoomed up the charts, occupying the top slot for seven straight weeks.

6. "BLUE SUEDE SHOES" BY CARL PERKINS, 1956

The rock & roll standard for which Perkins is best known was precipitated by one of those flashes of inspiration during which, no matter how unlikely the circumstance, you somehow *knew* something special was afoot—pun not intended. Carl Perkins was raised in abject poverty, and though he would end up successful enough, the lessons he learned at an early age never left him. One was that the little extravagances you allowed yourself were to be savored. To that end, a little vignette he witnessed struck home with him. When playing a dance one evening (December 4, 1955, to be exact—he never forgot it), Perkins noticed a couple dancing together near the stage. She was gorgeous, and he was sporting a pair of the highly coveted shoes made of blue suede. As they danced, Carl heard the boy caution his date: "Uh-uh . . . don't step on my suedes!" Though he could see the boy's point, he was still thunderstruck that a guy would value his footwear over a beautiful girl. That night in bed, Carl awoke at about 3 a.m. with a song idea buzzing in his head. Grabbing the nearest writing surface at hand (a brown paper potato sack), he jotted down the lyrics and went back to sleep. In a little less than three months, the song that made him immortal was racing up the charts.

7. "AT THE HOP" BY DANNY AND THE JUNIORS, 1957

Dance crazes being a pretty reliable way of drawing attention to your act, a Philadelphia doo-wop quartet called the Juvenairs sat down with their producer and a songwriter and came up with a concoction they knew would be their ticket to fame. *The* dance craze of the day was something called the Bop. Certain they were onto something, they demoed the tune, entitled "Do the Bop." At the behest of their label, the Juvenairs ditched their moniker—too evocative of "juvenile," as in delinquent. Danny and the Juniors shrewdly sought out the counsel of local rock & roll kingpin, the ubiquitous Dick Clark, and asked his opinion. He liked the tune, would dance to it if he could, and thought they had a potential winner on their hands, *but*—he cautioned them against using such a transient hook to build their name on. Once the Bop is dead, then what? Change it to "at the *hop*," he suggested. Bowing as they exited backward, they agreed. The release on Singular Records debuted late that autumn to less than stellar results. But Clark wasn't done with his benevolence just yet. In December, an act failed to appear for a taping of his *Bandstand* show; Danny and his boys being the proverbial kids down the block, they were quickly summoned, saving the day and their budding careers. "At the Hop," now picked up by a major label, went national and soon skyrocketed. Hitting number one, it remained there for five weeks, and what's more, became *the* best-selling record of the year. a sound-alike follow-up "Rock and Roll Is Here To Stay" would become their only other hit.

8. "RUMBLE" BY LINK WRAY, 1958

Though used as soundtrack fodder through the years as well as the theme song for locally produced horror shows, "Rumble" has the distinction of being the only *instrumental* single banned from the radio airwaves. Why? Because of its *title!* Radio station programmers somehow must have construed that a song with such a provocative name, and such menace to its power chords, could only spell trouble for impressionable listeners. Actually, the song was literally born in front of an audience. On July 12, 1957, guitarist Link Wray and his band, the Waymen, were playing a record hop in Fredericksburg, Virginia, hosted by actor Milt Grant. Part of the band's duties that night was to back up the Diamonds, stars of the day with their hit, "Little Darlin'." When Wray was instructed to perform a "stroll" backing to their tune, "The Stroll" (which had not yet been recorded), you might as well have asked him to perform a tarantella. Baffled by the request, his brother, who knew a thing or two, laid down the appropriate beat, and Wray, in a flash of inspiration he later described as a "zap from Jesus God," began striking a series of chords that mesmerized the assembled masses. The group would end the evening having performed what it dubbed "Oddball" four times.

Others, too, recognized that something special was happening, and the band was whisked into the studio to lay down a demo. The tape made its way to the head of Cadence Records, Archie Bleyer, who found it horrible, especially after Wray had punctured his speaker cones with a pencil in an effort to replicate the distortion he achieved naturally that night at the hop. But Bleyer's teenage daughter loved it, saying it reminded her of *West Side Story*. Caught up with inspiration himself, Bleyer renamed the track, "Rumble." Despite the ban, the song went on to sell four million copies.

9. "IT'S ALL IN THE GAME" BY TOMMY EDWARDS, 1958

Though known to most people as just another rock & roll oldie, this song has a distinction no other tune has so far matched: it is the only number one hit to be co-written by a U.S. vice president! (Though in all fairness, he wasn't VP when he wrote it—yet.) Charles Dawes was a banker and government official who dabbled in music. In 1911, he composed a tune he called "Melody in A Major." But for World War I and assorted duties under Warren Harding, he might have done something with it, but the added distraction of winning the 1925 Nobel Prize proved too much. Calvin Coolidge picked him for veep, after which he effectively retired from politics. The same year Dawes died, 1951, lyricist Carl Sigman added some words to the tune and it became "It's All in the Game." Four different versions charted that year, including one by R&B crooner Tommy Edwards. Though a fine singer with a smooth vocal style, Edwards didn't record anything during the next seven years that would approach the song's success. In 1958, just as his contract was about to expire, his label asked him to revisit some of his earlier recordings, this time to allow stereo mixes. As seven years is an eternity in the pop field, Edwards shrewdly agreed, but only if he could update the arrangement to a more current rock & roll ballad style. MGM acquiesced, and to everyone's astonishment the record bested the earlier version's charting, occupying the top slot for six weeks. Edwards never had such success again. Perhaps if he had hit up the then-veep, violinist and pianist Dick Nixon, for a tune, who knows?

10. "MACK THE KNIFE" BY BOBBY DARIN, 1959

The singer born Robert Cassoto had made it his goal to achieve greatness by age 25. This wasn't mere youthful arrogance, but knowledge of his own imperfect ticker—he'd been diagnosed with heart disease and he doubted he'd see

30. Brimming with ambition, he came into contact with the similarly hungry Don Kirshner. The two forged a partnership that resulted in contracts but few results. Finally, a deal with Atco bore fruit. "Splish Splash" made the top five, setting the performer on his way. A couple of popular but unremarkable hits followed ("Queen of the Hop," "Dream Lover"), but Bobby's desire to record something more meaningful gnawed at him. Inspired by Louis Armstrong's version, he began performing the Weill-Brecht chestnut, "Mack the Knife" as part of his live set. Although his Sinatra-like performance drew notice, even after Darin recorded it he remained uncertain of its merit. Luckily, his handlers at Atco recognized the shot at broader appeal the record could give him and pulled it as a single. The track garnered massive airplay; with kids *and* their parents picking up on his new, "sophisticated" sound, the disc camped out in the number one slot for nine weeks.

The roots of this hit went far back to another time and place. The *Threepenny Opera* premiered in Germany in 1928 and debuted in the United States five years later. Suffering from a poor translation, the show bombed, but one number, "The Legend of Mackie Messer," was singled out for special notice. Fast forward to 1954: the show, now recast with a new libretto that captured the wit of the German original, was a smash on Broadway (with a cast that included future TV stars Bea Arthur and John Astin). The dark story of criminality in 19th-century London features the bloodthirsty killer, Macheath aka "Mack the Knife." When Armstrong covered that signature tune, he evidently forgot or misunderstood the lyrics and inadvertently named the *actress* (Lotte Lenya, Weill's wife) rather than her character, whose name was Jenny. Darrin, in all innocence, repeated the error. The unlikely hit gave Darin some credibility as well as two Grammys.

Serendipity Doo-Wop

As a style within a genre, doo-wop has discernable traits that separate it from other forms of fifties tunes falling under the umbrella of rock & roll. (For those unclear on exactly what "doo-wop" is, sing the name aloud and listen. Get it? Surely everyone with ears has heard at least one song that fits that general description.) Rockabilly, Tex-Mex, and electric group sounds are easily distinguished from the street corner harmonizing that comprises the foundation of doo-wop. For anyone thinking about starting up a doo-wop revival, here are some important guidelines to help you on your way.

1. BIRD NAMES

The earliest favorite choice for groups of the doo-wop era was to pick a type of bird as its nomenclature. Why birds, one might ask? Because they *sing*, maybe. Think back on some of the biggest names of the era, and chances are they're named after a type of bird: the Orioles ("Crying in the Chapel"); the Penguins ("Earth Angel"); the Flamingos ("I Only Have Eyes for You"); the Crows ("Gee"); the Robins ("Smoky Joe's Café"—they later became the Coasters); the Jayhawks ("Stranded In The Jungle")—not to be confused with the Minnesota roots band of recent vintage, as if you would.

2. NUMBER NAMES

If the well of suitable bird names ran dry before you could get your act together, there was a suitable standby: names reflecting the number of members. Much the same way that randomly pulling a noun out of . . . the air became formulaic for bands in the nineties (Tool, Filter, Oasis, ad nauseum), so, too, did affixing an appropriate *something* after a member count become common practice in the fifties: the Five Satins ("In the Still of the Night"); the Five Sharps ("Stormy Weather"); the Six Teens ("A Casual Look"); and inverting the formula, the Jive Five ("My True Story").

3. CAR NAMES

Then there were those canny souls who might just decide to force an association with something they highly coveted: the Cadillacs ("Speedoo"); the Continentals ("Picture of Love"); the Edsels ("Rama Lama Ding Dong"); the Fleetwoods (a two-hit wonder: "Come Softly to Me" and "Mr. Blue"); the Skyliners ("Since I Don't Have You").

4. NONSENSE SYLLABLES, USE OF

Critical to meeting the established format of the genre was the use of ordinarily imbecilic language that, when sung, worked to great effect and made *complete* sense. The Monotones' "Get a Job," with its recurrent "sha na na na, sha na na na na" refrain is one example. (It also provided certain fifties revivalists with their name, but that's another story.) Another would be the haunting litany of "doo-bop sh-bop" that punctuates the verses of "I Only Have Eyes for You." Without that bit of business, what are you left with?

5. VOCAL PARTS

Tight harmonizing was key to the success of any doo-wop group, and the composition of the singers was essential to that end. Hence, a typical lineup would comprise a lead tenor (or castrato in the case of Frankie Lyman and the Teenagers, which is no reflection on Frankie—just the technical term for a falsetto singer), possibly a second tenor; a baritone, and a bass. The backup singers provided the bedrock of the group's sound, typically with ear-catching exhortations and complex sonic structures. If present, a bass singer usually had a least a small window to stand out, sometimes in intros, sometimes bridging one verse to another. Necessity being what it is, groups practiced where they could. Frequently, this meant in a bathroom somewhere; these areas of tiled walls and hard surfaces' natural echo could be used to refine and perfect the raw material that gave a group its unique flavor.

6. SUBLIMATION OF MUSIC

Even with up-tempo numbers, doo-wop wasn't about proving instrumental prowess. Your usual doo-wop number might contain a saxophone solo, but the instrumental backing as a whole was very definitely deemphasized, more than in a straight rock & roll outfit. A strong beat was perfectly acceptable, because when you think about it, these groups generally sprang from impoverished origins, where the luxury of an instrument didn't exist. Therefore, handclaps and finger snaps were the typical accompaniment for these performers—the vocals were everything. In the standard studio recording of this style, arrangements usually dictated some sort of instrumental break, which may or may not have supported some vocalizing. But the breaks wouldn't come at the expense or to the detriment of the vocal ensemble. This was not an idiom for showboating.

7. FALSETTO, USE OF

Possibly the biggest single element that the public identifies with doo-wop is the use of falsetto, which wasn't *always* present, but if it was, always made a lasting impression. Some groups included a singer who naturally could pull off this range most of the time: Frankie Lyman and Little Anthony (of the Imperials) being the two best-known examples.

Singers with that capability naturally had a short shelf life once puberty hit. Where the effect was most often used, however, was at the "tag" or ending phrase of a song. The final impression is sometimes the most lasting.

8. SYNCHRONIZED DANCE STEPS

It wasn't enough to be able to carry a decent tune; a successful doo-wop performer was also expected to perform *visually*. If you were the lead singer, you normally carried less of the burden. You could be out in front doing your thing and not worry about hitting your marks with the others. But if you were one of the four other guys supplying the backup, in addition to your vocal chores, you were expected to be in step with the others at all times. That usually meant extra time spent rehearsing the primitive (by present standards) choreography that made up the act. Also, you and your fellow performers were undoubtedly dressed in some sort of matching outfit, which you would be expected to keep pressed and maintained. Lead singers were permitted a little leeway to depart from the standard dress.

9. STRICT SEGREGATION

Typically by circumstance, doo-wop groups were comprised of neighborhood kids who grew up together. It was highly unusual for members to have come from disparate origins, unless the group came about through a forced proximity (for example, a military stint or college). Therefore, groups tended to included members of similar ethnicity: black groups were all black, Italians tended to stick with each other, and so forth. There were rare integrated groups, but these tended to have severely limited options, for one big reason: the realities of touring. Hitting the road in the South of the 1950s meant traveling in separate worlds and largely playing to separate audiences. As musicians in the Big Band era discovered, you integrated at your own risk. At best, black and white members in the same group could expect separate sleeping and meal accommodations; at worst, the offending band members would be expected to take a hike, lest the gig be canceled for the entire band. A few brave souls defied the status quo, but it usually took more clout than any one band had.

10. ONE DEATHLESS SONG

When reviewing the hit makers of the doo-wop era, one thing becomes clear: it was a rare thing for a group with one smash to follow up with another. A tiny minority managed two hits before disappearing. Although aficionados of the style will always have favorite tunes by the artists they follow, in terms of charting action, one-hit wonders were the rule. The exceptions were groups like the Drifters, who varied their style (and lineup) from record to record, or the Platters, who as careerists, had little commitment to rock & roll per se and as often as not would indiscriminately record safe "standards" from a generation earlier. The lack of longevity may be due in part to the relative youth and inexperience of the artists involved. When plucked from the street corner one day and ensconced on a tour bus the next, a certain amount of commoditizing took place, and most record labels saw you as disposable. Once all potential hit capability was thoroughly milked out, you were out on your bum with someone new to take your place. Still for many, one or two hits was enough. In time, a decent career could be had in the nostalgia market, with doo-wop groups (usually containing one original member, if that) hitting the road in package tours. For evidence of this, just check out your local PBS station during a pledge drive.

B-sides, This

As someone once pointed out, the flip side of a record was originally conceived simply to avoid the embarrassment of an artist putting out one-sided records. Whether this is true is neither here nor there—the point is, the nonhit side of a release, for time immemorial, was chiefly considered as a dumping ground. For some artists, coming up with a second recording to back the money song was an unpleasant chore; for others, it became an outlet for some noncommercial experimentation. Then there were those rare souls who, out of sheer pride, would back their hits with recordings that at least *aspired* to be as important as the A-side. In any event, the B-side was typically an afterthought. But once in a while, there existed flip sides of such shining quality that they were discovered by DJs, who would spin them *instead* of the intended hit side. This list calls attention to some recordings that, no matter what their fate, are worthy of notice.

1. "TZENA, TZENA, TZENA" BY THE WEAVERS, 1950

These folk revivalists never met an alien culture wherein they couldn't rework *some* melody to their style. When in the studio cutting Leadbelly's "Goodnight Irene," the Weavers chose to back it with a Jewish folk tune that had been "adapted" in the forties by Mitchell Parish (who seemed to have the knack for Americanizing exotic tunes, later working his magic on the Italian "Volare"). There were innumerable lyrical variations of this song, but the Weavers chose the most recent, which had been used as a sort of anthem by the newly created State of Israel. Their recording might have made a fine bonus to their classic performance on the A-side, but the phenomenal success of "Goodnight Irene" whetted the public appetite for more Weavers.

DJs flipped the disc and began spinning the celebratory sing-along, which in no time became almost as popular as the initial offering. No one was more surprised at the success of this unlikely pop smash than the Weavers themselves. Their popularization of the tune would make it a campfire staple for years to come.

2. "ROCK THE JOINT" BY BILL HALEY AND HIS COMETS, 1952

The early fifties saw bandleader Bill Haley in transition. His blend of western swing, country, and R&B, though unique, had a tough time connecting to an audience. Drifting away from the 10-gallon hats and toward the boogie sound he enjoyed would lead him to success, but he didn't yet know this. Instead, he dabbled in the new direction without completely leaving his country roots. This single, his first since burying the Saddlemen moniker, featured a weak rewrite of Hank Williams's "Cold, Cold Heart," entitled "Icy Heart" on the A-side. Backing it was the vastly superior "Rock the Joint," a ditty that truly lived up to its name before "rock & roll" as such existed. It much more accurately depicted the band's strengths, featuring both a pedal-steel break *and* a guitar solo, courtesy of studio ace Danny Cedrone, who would reprise the performance note for note two years later, to greater success. "Icy Heart" went unnoticed by programmers, who instead wisely picked up on the exciting sounds on its flip side. It went on to sell 75,000 copies, Haley's biggest success to that point. Correctly reading where the future lay, he followed up with "Crazy, Man, Crazy," this time scoring a national hit. But this would not be his last misstep in choosing single sides before he finally found stardom.

3. "THE LITTLE WHITE CLOUD THAT CRIED" BY JOHNNIE RAY, 1952

Poor old Johnnie Ray. Being deaf in one ear and sporting a humongous hearing aid wasn't a particularly time-honored tradition in show business, especially if you were a singer. And yet, this believed-to-be Native American, rumored bisexual, and emotionally charged performer dubbed the "Prince of Wails" occupied the number one pop single slot for then record-breaking 11 weeks in 1952. Though barely remembered today, to the fifties record buying public Ray was something of a former-day Leonard Cohen or a Morrissey, creating a body of work that was the very definition of depressionfest. With titles like "What's the Use," "Oh, What a Sad, Sad Day," and "Here I Am Broken Hearted," coupled with a stage show that was as emotionally draining as a revival meeting, Ray dominated the pre-rock & roll charts. But the shtick that became his trademark first surfaced here, on the flip side of his signature hit. "Cry" was written by amateur composer Churchill Kohlman, a night watchman at a dry cleaning plant. Though the Ray recording was a monster, Kohlman was said not to have liked it very much, as he envisioned his song to be treated as a honky-tonk weeper. He may have preferred the B-side, a maudlin offering penned by Ray himself about a meteorological entity that was so heartbroken at the world's seeming indifference, there was nothing left to do but weep. Moved by his own words, Ray did just that before the microphone, turning an otherwise arcane little ditty into a sob story. Like the Weavers, Ray, too, scored a double-sided hit single with his tear-streaked offering to the public. "Crying all the way to the bank" was a term custom-coined for Ray.

4. "MAYBELLINE" BY CHUCK BERRY, 1955

Here is an instance of an artist going into a studio, armed with what he expects will be the song that will put him on the map, only to find that the record company prefers his designated throwaway. Guitarist Chuck Berry had been playing with pianist Johnny Johnson's Sir John Trio since 1952, periodically breaking up their blues and ballads sets with country send-ups he'd dreamed up. White audiences took the hillbilly numbers at face value, while black ones, initially in on the joke, began to *request* them. By 1955, the band was ready to record some of its own songs. A chance encounter with Berry's idol, Muddy Waters, pointed the band in the direction of Chicago's Chess Records. There, Berry laid a smoky, self-penned slow blues tune, "Wee Wee Hours," on one of the owners, Leonard Chess. With its tin- kling keys and atmospheric vocal, it sounds like nothing else Chuck Berry would ever record, proving him to be a master of the idiom.

For the B-side, they decided to immortalize one of their "hillbilly" takeoffs, based on the country chestnut, "Ida Red." Chess, aware of the shrinking blues market, was receptive to seeing where this black bumpkin might take him. He made the second song, now renamed "Maybelline" (yep, after the cosmetics company), the plug side. To ensure its success, he brokered a deal with Alan Freed—in exchange for airplay, Freed and associate Russ Fratto were given co-credit, some- thing Berry didn't know at the time. One can speculate where Berry's career might have gone had "Wee Wee Hours" been released as planned. Might rock & roll have been denied its most important singer/songwriter/guitarist?

5. "ROCK AROUND THE CLOCK" BY BILL HALEY AND HIS COMETS, 1954

If further evidence was needed regarding the utterly clueless direction of this outfit, consider this: "Rock Around the Clock," a popular staple of the group's live show, was cut only as support for a postapocalypse R&B-style number, "Thirteen Women." The former concerned a guy who dis- covers the H-bomb has been detonated, leaving him as the sole man among 14 survivors. He blithely enumerates the ways in which the females will serve (or service?) him. Presumably, producer Milt Gabler's financial stake in the song was his primary motivation in getting Haley to squander studio time on it. "Rock Around the Clock," however, was allotted two takes at the end of the session. The first would have been the keeper, but for the Comets' habit of joining in on vocals and drowning out Haley's lead. The finished master was stitched together from the two attempts. The single was released, the first following the group's Decca signing. DJs found the A-side bizarre, to say the least, and in time began to turn it over in favor of the instantly catchy flip side. The Comets were booked on Milton Berle's popular TV show in May, finding themselves the butt of attempted comedy with an apparently inebriated old-time Hollywood actor upstaging their performance of "Rock Around the Clock" by dragging an old grandfather clock back and forth across the stage. All told, the single sold some 75,000 copies nationally—not bad, but not what was expected (ironically, matching the sales of "Rock the Joint"). The real windfall came the following year, when the film *The Blackboard Jungle* adopted the song as its theme, in turn sending the reissue all the way to the top of the charts. Nearly 50 years on, sales surpass 25 million.

6. "SIXTEEN CANDLES" BY THE CRESTS, 1958

These guys were a rare mixed doo-wop group (two black, one white, one Hispanic) that hailed from the Bronx. After releasing a pair of singles that achieved some local airplay, they cut a third, entitled "Beside You," an au courant R&B-style, harmony-laden song. Because it fit the prevailing tide at that time, the song was chosen to be the "plug" side. For the flip, the group cut a song the label had already picked out for them. "Sixteen Candles" was a little smooth compared to the local market norm, but the Crests actually liked it better. It wasn't for them to argue with their management, however. Fortunately for them, their opinion was echoed by the powerhouse DJs of New York City and Philadelphia, Alan Freed and Dick Clark, respectively. They, too, preferred the haunting birthday number and put it into heavy rotation. Other radio stations picked up on it, and an unplanned hit was launched. The only thing that might have enhanced its success was better timing; "Sixteen Candles" was shut out of the number one slot by, of all things, the Chipmunks' "Christmas Song"—who were the Crests to buck a holiday offering for kids? They never had a Top 10 record again, but their singer, Johnny Maestro, would score a number three 10 years later as vocalist on the maudlin "Worst That Could Happen" single by Brooklyn Bridge.

7. "CHANTILLY LACE" BY THE BIG BOPPER, 1958

Here's proof that DJs can be fallible in choosing hit material, even if the artist is—themselves. Radio personality J. P. Richardson, inspired in the summer of 1958 by a pair of novelty tunes from earlier that year, indulged his gift for satire by conceiving a comedic bit that would pair the two characters, the Purple People Eater and the Witch Doctor. The resulting record was entitled (what else?) "The Purple People Eater Meets the Witch Doctor." It might have stood a chance if radio programmers weren't already suffering from novelty fatigue. But what killed it in the end was the discovery of an even better flip: a randy frolic through the delights of phone sex. "Chantilly Lace" presented the boy's side of the conversation—though he's "got no money, honey," that's all right with this girl, because she *knows* what he likes. With barely contained lust, the Bopper looks forward to their 8 p.m. encounter—no further detail is needed; we know by now that the Bopper is one lucky stiff, getting some without even having to *pay* for it. "Chantilly Lace" put the Big Bopper on the map by going Top 10 that summer. Not bad for a recording done on such a low budget that the producer used *jingle bells* to simulate a ringing phone at the song's start. Bopper went on to immortality via the Winter Dance Party tour early the next year, but not before recording an album's worth of entertaining jump-swing and country-flavored tunes. In 1964, long past the point of any timeliness, Jayne Mansfield cut a reply record to Bopper's, purporting to be the *female* half of that phone call—it was called "That Makes It." Good thing Richardson never got to hear it.

8. "STAGGER LEE" BY LLOYD PRICE, 1959

On Christmas Eve, 1895, in St. Louis, Missouri, friends Bill Lyons and "Stag" Lee Sheldon, went out drinking together after work. At some point, the two got into a heated political discussion, which culminated in Lyons swiping Sheldon's hat off his head. After refusing to return it, Lyons was shot by an incensed (and armed) Sheldon, who snatched his hat back from the mortally wounded man and stormed off. From such entertaining vignettes are great records made. The story was turned into a popular song early in the 20th century, usually titled some variation of "Stack O'Lee Blues." The incident's locale changed with each telling, but the consistency was "Stag Lee" killing Bill "de Lion" after some dispute. Fast forward to the 1950s, when singer Lloyd Price was ready to stage a comeback: he'd successfully released a string of R&B singles before the Korean War disrupted his career. Once out of the service, he scored with the single, "Just Because," in 1957.

Casting about for a follow-up, he chose the similar-sounding ballad, "You Need Love." At a loss for an appropriate flip, he remembered a bit he used to perform in the Army to entertain his fellows. He had concocted a plot to go with the vague "Stagger Lee" story he'd been singing for years, enlisting some of his buddies to act it out as he sang. This worked just fine to support the money song he believed he had. Like so many others, he wasn't the best judge of his own commerciality, and "Stagger Lee" shot up the charts. This should have been enough, but industry giant Dick Clark had a problem with the song's graphic content. He couldn't very well ask his audience to judge the dance-ability of this tale of violent bloodletting. At Clark's request, Price returned to the studio to recut the tune, taking it from an "R" to a "G" rating, as it were, even throwing in a happy ending. (The two versions can be distinguished by their opening lines: the original starts "The night was clear . . . ," while the now more common remake begins "The night was *Claire*. . . ."

9.   "BE BOP A LULA" BY GENE VINCENT & HIS BLUE CAPS, 1956

One fine summer day in 1956, in a misguided attempt at a compliment that went unappreciated by its recipient, Gladys Presley told her son, Elvis, how much she enjoyed his new single. "What song is that, Mother?" he asked. "Oh, the Be Bop one. You know the one I mean, son?" "Do you mean 'Be Bop A Lula?'" "Yes, that's it. You've got another winner, son." "That's not me, Mother—that's Gene Vincent. Thank-youverymuch!" One couldn't blame Gladys for mistaking the record for a release by her son. Gene Vincent had in fact gotten his recording contract by winning a Capitol Records-sponsored Elvis soundalike contest. But in his body of work, he more than proved himself to be his own man.

The first recording sessions included the intended hit, "Woman Love." At the start of June 1956, the single was released, but before the month was up, DJs had flipped the record in favor of the song that would become Vincent's signature. "Be Bop a-Lula" would be co-credited to Vincent and his manager, Sheriff Tex Davis, but how it came to be written is in dispute. The most likely version is that Vincent co-wrote it with Donald Graves, a fellow patient he met in the hospital while he recovered from a motorcycle crash. Graves sold his rights to the song to Davis for $25.

10.   "THE TWIST" BY HANK BALLARD AND THE MIDNIGHTERS, 1958

Rock & roller Hank Ballard launched himself into notoriety with the underground success of "Work With Me, Annie," a marvelously smutty single that inspired a string of follow-ups and response tunes from others, including "Roll With Me, Henry," from Etta James and Buddy Holly's "Midnight Shift."

After the "Annie" song cycle had run its course, Ballard needed some novelty other than raunch to draw attention to his product. Whether he'd found it in the gospel-flavored "Teardrops on Your Letter" he didn't know, but to prepare it for release, he cut a disposable B-side, "The Twist." This little ditty was a reworking of a riff he'd originally lifted from a 1955 Drifters tune, "What 'Cha Gonna Do?," implemented to little success on his own "Is Your Love for Real?" in 1957. Now recycled as an up-tempo blues number, he found the solid if derivative piece of fluff utterly qualified to grace the nonplug side. "Teardrops on Your Letter" performed well, reaching number four on the R&B charts and flirting with the pop's Top 40. But the flip drew some attention also, reaching number 16 on its own merit. This did not escape Dick Clark, who thought it was the perfect vehicle to establish the portly Ernest Evans (rechristened Chubby Checker by Clark's wife, after Fats Domino). Clark's instincts proved to be correct when Checker hit number one *twice* with the song, in the summer of 1960 and again in the winter of 1962. As for Ballard, his version piggy-backed on Checker's, reaching the Top 30. It ended up as not a bad thing, for suddenly a string of dance records from Ballard began regular visits to the pop charts, something he hadn't managed doing on his own.

Rock & Roll is Here to Stay—Not!

B y the end of the 1950s, the tidal wave of innovation and creative energy that had marked rock & roll's origins inevitably petered out. The naysayers crowed that they'd been right all along, that the "fad" was a musical dead end, perpetrated by and for crude, talentless delinquents. Until the resurgence spearheaded by the Beatles would arrive several years hence, rock & roll underwent an undeniable fallow period where manufactured teen idols seemed to dominate the charts while the giants were out of the creative running. This is not to say that no classic recordings were released during this time, just that the independent artists had been marginalized while the market was co-opted by the corporate suits, eager for *their* share of teenagers' dollars. Still, such loss of momentum could be expected after the initial explosion. Given time to regroup, the next wave of artists, influenced mightily by their forebears, would soon regain control.

1. CARL PERKINS'S ACCIDENT, MARCH 22, 1956

After a pair of moderately successful singles, the 23-year-old Perkins was at last poised on the edge of greatness. "Blue Suede Shoes," his third release, represented the culmination of all his influences, and its sales reflected that fact, simultaneously racing up the pop, country, *and* R&B charts—a true crossover before the term had been coined. As Sun's first million seller flew off record store shelves, a trip East for some national exposure was in order. Booked on the *Perry Como Show*, Carl and his brothers set out for New York by car. Two days before their Saturday performance, the unthinkable occurred: clipping along on unfamiliar roads, the sleepy entourage nodded out to catch up on lost sleep. Unfortunately, so did their driver, manager Stuart Pinkham. The speeding car collided with a poultry truck and rolled down an embankment into a stream, just outside Dover, Delaware. The truck driver was killed; drummer W. S. Holland, miraculously unhurt, pulled an unconscious Carl out of the water. He awoke in the hospital three days later with a fractured skull. There he learned the rest of the party's fate: Pinkham suffered minor injuries; brother Clayton escaped with a few broken bones, but Jay Perkins had a broken neck—which led to his death two years later. Carl's recovery took a full six months, during which time he lay in bed watching helplessly as Elvis's rendition of his song stole his thunder. While Perkins was outwardly philosophical and temperate over the career setback, the trauma's damage to his soul became manifest in the coming years. He took the death of his brother hard, and with his bid for stardom thwarted, he turned to the bottle. Though he continued to release quality material, the momentum that had carried him to the brink of national success was dissipated. In time, the rockabilly sound he had pioneered fell from favor, and by 25 he'd become an anachronism. Among musicians at least, his place in rock's pantheon was assured, but as for the public, Perkins remained mostly a one-hit might-have-been. He deserved better.

2. BILL HALEY SUCCUMBS TO CHARISMA DEFICIT DISORDER, 1957

This journeyman musician just wasn't built for the stir he caused with "Rock Around the Clock." The aspiring cowboy singer spent some 10 years kicking around in various western swing outfits before settling on the name and style that put him on the map. A shift from his countrified boogie to rhythm and blues wasn't much of a stretch—1953's "Crazy, Man, Crazy" being the first result. This begat a string of Top 20 hits, notably "Shake, Rattle, and Roll." His bowdlerized 1954 version of Joe Turner's randy original demonstrated a command of the idiom, if not the lingo. Haley's innocence was evident with his assurance that he would never sing anything "suggestive"—exactly what did he think a "one-eyed cat peeping in a seafood store" was, anyway? "Rock Around the Clock" was released that same year, to fair success, but not until the following year when the film, *The Blackboard Jungle*, used it in its opening did the song explode. The resulting public demand for live performances gave America its first glimpse of the record's unlikely perpetrator—an aging, portly, spit curled professional, hardly inspiring to a generation poised to rebel. Still, the masses gamely accepted his follow-ups, "Razzle-Dazzle" and "See You Later, Alligator" among them. Even a film built around his career-defining hit did good business (although it finds him upstaged by a comely dancer throughout).

Haley and His Comets were sustained until the Memphis Cat exploded on the scene in 1956. From then on, no amount of sax solos and standup bass tomfoolery could spark the adrenaline Elvis so effortlessly commanded. Haley's last trip to the Top 20 was a juked-up version of "When The Saints. . . ." Defections from the Comets sapped their already diminished energies, and in trying to recapture their audience, Haley and his boys released an increasingly odd string of concept albums, ranging from rocked-up standards to instrumentals to songs featuring girls names (the last titled *Bill Haley's Chicks*, man!). Only in England could they still find audiences willing to party like it was 1955. Haley lived out his days embittered and paranoid, in a home with the windows painted black, before succumbing to a heart attack in 1981.

3. *AMERICAN BANDSTAND* GOES NATIONAL, AUGUST 5, 1957

Beginning in 1949, Philadelphia DJ Bob Horn hosted a popular radio show for teens. In this prerock era, his show offered an eclectic mix of pop singers, big band, and even some R&B. Three years later, publisher/media mogul Walter Annenberg decided to add an after-school dance show to WFIL's television lineup. After an initial tryout comprising record spinning and primitive music videos tanked, the show was retooled, adapting the format of a local radio program by bringing on teens and soliciting their opinions. The formula proved winning when it became clear that the youthful dancers were the real stars of the show. Viewers tuned in regularly to learn new dances and see their favorites. *Bob Horn's Bandstand* was a smash, but unfortunately, its host—a married man in his 30s who looked older—proved expendable following a series of drunk driving arrests and charges of too much intimacy with some of his female dancers. Enter Dick Clark, the eternally youthful 26-year-old who'd spelled Horn during his absences. Possessing an on-camera ease and a natural rapport with teens, the former disc jockey was a good fit. The fact of his near complete ignorance of rock & roll didn't particularly daunt him. Unlike for Freed, the inability to tell genius from garbage simply meant that the playing field was now leveled. Partial to crooners over authentic rockers, Clark gave made-to-order "singers" like Fabian, Tab Hunter, Frankie Avalon a tremendous platform and unprecedented exposure, leading in turn to overnight stardom. Performers chosen for their good looks over their ability became the rule, and the show's influence in creating careers could not be overestimated. The situation would repeat itself in 1981 when MTV hit the airwaves. An entire decade's worth of popular music was dictated by the most camera-friendly singers, and if you were videophobic or ugly, you may as well forget about stardom. As much as purists decried the situation, bad precedent had been set more than two decades before.

4. LITTLE RICHARD FINDS GOD—IN *AUSTRALIA!*, OCTOBER 10, 1957

Richard Wayne Penniman of Macon, Georgia, was a divided soul. Like his contemporary Jerry Lee Lewis, Penniman had been raised a God-fearing child of the church, yet a key part of his being was being claimed by the devil—the piano-pounding part. Add bisexuality to his burdens, and you have a man destined to hit a wall. As Little Richard, his outrageous persona and high-camp stage act came to define rock & roll's innate perversions. A flamboyant black man sporting a pencil-thin mustache *and* eyeliner was bound to attract some notice. This, coupled with a sound unmistakably primal in its inarticulate urgency, gave listeners as much cause to be repelled as attracted. By the summer of 1958, he had recorded a string of classics: "Tutti-Frutti," "Lucille," "Long Tall Sally," and "Rip It Up," among others. He had even appeared in several films, including performing the title song in *The Girl Can't Help It*. He was at the top of his game, yet something dark lurked beneath the pancake makeup.

In autumn 1957, Little Richard led an entourage that included Eddie Cochran and Gene Vincent to Australia. His popularity down under was unmatched, as out-of-control audiences caused near riots. (At Newcastle Stadium, a crowd inflamed at his stripping off articles of clothing dragged him over the footlights and onto the floor, as if to help him disrobe.) His deep internal divide finally surfaced in Melbourne a few nights later. At an outdoor concert, the sight of the newly launched Soviet satellite Sputnik in the night sky pushed him over the edge. Convinced it was a harbinger of the coming apocalypse, Penniman then and there announced the end of his rock & roll career. When his veracity was challenged, Richard peeled off $8,000 worth of jewelry and pitched it into Sydney's Hunter River. Back in the States, he announced his conversion to the Seventh-Day Adventist Church, and in January 1958 enrolled in the Oakwood Theological College in Huntsville, Alabama. That should have settled things definitively but it didn't. Specialty Records continued with business as usual, making "Good Golly Miss Molly" his next hit. His audience wasn't quite prepared to move on just yet. Richard stayed immersed in his Bible studies, taking time out only to record a series of gospel albums (the last one produced by Quincy Jones). Eventually, the pull of the secular world proved to be irresistible. In 1962 he attempted to reignite his career by touring in Europe, still a stronghold for fans of fifties rockers. Five years nearly to the day he had turned his back on his fame, he found himself headlining a five-and-a-half-hour extravaganza at the Tower Ballroom in England. Second-billed were some up-and-coming locals who had just released their first single, a little ditty titled, "Love Me Do." So it was that the torch was symbolically passed from one generation of rockers to another.

5. ELVIS PRESLEY IS INDUCTED INTO THE ARMY, MARCH 24, 1958

It is beyond argument that the most vital, enduring, and groundbreaking work Elvis ever did was in his pre-Army, Sun/early RCA years. It was also the era of his greatest influence. Never again in any incarnation did he exert so tremendous a sway on his peers. Henceforth, instead of leading trends, he followed them. (Had he survived another year or two, "Disco Hound Dog" would surely have become a reality.) This is not to say that the remainder of his recorded work was entirely valueless. In his much-ballyhooed 1968 comeback special, for example, he showed that given an opportunity and a challenge, he could rise to the occasion and shake off the Hollywood-induced stupor that informed the bulk of his film work. But surrounded by sycophantic lackeys, and with his career in the hands of a sideshow shill, it was beyond even Elvis's formidable command to pull out of the creative nosedive that began with his military service. Upon his return to civilian life, he marked his reintroduction to the public by dueting before a nationwide audience with renowned rock & roll hater Frank Sinatra. His frantic stage persona was mothballed as he entered into the ennui of assembly-line film production, churning out more than two dozen 90-minute commercials for anemic soundtrack albums. Too much of a professional to rock the boat, he amiably laid down vocals on whatever dreck was put before him, culminating in such classics as "No Room to Rumba in a Convertible" and "Do the Clam." The rock & roll animal that blindsided a generation in 1956 was gone for good. The death of his mother six months into his hitch, coupled with a taste for amphetamines cultivated while stationed in Germany, led him down a path best characterized by the malignancy upon his psyche. All that followed led to the King meeting his end, fittingly, on his throne. It would be left to former Beatle John Lennon to articulate what the cognoscenti had known for years. When pressed for a comment on the passing of his one-time idol, Lennon acidly remarked, "Elvis died when he went into the Army."

6.   JERRY LEE LEWIS RUINS HIMSELF, MAY 1958

Having proved himself on equal footing with Elvis at home, Lewis was set to carry his brand of showmanship abroad in person, something Presley could never do. Instead, it all blew up in his face when word of his marriage got out (see page 268). Following a disastrous reception in England, Lewis returned home to a country he didn't recognize and found himself a pariah overnight. Bookings were canceled, radio stations wouldn't touch his records, and he was held up as exhibit A in support of rock & roll's inherent iniquities. Momentarily speechless, he took out a full page ad in the trade papers, expressing hope that his fans wouldn't leave him over his current troubles. To no avail: with the fickleness of youth, kids found other performers to pledge their allegiance to, and Lewis was left to ponder the deep running conflicts within his nature that compelled him to pursue the path leading most directly to his own self-destruction. Though convincingly out of the running, Lewis could never completely shake off a sense of competition with Presley.

In 1961, with Elvis by now safely declawed and fixed, Jerry Lee still apparently viewed him as competition, although in career terms they were in different leagues. He released a bizarre single, "It Won't Happen with Me," in which he listed *by name* those whose love he could best: Elvis, Jackie Wilson, Fabian, and Ricky Nelson. In 1968, when Elvis was attempting to recast himself as a vital performer on television, Lewis cannily played up his bad boy image by portraying the Shakespearean villain Iago in a rock & roll treatment of *Othello* titled *Catch My Soul*. By the following year, with his segue into country music complete, he regained his artistic footing. "What Made Milwaukee Famous Made a Loser Out of Me" became a hit (though one wonders if buyers were surprised to discover it concerned drinking, not pedophilic incest). Lewis's talent for grabbing headlines never left him. Apart from the numerous tragedies that dogged him (two sons *and* two wives died prematurely) and assorted health scares, his most memorable moment in the news concerned a certain night in November 1976. Memphis police pulled him over for speeding and driving erratically. Though clearly drunk, he was let off with a warning. Within hours, police were called to Graceland, where Lewis had crashed his Cadillac into the gates and, waving a gun, demanded to see Elvis. This time he was led away in handcuffs, while inside, the King—doubtless aided by the contents of his medicine cabinet—remained blissfully unaware of anything awry.

7. BUDDY HOLLY DIES, FEBRUARY 3, 1959

All myth-making aside, it is nearly impossible to overestimate Buddy Holly's influence on all that followed. On every level, he inspired the legions tracing his footsteps, be it for his songwriting, his do-it-yourself methodology, his rock band blueprint (bass, drums, lead and rhythm guitar), or for making geekiness acceptable, even attractive. Holly was purposefully progressive with every recording, changing styles at his own commercial risk. This very unpredictability stalled his chart progress, setting him on the path that led to his own end. Giving the devil his due is necessary to understand Holly's career. The hit-making capacity he enjoyed with the Crickets was due in part to the production of Norman Petty. As producer, Petty gave free reign to Holly's fancies, allowing such unusual instrumentation as a celesta ("Everyday"), slapped thighs (also "Everyday"), a cardboard box ("Not Fade Away"), even full orchestration ("True Love Ways"). Experimentation didn't frighten him, and Petty and Holly's collaborations bore fruit. Where the deal went bad was with the price Buddy paid for such freedom. Petty also acted as manager and had power of attorney as well. His control of Holly's business interests was complete; all earnings were paid to an account he alone accessed, and the boys lived off an "allowance."

As Buddy grew in savvy, he chafed at the controls put upon him, gradually coming to see Petty's grip as restricting. Wishing to put the small-town limitations of Clovis, New Mexico, behind him, Buddy set his sights on New York. When push came to shove, his fellow Crickets sided with Petty, leaving Buddy to strike out on his own. Undeterred, Buddy continued to follow his muse, but hit records were getting scarcer. With so many of his songs familiar to us today, it's hard to believe that he had scored only one number one (and two Top 10s). The final single released in his lifetime, "It Doesn't Matter Anymore," alienated some with its air of pretension—string arrangements and the complete absence of guitar. At loggerheads with Petty over control of his finances and with hits hard to come by, Buddy felt he had no choice but to hit the road in the dead of winter to generate some cash flow. Signing onto the Winter Dance Party tour, he traveled the frozen Midwest during particularly rough conditions. In the end, exasperation with an unreliable bus compelled Buddy to charter a plane to make up some sleep and catch up on laundry, with devastating results.

8. THE PERSECUTION OF ALAN FREED, NOVEMBER 26, 1959

Having reached the height of notoriety as rock & roll's best known (self) promoter, by 1957 the thirty-six-year-old DJ Alan Freed had seen the top of the mountain. It was all downhill after that. His nationally aired dance show was canceled that summer, following outrage in the South when Frankie Lyman was shown dancing with a white girl. The following spring, a show in Boston ended disastrously when an overcapacity crowd broke into fights. The resulting melee and property damage resulted in Freed being charged with inciting a riot. Similar occurrences followed, despite several cities banning rock & roll shows. With more harassment to come, mounting legal bills ensured Freed's financial ruin. In 1959, when the congressional investigations into payola began, Freed's employers at WABC began to feel the heat. Seeking to indemnify themselves, or possibly just rid themselves of an asset that had become a liability, they asked to Freed to sign a statement declaring that he had never accepted payment to play a record. His predictable refusal justified their termination. With his empire crumbling around him, Freed maintained a righteous posture. Though a man of many flaws, principle was with him (particularly when being charged with a crime not yet illegal). Beset on all sides and judged unemployable, he began drinking heavily. By the time the whole sordid business reached a climax, Freed and his lawyers were ready to throw in the towel. In 1962, he pleaded guilty to the charges, receiving a suspended six-month sentence and a fine. The law wasn't quite done with him yet, however. Next, the Internal Revenue Service weighed in with tax evasion charges for underreporting his income due to added financial kickbacks. Before the penniless Freed could answer the indictment, he entered a Palm Springs hospital and died shortly afterward in January 1965. He was 43.

9. CHUCK BERRY IS ARRESTED, DECEMBER 21, 1959

An undeniably intelligent and articulate man, Chuck Berry was the closest thing rock & roll had to a poet laureate in the 1950s. Not for him the baby talk of "A-womp-bomp-a-loobop-a-womp-bam-boom"—he didn't want to be anyone's teddy bear, and little Suzy dozed beside him at the drive-in at her own risk. No, Berry was that rarest of things—a superb and innovative musician gifted with an instantly recognizable style and a talent for literate lyrics filled with humor and wordplay. His insightful observations neatly encapsulated the American teen experience—not bad for a married man whose first hit record came in 1955 at the age of thirty. No callow backwoods farm boy, he; Chuck was all growed up. Couple all of these qualities with a black skin and that certain air of confidence once called "uppity," and you'll find your-self marked. In addition to his red hot streak of teen anthems ("Johnny B. Goode," "Roll Over Beethoven," and "Sweet Little Sixteen," to name a few), his profile was raised further by his films and by his frequent headlining concert dates. The ubiquitous Mr. Berry even found time to open a club near his native St. Louis. Like his onetime mentor Allen Freed, high visibility coupled with carelessness led his ene-mies to seize the opportunity to bring him down.

Their chance came in the fall of 1959, when Berry crossed paths with a young Apache woman who happened to be a fluent Spanish speaker. In a moment of entrepreneur-ial insight, he saw her as just the person he needed to coach him in the language. He brought her from El Paso to St. Louis, employing her as a hatcheck girl at the club. But after two weeks he decided her skills were lacking and fired her. She was apparently able to parlay this career setback into a business of her own, operating out of a local motel. Authori-ties busted her for prostitution, but upon learning she was only 14, arrested her benefactor. Berry was charged with vi-olating the Mann Act, an ancient edict making it illegal to cross the state line with a minor for "immoral purposes." He had already done jail time as a teen, and following a more recent arrest for carrying a gun, the law was in no mood to cut Berry a break. He was convicted *twice*—his first conviction was vacated due to the judge's flagrant race-baiting—and in 1961 was sentenced to three years in prison.

Being taken out of the game at the height of his powers embittered Berry for life. Though he would again tour and release a few more singles, the damage was done. One of the first was "No Particular Place to Go," which evidently he'd forgotten he'd already recorded under the title "School Days" seven years before. (The latter, contrary to public perception, was written *before* the prison experience, despite containing the line "the guy behind you won't leave you alone.") Bizarrely, the only number one of his entire career came in 1972: a surreptitiously recorded stage performance of a schoolyard ditty extolling self-love, "My Ding-a-Ling."

10. THE RISE OF THE BRILL BUILDING, LATE 1950S

What exploded onto the cultural landscape in 1955 had sprung more or less spontaneously from any number of musical channels, primarily rural, Southern, and poor. Rock's earliest practitioners had been amateurs or low-level professionals—the real pros were still immersed in pop or jazz. However, once the new style began to show some staying power and the tidal wave that was Elvis demonstrated the fortunes that could be generated, the business world began to take notice. In the fifties, ground zero for this industry was contained in a structure located at 1619 Broadway. The Brill Building housed an entire stable of professional songwriters, music publishers, arrangers, demo singers, and virtually anything and anyone else needed to jump-start a career in popular music. Musicians were in residence; song-pluggers, radio contacts, and promoters were all within easy reach. When applied to rock & roll, the Brill Building gestalt could be summed up thusly: youthful rebellion commoditized, packaged, and sold back to the teens, to the tune of millions.

It should be emphasized that not every Brill Building product was entirely bloodless and mercenary. On the contrary, many rock classics were created through this system. What *is* notable is the pure business, assembly-line churning out of material specifically produced to capitalize on an existing market. (Its blueprint would not go unnoticed in Detroit by one Berry Gordy, Jr.) Control was shifted from the artist to the producer and songwriter, who, besides Buddy Holly, was rarely the same individual. Singers were tools implemented to present a song to its best advantage. Brill Building alumni would prove key in shaping the musical landscape in the next decade: Neil Diamond, Neil Sedaka, Jeff Barry, Ellie Greenwich, and the husband and wife teams of Gerry Goffin/ Carol King and Barry Mann/Cynthia Weil. One figure with less discernable gifts was Don Kirshner. His ear for commercial potential, eye for raw talent, and shrewd business dealings enabled him to cash out in five years for $3 million. (Later credits included the Monkees, the Archies, and in the seventies, *Don Kirshner's Rock Concert.*)

The effect of the Brill Building formula was to ramrod considerable muscle into promoting singers who were unremarkable and interchangeable. With rare exceptions, most of the resulting records were dispensable, formulaic fluff— musical junk food. With the market now so tightly controlled by such interests, and headquartered largely in Eastern urban centers such as New York and Philadelphia, what chance did someone from the sticks with genuine originality and freshness have?

Somewhere There's Music

S tardom in the acting world and its attendant arrogance can lead to a false sense of invincibility. Just because one *apparently* has mastered the skill of reciting someone else's words on camera and has learned to hit one's marks at the right time, doesn't necessarily mean that the world is clamoring to hear their musical talents. Occasionally, the successful thespian will come along who actually does possess some musical ability, but for every Sissy Spacek, there's a Don Johnson *and* a Bruce Willis. (And the reverse sin is certainly true—musicians attempting to act famously fall on their faces more often than not.) Granted, often a hot actor, usually a lucky lightweight, is rushed into a recording studio transparently to capitalize on the public's insatiable desire for *more*, without being too particular about what that *more* is. But far too often, success in one medium gives a star license to enact musical pretensions before a bewildered public. (Billy Bob Thornton, anyone?) With luck, these detours will be forgotten, if not forgiven. Here are some aberrations from the fifties. Be kind.

1. GLORIA SWANSON, *BOULEVARD!* (SONGS FROM THE 1957 MUSICAL)

This silent screen siren pulled off one of the more remarkable comebacks in film history as the unforgettable Norma Desmond in Billy Wilder's *Sunset Boulevard* (1950). Pity was, she didn't know when to stop. Buoyed by her nomination for an Academy Award for best actress (her third and unsuccessful), Swanson did what anyone with the means would do to seize the moment—in 1955, she commissioned a couple of Brits to create a *musical* treatment of her star turn to take on the road. Years before Andrew Lloyd Webber, the first Broadway-bound (she hoped) adaptation of the film classic was created in 1957. Believing she had Paramount's blessing, the showbiz veteran with just one singing role to her credit (and that 20 years earlier) opted to reprise her lead and thus handle the lion's share of vocal chores. Just turned 60, she gamely trotted out a preview on the *Steve Allen Show*. Those who loved the film were aghast, if not by her Cruella DeVil vocal stylings, then by the fact that the black comedy's original ending had been turned on its head, into a feel-good closer. This sat well with neither the film's creators, nor the studio, which had an eye to reissuing the original film. In these days before cross-promotion, they felt Ms. Swanson's musical would undermine their plans. Much to her shock and dismay, they pulled the plug on the project. Eventually, an LP of her performance was released quietly years later, the only documentation of the musical that never was. *Sunset Boulevard* proved to be the peak of her comeback, with only minor film roles and TV guest appearances left to her. Her lowered profile must have come as a relief to Joe Kennedy, who 30 years before had engaged in a torrid affair with Gloria and was not eager to have her resurface just as his son's political capital was rising. They'd dodged a bullet, but just for that day.

2. BETTE DAVIS, *TWO'S COMPANY* (ORIGINAL CAST RECORDING, 1953

It's hard to imagine what could possibly motivate a stab at Broadway from someone whose very speaking voice could curdle milk. But hubris knew no bounds when it came to Mother Goddamn, when in 1952, with the success of *All*

About Eve behind her, Bette Davis decided to turn her talents to a sketch comedy-musical entitled, *Two's Company*, co-written by Ogden Nash, Vernon Duke, and Sammy Cahn. (Perhaps all the backstage drama of her film role whetted her appetite to tread the boards for real.) Though surrounded with seasoned musical pros who would be expected to do most of the musical heavy lifting, the fact of Ms. Davis's vocal shortcomings in so prominent a role was apparently justified by her undeniable star power. Perhaps the show's producers were banking on the goodwill she'd generated throughout her career (!) as reason enough for audiences to be forgiving. The show opened in December 1952—showbiz lore has it that Davis fainted upon making her first entrance. "I've fallen for you," was her quick-witted ad lib before she began to warble a tune titled, "Turn Me Loose on Broadway." (Audiences may have expressed similar sentiments once she opened her mouth to sing.) The expected goodwill never materialized; scathing reviews greeted every road performance, and though the crowds still turned out (they'd obviously never seen a train wreck), the production quietly folded in early March 1953—ostensibly due to a tooth abscess Davis was suffering. Seems her mouth was generating pain in every direction.

3. ART CARNEY, (VARIOUS 45S, 1950S)

To the record-buying public of the 1950s, television star Jackie Gleason was well known for his excursions into the world of make-out music. His *Honeymooners* wife, Audrey Meadows, was likewise a veteran of musical theater. It therefore should come as no surprise that Art Carney, too, caught the bug for making music, but he wisely stayed in character rather than exceed his artistic grasp by actually attempting to sing. Most of his recordings consisted of narrations to children's stories, such as *Song of the South*, as well as some holiday offerings. However, he also waxed a series of novelty singles that fully articulated the Ed Norton experience in a way that television could not. One of them was a ditty titled

"Song of the Sewer," in which, as "Norton," he explains in so many words how he came to find himself in subterranean sanitation. The flip side offers a glimpse into Ed as a player—"Va-Va-Va-Voom," his come-on to the ladies he works beneath daily (so to speak). An even better release was "Sheesh, What a Grouch!" in which the narrator enumerates the latest string of annoyances he's inflicted on others and complains that he's being judged too harshly. A neat little three-minute *Honeymooners* theater of the mind—it's too bad these audio gems are so hard to find today. (Of course, a full album's worth might be a little hard to take.)

4. MARLON BRANDO, *GUYS AND DOLLS* (ORIGINAL CAST SOUNDTRACK, 1955)

In the most curious musical pairing until Clint Eastwood and Lee Marvin showed up for work on the set of *Paint Your Wagon*, Marlon Brando and Frank Sinatra found themselves signed to film the screen version of one of Broadway's most successful shows. Imagine everyone's surprise when the meatier role of Sky Masterson went to Brando, instead of to proven crooner (and certifiable bad boy) Sinatra! Instead, Ol' Blues Eyes was relegated to second lead Nathan Detroit. Brando, chosen for his box office appeal rather than his vocal talent, ended up performing the show's best-known tune, "Luck Be a Lady." "Performing" is the operative word here, because despite his protests that he was no singer (demonstrably true, as it happened), director Joseph Mankiewicz insisted. It took considerable time and splicing to patch together usable takes from all of Brando's attempts to nail the song. Meanwhile, Sinatra cooled his heels in the background, knocking off in a take or two the novelty tunes his role required. Although in no position to quarrel at that point in his career (he was, after all, still rebuilding after a fallow period), he let no one forget the musical snub, turning "Luck Be a Lady" into his own song in 1963. As for Brando, with many, many more embarrassing roles ahead, at least he wisely steered clear of musicals.

5. ROBERT MITCHUM, *CALYPSO . . . IS LIKE SO . . .* (LP, 1957)

For Hollywood tough guy Mitchum to have taken it upon himself to record an LP's worth of third world ditties may seem uncharacteristically whimsical at first glance, but this was no mere pipe dream for the convicted dope offender. As the liner notes had it, Mitchum developed a love for island music while on location in Trinidad. The fact that calypso (as embodied by Harry Belafonte) was all the rage in America at the time certainly couldn't have hurt his chances for a record deal. Despite what you might think, the album is an unexpected pleasure. Mitchum displays as good a command of the idiom as any Connecticut-born Caucasian can and is hardly the embarrassment one might expect. One can readily hear why an outsider would be taken with these engaging, ribald tunes. (Of course, since it was the fifties, Mitchum's versions were cleaned up considerably from the originals, but still. . . .) Though the kitsch factor is inescapable (Mitchum cannot refrain from "authentic" native phrasings like "dis" and "dose"), the musical backup is mightily impressive. Oldies fans might recognize the second cut, "From a Logical Point of View," as an earlier, rawer version of Jimmy Soul's 1963 hit, "If You Want to Be Happy." Capitol's high hopes for the album included releasing a single, "What Is This Generation Coming To?," a bewildered response to the kids and "dey rock 'n' roll." Its chart "failure" meant no calypso follow-up album from Mitchum, but he didn't give up music entirely. In 1958, he scored a minor hit with the theme to his film *Thunder Road*. An album's worth of what might be best described as "adult contemporary" tunes graced his 1967 release *That Man, Robert Mitchum, Sings*—the title tells you all you need to know. Amazingly, all of his recording studio output is readily available on CD.

6. JACK WEBB, *YOU'RE MY GIRL* (LP, 1958)

If anyone in the fifties had polled the public on which celebrity it would *least* expect to find gracing an album of romantic love songs, a good guess would place this man at the top of the list. So strongly was he identified with the role of Sergeant Joe Friday in *Dragnet* as the no-nonsense, hard-boiled cop, few suspected that Webb possessed any other emotions (although for the record, he plays a convincing dork in *Sunset Boulevard*.) So what can we expect from an LP of smooth grooves bearing his name? (And sporting a cover photo of "Jack Webb—the casual look": open collar, no tie, lit cigarette, wistful smirk, and with what appears to be a *ballerina* behind him!) To the great disappointment of kitsch aficionados, our boy does not sing. Instead, he "recites" the lyrics to a dozen pop standards over a bed of lush orchestration conducted by Billy May. The songs cover the range of romantic fervor, from "You Are Too Beautiful" to "You've Changed." Perhaps in his own way, he was seeking catharsis, having racked up two marriages by this time (including one to singer Julie London) and was about to embark on the third (to the first Miss USA, Jackie Loughery) of four. The liner notes offer another reason. Penned by writer Jim Bishop (author of *The Day Christ Died* and *The Day Lincoln Was Shot*; similar tomes on JFK, FDR, and Martin Luther King would be added to his credits, bolstering his credentials as a man who recognized tragedy when he saw it), who describes a man who "cannot sing a lick," but "yearns to be part of the world of music." Since Webb's accomplishments to that time included acting, producing, and directing, becoming a roadie was out of the question. This album presents the culmination of that yearning, as he presents a side of himself seldom seen in public: that of the deadpan poet. "Romantic Reflections," his credit reads. While there was no shortage of bittersweet ramblings over soft music in the fifties (remember Franklin McCormick?), what ultimately undermines this work is that Jack Webb is too known a persona. To hear him advise listeners to "Try a Little Tenderness" provokes nothing less than hilarity. One can admire his bravado in even attempting the project, but as a similar one-note Johnny would point out one day, a man has to realize his limitations.

7. HUGH DOWNS, *AN EVENING WITH HUGH DOWNS* (LP, 1959)

Though mostly known to younger viewers as the one-time co-anchor of *20/20*, Downs's history in television goes back to the forties, when he began as an announcer on *Kukla, Fran and Ollie*. His career usually involved hosting or announcing duties, with the occasional network news stint. Altogether, the image of a serious, responsible citizen emerges. So it seems somewhat jarring to find this same sober, no-nonsense grown-up strumming away at a guitar on an album jacket that proclaims, "Hugh Sings." (A similar effect might be had from a photo of Peter Jennings behind two turntables and a microphone emblazoned with "Peter Jams.") Not that anyone expects to hear "Blister in the Sun"—the album is in fact comprised of pretty much what you would guess: slow, folksy, ballads, with the odd introductory lesson thrown in. It is by no means awful, just vaguely disquieting. Unlike, say, Jack Webb's, Downs's performances are not particularly funny. He is too competent and earnest for any latent campiness to emerge, and he comes off no worse than the average guitar-brandishing folkster people are routinely subjected to at school, camp, or church—an inspired amateur. At least he steered clear of "Kumbaya."

8. WILLIAM FRAWLEY, *SINGS THE OLD ONES* (LP, 1958)

Hard to imagine that the actor best remembered by the public for his seamless personifications of crusty old codgers was once a viable vaudeville song-and-dance man. Doesn't say much for vaudeville, does it? Nonetheless, regular viewers of *I Love Lucy* were periodically treated to the old man's withering talents, as the scripts allowed. Given the tenor of the show's often mean-spirited humor, it's a wonder these musical diversions were ever taken at face value and not as a punch line to an insult. (It must be said in all fairness that similar attempts at night club entertainment periodically mar the otherwise perfect *Dick Van Dyke Show*.) Clearly, corn-ball stylings were Frawley's passion, and if you were the co-star of the hottest show on TV in the twilight of your career, wouldn't you want to recapture a taste of your salad days for public regurgitation? No? Okay, well Bill did, and with mo-tive, means, and opportunity at his disposal, he cut this LP for Dot Records, backed up with authentic vaudevillian arti-fice (banjo, ukulele, barbershop quartet). If your taste runs to arcane popular entertainment, and with minstrel shows being hard to come by, it can be said that this work is not bad. The real pity is that no visual record exists of the per-formances included here—it might be charming to see the old coot trot out a little soft-shoe routine or work that cane and straw boater like great-great-Grampa used to.

9. TONY PERKINS, "MOONLIGHT SWIM" (45, 1957)

Had Tony Perkins not become forever typed as Norman Bates in Alfred Hitchcock's *Psycho*, it would hardly be a source of wonder that he could claim impressive musical credentials. But like others on this list, so strongly is he iden-tified with a single role that the accompanying baggage seems to outweigh the merit of any other endeavors. It's easy to overlook that he was nominated for an Academy Award for his role in *Friendly Persuasion* (1956), or that he also had a successful Broadway background. But in those last few pre-*Psycho* years, the star-making machinery had its job cut out for it in spinning Perkins as a teenage heartthrob. Beyond all the normal press and fan magazine coverage, Perkins re-corded a series of singles to capitalize on his boy-next-door image, a sort of Pat Boone for more cerebral kids. His most successful stab (so to speak) was "Moonlight Swim," a cover of a song that barely cracked the Top 40 for Nick Noble in September 1957. One month later, Perkins's version made it to 24. Other 45s followed, including "The Prettiest Girl in School" and "Rocket to the Moon." When these failed to bet-ter his earlier chart progress, he was steered into a jazz-lite direction with a pair of LPs. Both his self-titled debut and

From My Heart failed to stir the record-buying public. His musical efforts concluded with the 1960 Broadway show *Greenwillow*, wherein he sings "Never Will I Marry." By the time his immortal Hitchcock showcase premiered that year, his musical career was as dead as Marion Crane.

10.   JACK LEMMON, *A TWIST OF LEMMON* (LP, 1958)

By reputation, this actor was one of Hollywood's true nice guys. His everyman persona lives on in through the work of his protégé, Kevin Spacey. Like Spacey, Lemmon, too, was blessed with latent musical ability seldom tapped for his film roles. As an outlet for his considerable skill on the keyboard, Lemmon contracted with Epic to present an album that would showcase his talents in an unironic way. Though he originally intended to deliver an instrumental LP consisting of his own songs as well as some standards, he was persuaded to *sing* two-thirds of the album. While enhancing the finished product's commercial appeal, it probably would have made for a more musically satisfying experience if he'd stuck to his guns. His singing is no embarrassment, but his playing is a revelation, offering a window into the artistic side of this talented actor. A follow-up album of twenties songs, released in the wake of *Some Like It Hot*'s success, falls more into the novelty category.

I'm Ready for My Close-Up

I t's interesting to note how many of the following actors and actresses are *still* making films, some over and some just under, 50 years on. Longevity in Hollywood was not something anyone could take for granted when these movies were made; after all, you could probably count on one hand the number of silent film stars still actively working in the fifties. Below is a role call of actors and actresses just starting out, scarcely daring to dream of the grand future awaiting, much less contemplate a screen career reaching into the 21st century. Also worth noting is how many of these performers were *featured* players, compared with those who fell more under the heading of unbilled extras. For some, their star quality was already evident—for others, years of grooming awaited.

1. JEFF BRIDGES, *THE COMPANY SHE KEEPS* (1950)—STARRING LIZABETH SCOTT AND JANE GREER

This potboiler centered on a love triangle between a recently paroled female con and a man (who doesn't know of her past) who just happens to be the beau of her *parole officer!* Largely forgotten by the public today, Lizabeth Scott was a talented, husky-voiced beauty. She starred in a string of film noire roles that fans of the genre appreciate, but with few exceptions she rarely did the kind of box office that her talent warranted. A former model and stage actress, Scott never had a high-profile marriage to enhance her star status (unlike Lauren Bacall, with whom she's often compared). She essentially retired in 1957 at age 35 after starring in Elvis Presley's second film, *Loving You*. By 1950, actor Lloyd Bridges had found a niche in motion pictures, mostly in supporting roles in westerns. Both he and wife Dorothy Dean did extensive stage work throughout the forties, while simultaneously starting a family. Younger son Jeff arrived in 1949, and within a year, he made *his* first screen appearance. He can be seen in this film as an infant in the train station scene in the arms of his mother. Not until 1971 would he make a more lasting impression, starring opposite Cybill Shepherd in *The Last Picture Show*.

2. CHARLTON HESTON, *DARK CITY* (1950)—STARRING LIZABETH SCOTT AND DEAN JAGGER

Producer Hal B. Wallis effectively functioned as Lizabeth Scott's champion, with the bulk of her roles coming in his productions. Here she appears as a sultry nightclub singer, providing smoky atmosphere to the tale of a man out for revenge against her boyfriend, a professional con man. That role, which essentially carried the picture, fell to newcomer Charlton Heston. Years before he ever parted the sea, was imprisoned by apes, or fell in love with guns, he was cast on the strength of some TV roles. In the film, he and his group of cons (which included future *Dragnet* police partners Jack Webb and Harry Morgan) fleece a businessman (played by Don Defore, known to many later as the perpetually bewildered Mr. B on *Hazel*) in a rigged poker game. As the money was not his to lose, the businessman kills himself. His brother sets out to track down those responsible for the death just as Heston tries to discover who is taking out his gang, while both try to elude the police. Heston's performance is adequate in a predictable film, while Webb and Morgan, functioning as comic relief, virtually steal the movie. Still, his lead was good enough to draw the attention of Cecil B. DeMille, who cast Heston as the star of his next extravaganza, *The Greatest Show on Earth.*

3. MARLON BRANDO, *THE MEN* (1950)—STARRING TERESA WRIGHT AND EVERETT SLOANE

The hard realities facing vets returning from World War II had seeped into Hollywood films almost as soon as hostilities had ceased, most notably in *The Best Years of Our Lives* (1946). Another take on the difficulties that battle-scared soldiers endured came from producer Stanley Kramer, later known for his "message" films. The message here was the plight of young men in their prime trapped in crippled and wounded bodies. The action takes place in a rehabilitation ward showing the daily agonies from mental as well as physical trauma. A noble enough purpose, later ratcheted up with such post-Vietnam films as *The Deer Hunter* (1978) and *Born on the Fourth of July* (1989). It's too bad that the film's makers were apparently so insecure about the compelling nature of their material that they tarted it up with intrusive music cues and heavy-handed dialogue. As the wheelchair-bound Ken, Brando battles not only his body's limitations, but the impact of his condition on his relationship with his fiancée, Ellen (Teresa Wright). The film's antiwar message might have fared better with audiences had the movie not opened the same month that hostilities erupted in Korea.

Brando had forged quite a successful career on the stage in New York, first gaining notice on Broadway in *I Remember Mama.* His performance as an embittered veteran in the play *Truckline Café* first drew Stanley Kramer's attention, but after taking on the role of Stanley Kowalski in Tennessee Williams's *A Streetcar Named Desire* in 1947, he was impossible to ignore. Before the film version got underway, Kramer signed the actor for his own project. As perhaps *the* actor most identified with the "Method" school of performing, Brando was true to form, spending a month bedridden at a veteran's rehab center in California and eschewing the luxury accommodations provided for the actors during filming for more modest housing at a relative's home. It wasn't all despair and deprivation, however. During filming, Brando agreed to go out to a bar with some of his cast members but insisted on remaining in his wheelchair. While on the outing, a woman preaching the Gospel came upon the actor and took pity on his plight. She kindly advised him that perhaps some prayer could alleviate his suffering. Brando thanked her and began on the spot. Within moments, he slowly began to rise from the chair, and when he stood up and broke into a tap dance, the woman fainted dead away.

4.   SIDNEY POITIER, *NO WAY OUT* (1950)—STARRING RICHARD WIDMARK AND LINDA DARNELL

In an era when black film actors inevitably were relegated to minor roles, or expected to stay true to stereotype in the background, Poitier's rise was truly groundbreaking. Born in Florida in 1927 to Bahamanian parents, he found his only escape from the crushing poverty of his youth in movies. Here he learned how the world worked, but he would later observe how there was virtually no role model for himself. Lacking any better direction, he served briefly in the Army but soon found himself unskilled, out of work, and in bad company. A spontaneous decision to audition for a Negro theater group sealed his destiny—so severe was his rejection that he steeled his determination to overcome his limitations and be accepted. He found work understudying for Harry Belafonte, which led to a role on Broadway in *Lysistrata*.

The next few years saw Poitier honing his craft in a wide array of plays, from farce to classics. *No Way Out* was a realistic look at race relations in postwar America. A pair of racist crackers, the Biddle brothers, are shot during an attempted robbery. When the two are brought to the county jail hospital, Ray Biddle (the ever-reliable Richard Widmark) vows revenge if the young resident (Poitier) is unable to save his brother. When the brother dies, Biddle escapes and exacts payback. To cast an inexperienced unknown in such a pivotal role could have been disastrous, but writer/director

Joseph Mankiewicz was no ordinary filmmaker. By 1950, he had already won a pair of Oscars for *A Letter to Three Wives* in 1949, a feat he repeated in 1950 with *All About Eve*. He had also many writing and producing credits, including *Fury* (1936) and *The Philadelphia Story* (1940). Poitier displayed the dignity and self-assurance that would become his stock-in-trade for the next four decades—calm and cool under horrendous pressures, but fiery and passionate if pushed. Having such a marvelous initial showcase for his talents led to quality roles in films such as *Cry, the Beloved Country* (1952) and *The Blackboard Jungle* (1955). Kramer tapped Poitier's talents again to even greater effect in 1958's *The Defiant Ones* opposite Tony Curtis. Revisiting the racial conflict theme, the work stands up very well as an action film, as long as the heavy-handed "message" doesn't get in the way.

5. ANNE BANCROFT, *DON'T BOTHER TO KNOCK* (1952)—STARRING RICHARD WIDMARK AND MARILYN MONROE

This future miracle worker, born Anna Maria Italiano in the Bronx, entered show business via television. For two years as Anne Marno, she worked at her craft, mostly in TV adaptations of radio mysteries. Through a bit of luck, she caught the eye of producer Darryl F. Zanuck, who renamed her Bancroft. His first Hollywood project for her was as a supporting player in a drama intended as Marilyn Monroe's breakthrough film. The movie concerns an airline pilot (Widmark) whose girlfriend (Bancroft) is a lounge singer at the hotel where he stays while in town. Also at the hotel is a recently discharged mental patient (Monroe) employed as the in-house babysitter. After being dumped by Bancroft, Widmark is drawn to Monroe, before realizing what a head case she is. It's a shame the film is so badly written, because the potential for an intriguing story is certainly there. It's interesting to witness Bancroft, not particularly known as a singer, pull off the performance. As Lyn, she is suitably cynical and world-weary. This seen-it-all persona would work very well years later in her most memorable role as Mrs. Robinson in *The Graduate*.

6. CLINT EASTWOOD, *REVENGE OF THE CREATURE* (1955)—STARRING JOHN AGAR

After their initial heyday of horror films (*Dracula*, *Franken-stein*, *The Wolf Man*, or any combination thereof) petered out in the early forties, Universal Studios wouldn't successfully rework the formula until the arrival of the "Gill Man" in 1954. Though by this time the studio was no longer capable of re-producing the timeless atmosphere of the classics, the crea-ture still had its strengths. As a sort of underwater King Kong, both the "beauty and the beast" tale and "man tampering with nature" themes survive intact. Being a successful new franchise made sequels a must. *Revenge of the Creature* (1955) and *The Creature Walks Among Us* (1956) rounded out the series, but diminishing returns being what they are, they cannot be regarded as must-sees. That is, unless one is an Eastwood fan, for in the second film we are treated to a bit part from the future Dirty Harry. In a laboratory scene, he plays a stereotypical bumbling assistant. Summoning his boss to alert him that a lab rat has gone missing, he inexpli-cably reaches into the pocket of his lab coat and produces the errant rodent: "Now how'd he get in there?" The years to come would provide him with far more memorable dialogue, but one has to start somewhere. "Somewhere" for him began as a series of dead-end blue-collar jobs.

A stint in the Army placed him in the company of David Janssen and Martin Milner, both of whom scored big in tele-vision down the road. They encouraged the six-foot-four Eastwood to give acting a shot, and following his hitch he did. Eventually he was able to enlist a cinematographer friend into getting him a screen test before director Arthur Lubin. Although known primarily as a director of comedy (Abbott and Costello, Francis, the Talking Mule), Lubin rec-ognized a certain something and gave Eastwood his start. A year and a half later, his contract was canceled, but Eastwood was nothing if not lucky. While visiting a friend at CBS studios, an exec stopped him in the hallway and asked him, "Are you an actor? You look like a cowboy." Thus was Rowdy Yates cast for the *Rawhide* series, setting Eastwood on the path that would lead to The Man with No Name.

7. PAUL NEWMAN, *THE SILVER CHALICE* (1955)—STARRING VIRGINIA MAYO AND JACK PALANCE

Possibly the most embarrassing film debut featured here is this bomb, less from any fault of Newman's than from a directionless script and inept execution. While adept at crime stories and melodramas, Warner Brothers lacked the knack for historical epics, as it proved with *The Story of Mankind*. Sword-and-sand pictures were perfected over at 20th Century Fox, Paramount, and MGM, but this didn't stop lesser hands from taking a stab at the genre. So traumatized was Newman from the experience that in later years he actually took out newspaper ads begging people not to watch the film on TV (which, of course, only achieved the opposite result). Clearly out of their league and perhaps recognizing it, the film's makers used the time-honored ploy of stacking the movie with familiar faces. Thus you have Jack Palance camping it up as a wizard (complete with pointy hat), Natalie Wood (as a *blonde*), Pier Angeli, Lorne Greene, and E.G. Marshall all populating ancient Rome. The sets used were likened to giant Legos, more akin to sci-fi than the first century. Even the costumes were laughably bizarre. One cannot fault the budget, however; Warner's spent $4.5 million, even shooting the film in CinemaScope. Newman arrived by way of Broadway and television. Fifties TV was heavily populated by teleplays, and many future silver screen personalities apprenticed there. Having left the running of his family's sporting goods store behind, he studied theater, attaining a master's degree from Yale in 1952. Unlike so many others', his family background did not include squalor. Though Newman was highly regarded as an actor on entering films, reviews for this turkey referred to him as "wooden" and uncomfortable. Given the material he had to work with, this is understandable. He beat a hasty retreat back to the stage, scoring in *The Desperate Hours*, before the call of his contract summoned him for the Rocky Graziano biopic *Somebody Up There Likes Me* (1956). He would fare much better with the second go-round.

8. SHIRLEY MACLAINE, *THE TROUBLE WITH HARRY* (1955)—STARRING EDMUND GWENN AND JOHN FORSYTHE

This uncommon black comedy from Alfred Hitchcock would take years to become fully appreciated. Sandwiched between the director's more popular *To Catch a Thief* (1955) and *The Man Who Knew Too Much* (1956), the film tends to be overlooked in the shuffle. But its lightness (for Hitchcock) may have been influenced by his television program, which began around the same time. The trouble noted in the title is that Harry is dead, and everyone in town seemingly had a motive to put him that way. Newcomer Shirley MacLaine (she'd renamed herself from her given name of Shirley Mac-Lean Beaty, after a producer continually mispronounced it; brother Warren, with a slight modification, kept his) arrived by way of Broadway where she was a singer/dancer. While working as understudy to Carol Haney in *The Pajama Game*, both actresses unexpectedly got a break—Haney to her ankle, and MacLaine by moving to the lead role. There she was spotted by Hal Wallis, who offered a studio deal. MacLaine's performance in *Harry* set the tone for her initial string of films: words like "sassy" and "pixie-esque" come to mind. As Harry's ex-wife, Jennifer, MacLaine approaches an apparently tragic situation with complete nonchalance. Like all of the film's leads, she is less concerned that the man is dead than how it might reflect on her if she is revealed to be responsible. Hitchcock purposely cast his film without big stars, creating an ensemble that could convey believability without the distraction of Hollywood baggage. All have presence (including future Beaver Jerry Mathers) without too much sparkle, enhancing the film's innate charm. MacLaine required a few more films to really hit her stride, finally putting it all together in Billy Wilder's *The Apartment* (1960). In it, she at last received the perfect combination of story, cast, and direction to fully use her gifts.

9. SEAN CONNERY, *NO ROAD BACK* (1957)—STARRING SKIP HOMEIER

Long before he sang to leprechauns for Walt Disney in *Darby O'Gill and the Little People* (1959), or had a license to kill even, this young Scot was cast in an Errol Flynn musical entitled *Lilacs in the Spring* (1955). However, since his role was practically nonexistent, his next film is considered to be his debut—as a low-level gangster. *No Road Back* is about a medical student (Homeier) who, after studying in the United States, returns to England to discover that his elderly mother had paid for his education through ill-gotten means. Connery plays Spike, a member of group of toughs who commit robberies. Though Connery's role barely required 15 minutes of screen time, his menacing presence made an impression. He came off as the scowling, intimidating figure whom everyone would come to know so well in the years that followed. From a destitute Edinburgh upbringing (which rivaled Poitier's for deprivation), Connery entered into the profession by pure happenstance. Poorly educated and with limited resources, he possessed one tangible asset: his superb physique.

Following a stint as a coffin polisher, Connery decided to try out for a Mr. Universe competition, where he won the slot to represent Scotland. Though he finished third, he did learn from some of the other contestants of openings in a London-based touring company of the musical *South Pacific*. He auditioned and won a part as one of the sailors providing vocal backup. This led to other stage work, and by 1956 he'd scored some television roles, including the lead in a BBC production of Rod Serling's *Requiem for a Heavyweight*. *No Road Back* was his first credited film role, though as the newcomer, he naturally drew the brunt of on-set jokes. Early on in the production, when he was heard complaining about the speech impediment his character was given, some of the crew pointed out a man high up in the production to take his grievance to. While relating his beef, Connery discovered that the director had the same speech defect.

10. JACK NICHOLSON, *THE CRY BABY KILLER* (1958)—STARRING BRETT HALSEY AND CAROLYN MITCHELL

A true B exploitation picture marked the big screen debut of future Oscar winner Jack Nicholson. Roger Corman, famous for his low budgets and equally low production values, cast the 21-year-old as a teenager who inadvertently shoots two of his tormentors, then holes up in a shop while surrounded by police. Though his persona hasn't yet found its voice, there are glimpses of the Jack Nicholson-to-be, especially when he has a gun in his hand. Corman cast Nicholson three more times in the early sixties in small roles within his usual low-grade schlock; *Little Shop of Horrors* is the best known. After he spent some time doing a bit of script writing and more bad films, Nicholson's career finally kicked in with *Easy Rider* in 1969.

Cry Baby's director, Jus Addis, also went on to bigger and better things, and was steadily employed in television throughout the sixties with shows like *Combat!*, *Lost in Space*, and *The High Chaparral* to his credit. *The Cry Baby Killer* was his only feature film. A sad tale connected to this release concerns the female lead, Carolyn Mitchell. A California beauty queen born Barbara Ann Thomason, she appeared in only two films and in 1958 became the fifth wife of actor Mickey Rooney. Theirs would be a stormy relationship, due to his wandering eye and her emotional instability. In time, she bore the star four children, but things remained rocky. In 1965, while Mickey was away filming, she began an affair with a Yugoslav actor. Upon his return, things were brought to a head and Mickey moved out. Just as they began to sort out their troubles, her boyfriend, angry over her apparent decision to break off the relationship, shot her dead and then himself in the Rooney's home. She was 29.

The Next Film You See

The following films defy classification. Some are noble experiments gone awry; others are totally creatures of their time that may be laughable outside of their context; and still others are actually quite good works that are just a little . . . different. Out of the ordinary. Not what you'd expect. A valid response to all might be, "What were they *thinking*?" For better or worse, this collection of Hollywood films presents unparalleled insight into the fifties experience.

1. *THE NEXT VOICE YOU HEAR . . .* (1950), DIRECTED BY WILLIAM A. WELLMAN AND STARRING JAMES WHITMORE AND NANCY DAVIS

In an era dominated by heightened paranoia, what could be more frightening than tooling around in the family sedan, going about your business, when suddenly the voice of the Almighty Himself starts issuing forth from your radio speaker? Once your trousers dry, then what? Such was the moral dilemma facing citizens of the world in this curio, as embodied by the Smith family. Cannily cast as regular Joe was journeyman actor Whitmore, who in true Everyman fashion, proceeded to get drunk. Wife Mary, the very embodiment of Plain Jane, was with child at the time of God's broadcast, and therefore denied that luxury. Instead, she gets to look earnest, frightened, pious, and adoring, skills

143

that would prove to be invaluable to Davis soon enough with her marriage to a certain divorced B-list actor at Warner's, whose acting career was in its twilight. Perhaps the most shocking aspect of the entire production is that, despite the embarrassment of quality talent behind the project (director Wellman, producer Dore Schary), the film somehow managed to make it past quality control. The cinematic equivalent of a car wreck, you felt guilty for being sucked in, yet you couldn't turn away. Without coming down on any particular side of the issue, the film tries to tread a middle ground, ultimately deciding that a return to traditional values in a world gone mad is good (or at least can't hurt). Sadly, the voice of God is never actually heard in the film, owing to artistic effect and the fact that James Earl Jones was only 18 at the time (and a stutterer in any event). If ever a film cried out for an update, God knows it's this one. Fire up the Crown Vic and let's go! *The* Last *Voice You Hear* . . . , anyone?

2. *MY SON JOHN* (1952), DIRECTED BY LEO MCCAREY AND STARRING HELEN HAYES, ROBERT WALKER, AND VAN HEFLIN

Though heavy-handed cinematic polemics were abundant in this decade, rarely were they assembled by such skilled hands. Once again, we have a richness of talent pooled together to create—what? This film is a blemish to all involved, a shrill, brainless propaganda piece whose sole purpose in being may have been to deflect suspicion away from its makers then under scrutiny by the witch-hunters in Washington. By offering up this tripe, they might somehow be seen as doing their patriotic duty by validating the rampant suspicion and mistrust of nonconformity that was then in vogue. Alternative theory: perhaps it was intended as a *satire* of what was going on in America, an attempt to hold a mirror up to society and scream, *wake up!* If so, the first rule of black comedy is to be funny, and this bleak time-waster takes itself far too seriously to entertain even that notion of self-awareness.

Leo McCarey was a first-rate director, with two Academy awards to prove it. Among his screen gems were the Marx Brothers' *Duck Soup* (1934), a tribute to anarchy if ever was; the screwball classic, *The Awful Truth* (1937); and Bing Crosby's shining moment (no, not the one with Bowie), *The Bells of Saint Mary's* (1944). Further bolstering McCarey's bona fides was his pairing of Stan Laurel and Oliver Hardy as a team back in the twenties. By the fifties, however, he was solidly right wing, and this film demonstrates how much he was willing to sacrifice his reputation to score some political points. As for Helen Hayes, first lady of American theater, what can you say? She was willing to come out of nearly 20 years self-imposed retirement from motion pictures for *this?* She plays a mother whose two youngest sons enlist to fight in Korea. Firstborn John (Robert Walker), however, seems to be less than respectful of the things Hayes's character holds dear: the Bible and the American Legion among them. On learning that John is being investigated as a *possible* security leak, and that he is dating a woman who *might* be a spy, well, suspicion is as good as guilt. The screenwriter (McCarey!) ends the movie by showing that her fears are well founded. A shabby end to a promising career for Walker, who died at age 32 before completing the film. (The picture was finished by cobbling together bits from *Strangers on a Train* and the use of a double.)

3. *THE THIEF* (1952), DIRECTED BY RUSSELL ROUSE AND STARRING RAY MILLAND

Finally, some good news! This curiosity represents a rare Hollywood experiment: a topical tale of espionage wherein all plot is forwarded strictly through facial expressions and sound effects. That is to say, *there is no dialogue!* Plot-wise, the film is fairly routine; it concerns nuclear scientist who decides to sell secrets to a foreign power before having second thoughts after events are set in motion. The film's real innovation comes through in the editing, score, and photography. Shades of Hitchcock, Welles, and Serling come to mind;

if silent films had not ceased production after 1927, the results might look like this. Ray Milland fully communicates his character's conflicted emotions and torment. A reliable second lead for most of his career, Milland saw his fortunes take a quantum leap forward in 1945 when Billy Wilder cast him as an alcoholic writer in *The Lost Weekend*. His unexpected bravura performance in that role won him an Academy Award, and from then on Milland wisely used the cachet it gave him to take the occasional risk in his work. *The Thief*, though hardly a box office blockbuster, admirably challenged the audience without pandering, craftily instilling a dread that mere words fall short of. A ringing telephone never sounded more ominous.

4. *THIS IS CINERAMA* (1952), DEVELOPED BY FRED WALLER AND NARRATED BY LOWELL THOMAS

A true oddball feature, this 115-minute billboard purporting to showcase the future of filmmaking unwittingly defines "period piece." For the uninitiated, Cinerama represented an opening salvo in a long line of motion picture innovations implemented throughout the fifties as the industry desperately sought to maintain its stranglehold on audiences in the face of the television threat. Its competition included CinemaScope, VistaVision, Todd-AO, and something called WarnerSuperScope. All this tinkering was intended to give audiences an overwhelming, larger-than-life, filmgoing experience. With Cinerama, special cameras with multiple lenses shot three images simultaneously, intending to capture not just the central subject, but peripheral ones as well. This meant that theaters had to be equipped with a mammoth curved screen and projection gear capable of running the three 35mm images simultaneously *and* in sync, along with a fourth strip that contained a seven-track sound accompaniment. (Too much to go wrong just invited trouble.) Special projectors ran 26 frames per second rather than the usual 24 to smooth out the discernible flicker of an image now spread out so far and wide. Decades later, all the effort to present a seemingly three-dimensional image with louder-than-life sound culminated with something called IMAX.

The film began with a preamble—veteran newsreel narrator Lowell Thomas offers a black-and-white recitation of the origins of captured motion and the many efforts to advance the art. Then followed what the audiences came for: a front seat ride on the Atom Smasher roller coaster at Rockaway's Playland, as seen through the lenses of Cinerama. Predictably, those fainter of heart responded to what they saw with dizziness and nausea, much to the dismay of theater managers (not to mention those employees at the bottom of the food chain). It was all downhill from there. The remainder of the film was devoted to something for everyone, provided everyone was a middlebrow. Among the spectacles seen: an *Aida* production from La Scala in Milan; Niagara Falls; excerpts from Handel's *Messiah*; Venetian canals by gondola; a bullfight; the Vienna Boys Choir; waterskiing from Florida's late, lamented Cypress Gardens. (The last inclusion was no accident, as Fred Waller, the developer of the Cinerama process, also invented waterskiing. No kidding.) Meanwhile, a literally unheard of sound system ("stereophonic") blasted the audience in all its teeth-rattling glory.

The film's big finish played out to strains of "America, The Beautiful," as the audience was taken on an aerial tour from the Great Plains to New York City, shot from a low-flying B-25. Not for the last time, state-of-the-art technology was employed in the service of pure, unvarnished hokiness. (Latter-day examples include James Cameron's *Titanic* and any *Star Wars* flick.) Though it only played on 30 screens nationwide, the release did extremely good business over the next 10 years wherever it appeared, before the inherent unwieldiness and obsolescence of the technology sealed the movie's doom.

5.   *5,000 FINGERS OF DR. T* (1953), DIRECTED BY ROY ROWLAND AND STARRING HANS CONRIED AND TOMMY RETTIG

Common sense dictates that the surrealism of Dr. Seuss's oeuvre defies a live-action cinematic approach. (Recent

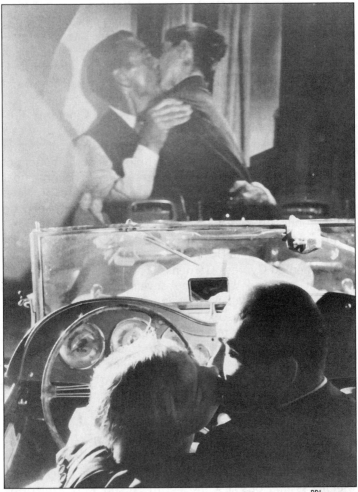

With so many of the bad movies on this list playing at drive-ins, couples could concentrate on more important subjects.

works by Jim Carrey and Mike Myers prove the point.) That is why the most enduring rendering of a Dr. Seuss work is commonly held to be the 1966 televised animation of *How the Grinch Stole Christmas*. Couple that timeless Seuss tale of anticommercialism (hear that, Ron Howard?!?) with a simpatico director (Chuck Jones, the genius/madman behind Looney Tunes), and you create an unsurpassed classic. It may be of some surprise to discover, therefore, that Dr. Seuss (Theodore Geisel, actually) *himself* joined forces with Stanley Kramer (!) 50 years ago to create a wildly subversive live-action musical—a film that stands as the direct precursor to *Willy Wonka and the Chocolate Factory*. *5,000 Fingers* easily deserves a place alongside that film, and maybe *The Wizard of Oz*, too, as an appealing work of cinematic fantasy ostensibly for, but not limited to, children. For a variety of reasons, the film is all but forgotten.

A veritable subcult has sprung up around this movie, which concerns the adventures of 10-year-old Bart (played by Tommy Rettig of *Jeff's Collie* fame), who chafes against the tyranny of forced piano lessons from the oppressive Dr. Terwilliker (Conried). Bart's mother is widowed (the war, we assume), and the only other father figure present is the unpretentious plumber next door (played by singer Peter Lind Hayes). The bulk of the action takes place in Bart's dreams, where he is spirited away to Dr. T's fiefdom, a prison camp dominated by an enormous piano where 500 similarly tormented boys are forced to practice eternally. Their only salvation lies in Bart's leading a revolt. The film does a fine job of presenting the situation exactly as a 10-year-old would imagine it, without ever resorting to condescension. Conried, a successful radio actor (who later would voice Snidely Whiplash on the *Dudley Do-Right* cartoon) is superb as the menacing overlord, who also has designs on Bart's mother. Mr. Zabladowski (Hayes), a simple man who understands the mind of a young boy, is Bart's choice for new dad. Though this subversive film works on a number of levels (totalitarian allegory, Freudian study, cultural conflict), the finished product was not what its makers intended. Producer Kramer always allowed that it was his biggest disappointment, gutted by budget constraints and a director he came to regret choosing. The studio substantially reedited the film following preview audience feedback, and a number of scenes and musical interludes were dropped entirely. Nonetheless, what remains is a highly imaginative, dark, and wittily surreal film. A book detailing the story of this film awaits writing.

6. *HELL AND HIGH WATER* (1954), DIRECTED BY SAMUEL FULLER AND STARRING RICHARD WIDMARK

Though topical action films weren't in short supply at this time, this one takes an unusual twist, which made for particularly unsettling viewing. Fresh on the heels of the real-life announcement from the White House of a nuclear explosion outside our sphere of influence, 20th Century-Fox rushed into production a film capitalizing on the event, providing an explanation for the atomic blast. The effect was to exacerbate tensions while simultaneously reassuring audiences that things were under control, if not by our government. *Hell and High Water* begins as a pseudodocumentary, presenting the facts as known before purporting to offer "the story of that explosion!" Not since Orson Welles's *War of the Worlds* broadcast of 1938 had such bald-faced hoodwinking been contrived. Film noire veteran Richard Widmark was cast as a jaded mercenary submarine commander, hired by a cadre of concerned scientists. Dismayed at the failure of politicians to seriously take on the rogue nations in possession of the bomb, they set about doing it themselves. Along the way, the predictable conflicts and romantic interludes unfold. Plot giveaway: The scientists, aided by a motley group led by Widmark, uncover evidence that the unnamed enemy's intent is to bomb North Korea, so that America will be blamed and World War III will commence. In the end, they manage to track the warhead to a salvaged B-29 in the enemy's possession. Left with no choice but to bring down the plane, they inadvertently set off the nuke in doing so, causing the explosion detected near the Arctic Circle. Much credit must be given to the film's writers and creators for even coming up with such a wild premise. Imagine—a go-it-alone, extralegal action taken to disarm a foreign power's weapons of mass destruction? Only in a fictitious world.

7. *THE CONQUEROR* (1956), DIRECTED BY DICK POWELL AND STARRING JOHN WAYNE, SUSAN HAYWARD, AND AGNES MOOREHEAD

Here it is—the infamous camp classic, unintended though that was. There is so much to say about this movie (and much has been said) that it serves no purpose to beat the horse further. For those who've remained in the dark until now, a synopsis is in order. Infamous flyer/billionaire/recluse Howard Hughes had dabbled in film producing since the 1920s, with fair to middling results. *The Conqueror* finished his film career for good and brought down RKO Studios as well. Those feeling charitable called it "an Eastern Western," as if Indians and Mongol hordes were interchangeable. The fact is, that was exactly how John Wayne approached perhaps the biggest misstep of his career, playing Mongolian warrior Genghis Khan. In a role originally conceived for Marlon Brando (who wisely begged off), Wayne, made up in Fu Manchu moustache and taped "Oriental"-like eyelids, was also required to deliver appallingly stilted dialogue. The lines as written come off as someone's earnest translations from an unfamiliar language, much like the dubbing in Asian martial arts flicks. "I feel this Tartar woman is for me. My blood says: take her!" The (at first) unwilling recipient of his lust, Susan Hayward stars as a redhead inexplicably native to the Far East and a member of the opposing tribe. Despite the murder of her father and her people at the hands of Temujin (as Wayne's character is known throughout most of the film), the spirited lass eventually comes around to his worldview to rule the new empire at his side.

Hilarious miscasting, racial stereotyping, and tortured

dialogue aside, another aspect to this film warrants notoriety. Since location filming in Asia was out of the question at the height of the Cold War, "safe" locales had to double for Mongolia. So it was that *The Conqueror* was filmed in Utah near the desert town of Saint George. There, the cast and crew lived for the three months that it took to shoot the principal photography. No one thought to question the fact that the U.S. government had been conducting atomic testing about 100 miles upwind. That is, until the body count began. A run-through of the principals: Wayne, Hayward, Moorehead, director Powell, all dead of cancer and Pedro Armendariz, a suicide while battling cancer. In a 1980 article, *People* magazine cataloged 91 cancer victims among cast and crew, half of whom succumbed. (They never bothered to check the thousands of Native Americans recruited to play the Mongol hordes.) The population of Saint George likewise was wiped out. Thus, in every measurable aspect, *The Conqueror* was a disaster, though not an unmitigated one. For those whose cinematic taste runs to the bizarre, it still delivers the comedic goods.

8. *THE BAD SEED* (1956), DIRECTED BY MERVYN LEROY AND STARRING PATTY MCCORMACK

This entry underscores the peril of turning plays into films. Though the movie was based on a hit Broadway show exploring nature versus nurture, the decision to pull its punches and contrive a feel-good ending gutted the work of any value its creator might have intended, leaving only unplanned hilarity. The story portrays eight-year-old Rhoda (McCormack), a model child, and her nervous mother (played by Nancy Kelly). The two form an especially close bond, as the father is often away on business. But something dark lurks beneath their domestic tranquility—the mother is plagued by suspicions, fearing that her daughter hides an evil, amoral side capable of any abomination. Her worries are further inflamed by the discovery that Rhoda, adopted as a baby, was actually mothered by a murderess. Whatever innate evil her daughter possesses surely was transmitted biologically. Nowadays, with demon spawn a hackneyed plot device (*The Exorcist, The Omen, The Good Son*, etc.), *The Bad Seed* must have been groundbreaking stuff. McCormack is quite chilling in turns as her moods swing from sunny to black. But too much of the film is squandered with stagy expository scenes: audiences need to be shown and not told. Without giving away any particular plot points, the play's original unsettling ending is far preferable to the tacky, contrived divine retribution scene so jarringly slapped onto the film's end. It gets worse. Just when theater patrons could be expected to offer each other their critiques as the credits roll, a hokey curtain call occurs. Actors onscreen file out and take their bows. Next, we are treated to the sight of mother and daughter, still in character, giving ticket holders what they've waited two hours to see: Mom administering a spanking to her bad, bad girl. What in God's name are we to make of *that*? Playwright Maxwell Anderson's opinion of what had been done to his work is not recorded, but some things are better imagined.

9. *THE STORY OF MANKIND* (1957), DIRECTED BY IRWIN ALLEN WITH A STAR-STUDDED CAST THAT INCLUDES RONALD COLMAN, THE MARX BROTHERS, VINCENT PRICE, PETER LORRE, DENNIS HOPPER, AND AGNES MOOREHEAD

In a decade fond of cinematic spectacle, an ever more grandiose moviegoing experience was always just around the corner. Since biblical films and costume dramas had always done well, this film's makers must have reasoned: why limit oneself? Why not tell the *entire* story of mankind? Such a colossal undertaking required a focus. So it was that the undertaking was framed by a celestial courtroom drama, wherein the Almighty must decide if the human race, having discovered the H-bomb, should be allowed to live, given its history of carelessness. Representing the "Spirit of Man" was the eloquent and genteel Ronald Colman. Playing the prosecution (as "Mr. Scratch"), Vincent Price was at his diabolical best. In his usual charming manner, he made the case for man's destruction by trotting out history's ugliest moments. Rebuttals came in the form of somewhat more inspiring scenes from the past. Given thousands of years to cover, the film had to be made on the cheap. With dozens of stars appearing in what amounted to cameo roles, the film library at Warner's was plundered for relevant stock footage to fill in the gaps. Where the concept gets wobbly is in the inability to make up its mind about what its intent is—serious, thoughtful history or vaudevillian broad comedy? Attempting to have it both ways ensured the failure of both. The gags are lame, especially when sandwiched between truly dark moments. As is usual in these sorts of situations, the devil makes the more convincing case. Then there is the matter of casting: Dennis Hopper as Napoleon? Harpo Marx as Isaac Newton? Peter Lorre as Nero? Decadence never looked so creepy. Director/producer Allen made a name for himself with television fantasies (*Lost in Space*, *The Time Tunnel*, *Voyage to the Bottom of the Sea*) in the sixties and with disaster films (*The Poseidon Adventure*, *The Towering Inferno*, *The Swarm*) in the seventies. Many would suggest that he achieved both goals with this fantastic disaster. Consider this: despite the big names involved and the compelling theme, the film has never been available on video or DVD. Can a film be *that* bad?

10. *WIND ACROSS THE EVERGLADES* (1958), DIRECTED BY NICHOLAS RAY AND STARRING BURL IVES, CHRISTOPHER PLUMMER, AND GYPSY ROSE LEE

Now *here* is an oddity, albeit a good one. Its makers had been on a roll: director Ray fresh off the heels of *Johnny Guitar* (1954) and *Rebel Without A Cause* (1955) and writer Budd Schulberg from a string of successes, including *On the Waterfront* (1954), *The Harder They Fall* (1956), and *A Face in the Crowd* (1957). Add a supporting cast unmatched in variety (burlesque legend Lee, writer McKinley Cantor, Israeli model Chana Eden, clown Emmett Kelly, and Peter Falk in his big-screen debut) to a forward-thinking environmental theme, and you have a lost masterpiece—a beautifully shot film that is largely forgotten today. Filmed on location, the movie concerns efforts by an alcoholic Audubon Society worker (Plummer) to stop the slaughter of endangered native birds. Playing the heavy for not the first time was folk singer Burl Ives, as Cottonmouth—a long way from his holly, jolly future. The film has a moody, atmospheric feel to it. In some ways it resembles nothing less than a fifties *Apocalypse Now*, as the audience is led into Cottonmouth's bizarre world, where—as a Kurtz-like figure—he lords over a secret band of fringe dwellers considered to be rogues by society. As Murdock, Plummer grapples with his own demons, but they are sublimated to his quest. When the two cultures meet the seeming opposites recognize their commonalities. Though a strained mutual respect develops, they never fully forget their adversarial relationship. That Plummer and Ives were never better is a fair assessment, making the film's unavailability all the more frustrating.

YOU!!! Are a Blabbermouth!

In a time that demanded guts and principled action, these 10 individuals revealed themselves to be self-righteous, ignoble, and mean. When the recently reactivated House Committee on Un-American Activities (HUAC) decided to launch an inquisition of Hollywood leftists, some within the industry went along happily. The cover of "national security" was used to justify the settling of scores and silencing of dissent. Until and unless any of the accused were found guilty of working to overthrow our government or commit espionage, these misanthropic zealots had no business ruining people's careers—period. Being a lefty, or even a member of the Communist Party, was not illegal, then or now. The following people revealed a perverted sense of patriotism while acting as accessories to the persecution of their fellow Americans.

1. EDWARD DMYTRYK, DIRECTOR/WRITER

Dmytryk's career was off to an impressive start with two politically charged films under his belt—*Hitler's Children* (1944), an anti-Nazi film, and *Crossfire* (1947), a study of anti-Semitism—when he was called before HUAC. Pegged as a leftist and ex-party member when pressed to name names, he at first invoked his constitutional rights. This did not impress the courts then intent on trampling civil liberties, and along with nine others known as the Hollywood Ten, he was sentenced to 12 months for contempt of Congress. Upon his release, he worked in England, but financial necessity compelled him to rethink his principles. In 1951, he revisited HUAC, this time giving them everything they wanted to hear. As three of the people he sold out were among the Hollywood Ten and involved at that moment in litigation, his charges were particularly damaging. Dmytryk went on to direct for another 20 years, but he never again reached the creative heights he had attained in the forties.

2. ELIA KAZAN, DIRECTOR

The 1999 decision of the Academy of Motion Picture Arts and Sciences to honor Kazan with a lifetime achievement award stirred deep emotions. In the almost 50 years since he named names before HUAC, no one man so embodied the bitter taste of the era. One reason might be that of all the former lefties to turn on their fellows, he was in the greatest position of strength when he did it. Unlike so many others, Kazan had other options: working in Europe and returning to the stage (where no blacklist existed) among them. He certainly had the financial wherewithal to take a hit, with the much acclaimed *A Streetcar Named Desire* (1951) under his belt. Even apologists sympathetic to his actions noted that if anyone could have broken the power of HUAC, it was Kazan. Instead, he volunteered names of people in no position to survive the damage, while merrily continuing his career. Without so much as a pang of regret, he took out a full page ad in the *New York Times* in 1952 encouraging others to step forward with what they knew. His widely touted *On the Waterfront* (1954) followed his testimony. If intended as an allegorical defense of informing, the comparison to his own situation is not well taken. He went on to make other acclaimed films, but he could never outrun the stench of his actions.

3. BURL IVES, SINGER/ACTOR

Years before being cast as a snowman in the sixties' *Rudolph, The Red-Nose Reindeer* special, Ives displayed a heart of ice when called before HUAC. The rotund folkie had in fact been quite the supporter of many progressive causes, along with many of his fellow performers. But publication of *Red Channels* would find him brushed with the taint of subversion. He found himself before the committee, alongside friends Pete Seeger and Richard Dyer-Bennett. The latter two refused to dignify the charges before them and were duly blacklisted. Ives, however, was quite prepared to sing. He went on to enjoy employability in some high-profile films, including work for Elia Kazan and Budd Schulberg. Go figure.

4.   ROBERT TAYLOR, ACTOR

This lightweight journeyman actor was among the first to testify before HUAC. He obligingly supplied them with names, even helping with their spelling. He continued his mediocrity in Hollywood, eventually replacing pal Ronald Reagan as host of *Death Valley Days* on TV.

5.   RONALD REAGAN, ACTOR/SAG PRESIDENT

The metamorphosis effected by this contract player from New Deal Democrat to staunch right-wing Republican had powerful reverberations throughout the industry. The change coincided with his bottoming out as an actor, appearing in such dreck as *That Hagen Girl* (1947) and *Bedtime for Bonzo* (1951). According to Reagan's biographers, his position as Screen Actors Guild president gave him direct insight into the influence that Hollywood Communists were having on the industry. Critics point out that being a Democrat is not the same thing as supporting Stalin, and even people who at one time may have been party members no longer were, and in any event they were hardly a national security threat. Flushing out subversives made a convenient cover for union-busting. As SAG president, Reagan was among the first to appear before HUAC and cheerfully continued to supply names to the FBI even afterward. His actions during this time solidified his conservative credentials, just in case he was considering a career change.

6. LARRY PARKS, ACTOR

Larry Parks's name is largely notable for the public whipping he endured at the hands of HUAC. Two days after his initially courageous stand, the committee took testimony from him again in a closed-door session. Word leaked out soon enough that the *Al Jolson Story*'s star's valiant stand lasted only as long as he remained in the light of day. As Jolson himself might have said, "You ain't heard nothing yet!" Despite giving HUAC members what he thought they wanted, his acting days were essentially over. During a second wave of hearings, he literally begged to reappear for another shot at getting back into their good graces. Had he donned white gloves and some blackface, he might have stood a better chance. Parks's career was as dead as Jolson's, despite these efforts.

7. ROBERT ROSSEN, WRITER-DIRECTOR

As the filmmaker responsible for *Body and Soul* (1947) and *All The King's Men* (1949), Rossen could claim some impressive credentials, including Oscar-winning director. Yet another was as a card-carrying member of the Communist Party from 1941 till 1945. Some said he felt privately slighted when *not* called before HUAC as part of the Hollywood Ten in 1947. He was finally brought in four years later, in 1951. At that time, perhaps out of spite for not being called up sooner, he refused to name names. After mulling the matter over (and not working) for two years, he reappeared, this time with a list of 57 names. He explained his lapse in 1951 as his not wanting to be a stool pigeon, something he was now okay with. His career proceeded accordingly; he would go on to write, produce, and direct *The Hustler* in 1961.

8. FRANK TUTTLE, WRITER/DIRECTOR

Despite a long career going back to the silent era, Tuttle really only had one truly memorable work to his credit: the

1942 film noir *This Gun's for Hire*, starring Alan Ladd. A favorite of Bing Crosby, whom Tuttle often directed at Paramount during the thirties, he was widely known as a supporter of left-wing causes and for his Communist Party affiliations. It was the early fifties before HUAC got around to bringing him in, and Tuttle, by now prepared to disavow his past affiliations, began naming names. His cooperation, coming on the eve of his retirement, seems rather pointless in retrospect. After a four-year lull, he completed three more films before calling it a career.

9. BUDD SCHULBERG, WRITER

As an uncredited staffer working on scripts throughout the thirties at Paramount, Schulberg was in a fine position as a fly on the wall to observe the workings of a major Hollywood studio. All of this would end up in his first novel, *What Makes Sammy Run?* (1941), the story of a corrupt studio head. Like his good friend Elia Kazan, he had been a party member and supporter of left-wing causes as well. Also like Kazan, his seeming disenchantment with his past politics led him to name names quite willingly. After being "outed" by a fellow screenwriter, Schulberg wired the committee, offering his services. While the tempest brewed, Kazan began to move forward on a story idea he'd been mulling over for some time about the corruption and organized crime control of New York Harbor's dockworkers. As planned, it was to be a collaboration with playwright Arthur Miller. But Miller, disgusted with Kazan's performance before the committee, refused to work with him. No problem, Kazan reasoned, knowing that he'd have a more receptive partner in Schulberg. They set to work on what became *On the Waterfront*. They disagreed later, however, about whether or not it was intended as a commentary on recent events.

10. WALT DISNEY, PRODUCER

As a studio head, Disney regarded labor unions the same way mice regard cats. When HUAC summoned him, the first name he supplied them with was that of a Hollywood labor organizer who had bedeviled him for some time. In his mind, unions were nothing more than Communist tools, and he told the committee as much. Labor strikes, to which his studio had been subjected, were staged to the benefit of "the commies." Like Reagan, Disney continued to inform on anyone who incurred his wrath. His enlightened labor practices live on with the overseas sweatshops churning out products bearing his name. It *is* a small world, after all.

Hello, Norma Jeane

A nd it seems to some she lived her life like a scandal in the wind. What would a fifties book be without a little bit of MM? Actually, here's an opportunity to clear up a few misconceptions: Yes, she could act; yes, she could sing; and though known to dispense sexual favors the way some people write thank-you notes, she was not a "ho." Elevated to icon status, Marilyn Monroe was a study in contradictions: emotionally fragile, but steely determined; chronically tardy, but reliably professional; the biggest star of the fifties, but in person, the least starlike. This archetypical "dumb blonde" was intellectually insatiable, and it is a tribute to her drive that from such humble, dysfunctional beginnings she willed herself to become one of Hollywood's most enduring legends, with equal appeal to both sexual orientations.

1. *ALL ABOUT EVE* PREMIERS, OCTOBER 1950

Scarcely three years after her fleeting film debut in the epic mule showcase *Scudda Hoo! Scudda Hay!*, the former Norma Jeane Baker suffered through a series of insipid, undemanding roles before securing a piece of the much-acclaimed *All About Eve*. Though hardly a star-making part, the role put her in the august company of Bette Davis, Ann Baxter, and George Sanders, making it the most important of her *six* film appearances that year. Widely regarded today as one of Hollywood's greatest pictures, *Eve* was honored by its then-record-setting 14 Academy Award nominations. Not bad for a struggling contract player whose studio, 20th Century-Fox, seemed barely aware of her potential. This part, coupled with her small but glittering role in John Huston's *The Asphalt Jungle* that same year, slowly but surely found her name getting some ink in the press.

2. MAKES COVER OF *LIFE* MAGAZINE, APRIL 7, 1952

While tending to the publicity accompanying the buildup to her first *lead* role, in *Don't Bother to Knock*, Marilyn and her handlers found themselves momentarily blindsided. In March, the revelation aired that the buxom model posing in the altogether for a best-selling calendar was none other than Monroe herself, photographed three years earlier. Caught in a potentially career-destroying situation, Marilyn cleverly disarmed her critics by implementing a bit of spin combined with frank and unapologetic candor. Rather than tearfully repenting her actions and pleading for forgiveness, as might have been expected, she matter-of-factly related the financial necessity of being homeless and hungry in 1949 that led her to doff her drawers. When asked by a "sob sister" reporter, "Didn't you have *anything* on?" Monroe dryly responded: "Sure, the radio." The fact that she was neither hungry nor homeless at the time mattered not. What did was the stamp of approval issued by the country's leading weekly. *Life* featured her in that familiar come-hither pose, in an off-the-shoulder white dress, and admiringly reported on the innocent waif's career progress in such a cutthroat business. All perceptions of naïveté to the contrary, Monroe demonstrated a firm grasp on the exploitation of her public image.

3. APPEARS IN FIRST ISSUE OF *PLAYBOY*, DECEMBER, 1953

Before explaining the acquisition by Hugh Hefner of his first centerfold, let's backtrack to the session. In late 1948, young

Marilyn, on her way to an audition, got into a fender-bender that rendered her car undrivable. As passersby gawked at the vision in tight dress and heels, some gentlemanly types proffered their business cards to the lady in distress, including noted Hollywood photographer Tom Kelley. He lent her $5 for cabfare, and although the tryout didn't go very well, she never forgot the kindness. Forward to the following spring, when jobs were scarce, and padding her modeling resume seemed a canny move. Monroe showed up at Kelley's studio, $5 in hand, and asked if Kelley had any work. As it happened, a model for a beer ad had called in sick, so she happily stepped in. Pabst was pleased with the results, as was a Chicago calendar maker who saw them. Word got to Marilyn through Kelley: would she be interested in a nude modeling project? She agreed and returned to the studio in late May. As his wife dressed the set, Kelley put on some music, set up a ladder, and began arranging the poses. Marilyn left with 50 of the $500 Kelley was paid and never returned.

Come 1953, aspiring publisher Hugh Hefner was casting about for something electrifying to jump-start his new enterprise. While word that the star of that year's *Niagara* and *Gentlemen Prefer Blondes* had posed bare a few years before was common knowledge, the images had only been available on a calendar, not in any magazine. Hefner discovered that a local firm held the rights, and for a $500 investment, he secured not only alternative poses but the color separations as well. Lest anyone miss the point, a black-and-white shot of Marilyn in a low-cut dress looking positively exuberant graced the cover of that first issue. The event proved mutually beneficial to both parties—*Playboy* was launched, selling an impressive 10,000 copies first time out, and Marilyn's photos were presented somewhat more respectably than on the wall of some garage. Curiously, the century's two biggest boosters of sex-as-nothing-to-be-ashamed-of never met. (Years later, Hefner would buy himself a crypt adjoining Monroe's.)

4. MARRIES JOE DIMAGGIO, JANUARY 14, 1954

Characteristically, his girlfriend's image being splashed in the center spread of the new men's magazine gave the former slugger further cause to stew. Though they'd been dating for two years by this time, the Yankee Clipper never seemed to get it through his head that his beloved was the embodiment of every American male's fantasies, and furthermore it was a role she relished. His wishful thinking saw her ending her career and settling down to the role of homemaker, something that even had she desired to, was ill-equipped to deliver. They had met at his request after Di-Maggio spotted Monroe in a cheesecake photo posing as a batter—he took it at face value that she was a fan. That she'd never been to a game, and sports bored her, should have hinted at future troubles, but it didn't. DiMaggio, on the other hand, had nothing but contempt for Hollywood and all of its attendant glitter. Nonetheless, a definite chemistry was ignited by early 1952, and the two quietly began dating. DiMaggio remained consistent in his Old World view of women. They fought bitterly over any attention she received from other men, the clothes her career called for, and his overall air of condescension. According to the available evidence, his success as a hitter didn't end with baseball. They weathered nearly two years of a roller-coaster romance before stunning friends and public alike with their wedding at City Hall in San Francisco. Before leaving the premises, the bride secured a promise from her husband: gazing at her wedding bouquet, she invoked Jean Harlow, her idol, whose fiancée placed fresh flowers on her grave every week. If she died before he did, would he do the same for her? Joe DiMaggio assured her that he would.

5. ENTERTAINS TROOPS IN KOREA, FEBRUARY 16, 1954

The two, accompanied by DiMaggio's business manager, went to Japan, ostensibly on their honeymoon. While there, Marilyn received an invitation from the Army to perform in a

USO show for the Allied troops. Despite her husband's strong disapproval, she jumped at the chance. For four days, she traveled to an assortment of makeshift outdoor venues in bone-chilling cold, in each instance greeted by tens of thousands of men who had never seen her films but certainly knew her from pinups and magazine photos. The contact was life-changing on both ends: the men would never forget the star who seemed so happy and giving, obliging all photographers, blowing kisses, and projecting genuine joy at performing for them. For Marilyn, unscripted and completely bereft of any stage experience, a live audience of grateful men cheering her every move touched her deeply. She went back to her husband, bouncing with excitement: "You never heard such cheering!" "Yes, I have," he noted, taking measure of the fate that placed the former baseball star with his glory days behind him in a marriage with an actress whose best was yet to come.

6. DIVORCES JOE DIMAGGIO, OCTOBER 27, 1954

In the months following their overseas sojourn, events unfolded true to form. Friends told of late-night phone calls from Marilyn following violent fights; DiMaggio periodically haunted her film sets, berating her in public before storming off, and his jealous rages continued toward any man compelled by work to spend time with her. For Monroe's part, try as she might, DiMaggio's lowbrow interests bored her. She found fishing tedious, his absorption in televised sports unfathomable, and his attempts to control her intolerable. While she sought to engage him intellectually with the culture she immersed herself in, he turned a deaf ear. When they fought, he sometimes went days without speaking to her. All in all, it was a pretty good recipe for disaster. The final straw came when newsman Walter Winchell practically arm-twisted DiMaggio to witness some location shooting his wife was engaged in. Upon arriving in New York, he was greeted by the sight of throngs gathered to witness the filming of the immortal scene in *The Seven-Year Itch* where Marilyn (cast as The Girl) pauses over the subway vent while her skirt billows upward in the breeze. The unmistakable sounds of a major battle erupted from their hotel room that night. The next morning on the set, makeup was applied to cover up several bruises. The couple returned to California, and two weeks later, Monroe filed for divorce. The star's personal dramas made work on the comedy even more challenging, though there were offscreen moments of unexpected levity that rivaled anything found in a film script.

The incident that became known as the "wrong door raid" demonstrated that, despite their legal breakup, DiMaggio was still intent on keeping tabs on Marilyn, to a degree that bordered on sociopathic. Before their divorce, he'd hired a pair of private investigators to gather evidence of any infidelities. Now, nearly two weeks after the marriage had ended, the Yankee Clipper stuck to his task. On receiving word that his former wife had been followed spending several evenings at the same address, an enraged DiMaggio gathered his posse. Accompanied by pal Frank Sinatra and two muscle men, he banged on the apartment door, demanding entrance. Getting no response, they quickly busted down the door, only to find 37-year-old Florence Kotz in bed, screaming. The residence they'd been seeking was nearby—the home of one of Marilyn's classmates from an acting study group. Despite the efforts to cover up the embarrassing event, *Confidential* magazine reported it in great detail a year later.

7. QUITS HOLLYWOOD TO STUDY ACTING IN NEW YORK, FEBRUARY 1955

Disillusioned by marriage and her shabby treatment at Fox, Monroe knew she needed a break. Tired of the continual grind of unimaginative roles, she took the first step toward autonomy by forming Marilyn Monroe Productions, a company that would give the actress complete control of her projects. As Fox and her lawyers duked it out, she chose this time of reinvention to relocate and realize a lifelong dream:

to study under the famous Lee Strasberg, the father of "Method" acting. Though sometimes derided as a fad that resulted in performances riddled with tics, the Method turned out some undeniable greats: Brando, Dean, Newman, and Poitier among them. Monroe's drive to hone her art also included a desire to broaden her self-education. Like many whose academic backgrounds are spotty at best, she tended to overcompensate, tackling weighty works that most would shun. Her pursuit of culture also put her back into close contact with famed playwright Arthur Miller, author of *Death of a Salesman* as well as the recent allegory *The Crucible*. At the same time, DiMaggio, who apparently was only capable of behaving when he *wasn't* married to her, continued to squire her around. Keeping the two dalliances separate involved considerable juggling.

8. LEGALLY CHANGES NAME TO MARILYN MONROE, FEBRUARY 23, 1956

The end of 1955 saw two major developments: a successful conclusion to her battle with Fox, and her liaison with Miller resulting in FBI suspicion that she was a "fellow traveler" with the "known Communist sympathizer" playwright. As a result unbeknownst to her, the government began compiling a voluminous file on her every move. As filming began out west on *Bus Stop*, Miller relocated—partly to be near her, partly to establish Nevada residency for his upcoming divorce. Any chance of reconciling with DiMaggio at this time was dashed. With new beginnings in the air, Marilyn formally retired the name "Norma Jeane," with which she'd usually signed documents. Though generally clear-headed in her decision making at the time, her reliance on sleeping aids, enabled by their easy accessibility and the toll that her assorted traumas were taking on her, had become manifest.

An interesting chapter in Red-baiting played out that summer. Walter Winchell, a close friend of both DiMaggio *and* J. Edgar Hoover, put the word out in his column that America's most beloved blonde was dallying with "a longtime pro-lefto." Miller was duly summoned to testify before HUAC. Despite all of its surveillance and snooping, the FBI was at a loss to provide any evidence that Miller had ever been a member of the Communist Party. Thus it was from a position of strength that he appeared before the committee, denouncing its work and refusing to name names. Contempt of Congress charges were a certainty, even likely, after Miller rejected a deal wherein all charges would be dropped if he simply allowed himself to be photographed *shaking hands with Walter Winchell!* (Only in America, folks.) This didn't happen, but with enormous hubris and more than a hint of self-serving drama, the playwright declared before the world (while demanding the return of his passport) his intent to "marry Marilyn Monroe," who was leaving for England on her next project. The press and much of the country were shocked, no one more so than Marilyn herself.

9. MARRIES PLAYWRIGHT ARTHUR MILLER, JUNE 29, 1956

So it was while watching the proceedings on television that Marilyn heard Miller's proposal of marriage. Any reservations she had (and there were plenty) had to be brushed aside in the rush to change the story from "noted playwright under suspicion" to "suspected playwright cleared as love conquers all." So valuable was the cachet of goodwill from being associated with Marilyn that Miller found himself the recipient of much-needed public support (as he had no doubt banked on). Winchell's efforts to punish the star merely won both of them sympathy. Events tumbled head-long with little pause for clear thought. Miller and Monroe made arrangements to meet the press on the afternoon of their planned civil ceremony. An overzealous reporter, eager to scoop the competition, engaged in a chase with the couple's car. It ended when the press vehicle smashed into a tree, killing the young journalist. Always sensitive to portents, Monroe wept—this surely was a bad omen. Two days later, a religious ceremony with friends and family was held. The festivities were held up by the bride's cold feet. Assured by her people that this second wedding need not take place, she first agreed, then paused and finally said, "We can't disappoint [the guests]."

10. *SOME LIKE IT HOT* PREMIERES, MARCH 29, 1959

The soap opera that was Monroe's new marriage never had a chance. Now in England filming *The Prince and the Showgirl* opposite Laurence Olivier (who also directed), she found herself in the company of *two* men who continually condescended to her, mistaking her lack of cynicism for a lack of sophistication. To Freudians, Miller's casually (or carelessly) leaving open a personal journal where his wife could find it was no accident. Happening upon it, she glanced down to discover in detail his own considerable doubts about their union and his expressions of disappointment and pity for her. To someone of her particular psyche, the revelation was devastating. In less than a month, the marriage had been dealt a blow from which it would never fully heal. Further complications arose from her subsequent pregnancy, followed by a miscarriage. Despite, or maybe because of, this inner turmoil, her performance in *The Prince and the Showgirl* shines. Her next outing, which she undertook after a two-year lull, would prove to be her most lasting comedy.

Of all people, Billy Wilder, who had directed Monroe's triumphant performance in *The Seven Year Itch*, had reason never to want to work with her again. She gave him fits with her pathological tardiness, her dependence on acting coaches, and her desire for endless retakes to nail lines just so. Still, he couldn't argue with the results and offered up extravagant praise for her nuanced performances, declaring all the effort to be worth it. After all, he said, "anyone can memorize lines." Tony Curtis, exasperated and exhausted by her "method," was less forgiving, likening his love scenes with Marilyn to "kissing Hitler." The antipathy was mutual. That being said, the roaring twenties farce is a surprisingly "modern" film, with its casual violence, cross-dressing, and implied homosexuality. The casting is perfect, with Jack

PDImages.com

Newlyweds Marilyn Monroe and Arthur Miller revel in marital bliss.

Lemmon responsible for the lion's share of laughs. Monroe's final two and a half films (*Let's Make Love*, 1960; *The Misfits*, 1961; and the unfinished *Something's Got To Give*, 1962) disappoint by comparison, making *Some Like It Hot* an enduring epitaph.

You Can Say That Again

There are any number of famous movie lines from some of the decade's biggest films that culturally literate people are familiar with: "Stella!!!"; "I'm ready for my close-up, Mr. DeMille"; "I coulda been a contender, Charley"; "Shane, come back!"; "Nobody's perfect." We won't concern ourselves with the obvious, opting instead for some great cinematic quotes that have stood the test of time. The following quotations cover a lot of ground, yet in some way, seem to resonate within our own day. No other commentary is necessary, other than: use them wisely.

1. *SUNSET BOULEVARD* (1950)

Gloria Swanson (as Norma Desmond): "They took the idols and smashed them, the Fairbankses, the Gilberts, the Valentinos! And who've we got now? Some nobodies!"

2. *BORN YESTERDAY* (1950)

William Holden (as Paul Verrall): "A world full of ignorant people is too dangerous to live in."

3. *THE BIG CARNIVAL* (1951)

Kirk Douglas (as Chuck Tatum): "Bad news sells best, 'cause good news is no news."

4. *HIGH NOON* (1952)

Lon Chaney, Jr. (as Martin Howe): "People gotta talk themselves into law and order before they do anything about it. Maybe because deep down they don't care. They just don't care."

5. *SHANE* (1953)

Alan Ladd (as Shane): "A gun is as good or as bad as the man using it. Remember that."

6. *THIS ISLAND EARTH* (1955)

Rex Reason (as Dr. Cal Meacham): "Our true size is the size of our God!"

7. *BAD DAY AT BLACK ROCK* (1955)

Walter Brennan (as Dr. T. R. Velie, Jr.): "I feel for you, but I'm consumed with apathy."

8. *FRIENDLY PERSUASION* (1956)

Walter Catlett (as Professor Waldo Quigley): "I want you to know, sir, I honor your prejudices—um, uh, convictions."

9. *OLD YELLER* (1957)

Fess Parker (as Jim Coates): "Now and then, for no good reason, life will haul off and knock a man flat."

10. *ON THE BEACH* (1959)

Ava Gardner (as Moira Davidson): "I love Americans. They're so naïve."

And Now, a Word From Our Sponsors

Back in the day, commercials featured two kinds of showbiz folk: the up-and-comers who sometimes made it big in the future (like Martha Stewart) or veteran performers in the twilight of their careers (for example, Buster Keaton, the Marx Brothers). To find a financially set Hollywood star in her prime, with a healthy career (married to an even bigger actor/producer, for instance) flogging products (for example, cell phones) on TV would have been unthinkable and a little crass. (Nor would you find bankable personalities slumming by doing ads that aired only in Japan or Europe.) In the fifties, certifiable legends had a healthy enough sense of self-worth to do their shucking and jiving in the light of day, while newcomers often got their start as human props. Here are a few.

1. JAMES DEAN FOR PEPSI

In December 1950, this UCLA theater major responded to a posting seeking aspiring actors for a television ad audition. Out of the hundreds who turned out, Dean was among the 12 selected to represent typical teenagers. Though older than his peers, he looked younger. The producers liked what they saw in his rough-hewn but well-scrubbed appearance. On December 13, they spent the afternoon filming at Griffith Park, where Dean was the subject of numerous close-ups among the gang riding the carousel and drinking Pepsi. A later sequence had him snap his fingers and lead the revelers to the malt shop, where they partook in a veritable Pepsi orgy while dancing around a jukebox, singing, "Pepsi Cola hits the spot!" The shoot, for which Dean received the princely sum of $10, represented his first paid acting job. A departure from his accustomed stage work, this first filmed performance found the 19-year-old cast as a rebel without applause.

2. MARILYN MONROE FOR UNOCAL

It's uncanny to find that so early in her career, Monroe's character was more or less established when she filmed a commercial for United Oil of California. She's cute, whimsical, and projects the persona that begs for someone to protect her. The spot shows her at a service station (remember those?), whereupon she informs the attendant that "Cynthia" is her first car, and that she wants her to be the best cared for car ever. "Put Royal Triton in Cynthia's little tummy!" "Right, lady!" The innuendo is unmistakable—you know exactly *what* the attendant wants to offer and *where* he wants to put it. Still, the feigned innocence is something to behold.

3. CHARLTON HESTON FOR CAMEL CIGARETTES

Given the name Heston would make for himself as National Rifle Association spokesman decades later, there's no surprise finding the young actor promoting another deadly product. What made for tragic irony was the smoking-related deaths of his father and sister years later, after which Heston would bitterly rue his years pushing tobacco products. At the time he filmed this particular ad though, he was probably in no position to turn down any opportunity for exposure. In the spot, he comes at the end of a line of established showbiz personalities who are outed by an unseen narrator as "Camel smokers": Tony Curtis, Jane Greer (who?), John Wayne (d'oh!), and so forth, until the newcomer comes into view. Distinctly uncomfortable-looking as the narrator demands of him, "What makes *you* a Camel smoker?" Heston stammers an explanation about not knowing what the scientific data say—all he knows is that he likes the "mild" taste. And compared to whatever smoking materials he evidently must have been indulging himself with, Camels probably *were* milder.

4. BUSTER KEATON FOR ALKA-SELTZER

The consensus among those who know about such things is that twenties film audiences were blessed with a trio of bona fide comic geniuses. Charlie Chaplin, Harold Lloyd, and Buster Keaton composed the silent cinema triumvirate of innovative, groundbreaking filmmakers whose work would influence film comedy for generations to come. By the time sound came along in the thirties, each of these actor's glory days were largely over: Chaplin kept most of his cachet the longest before personal and political issues caught up with him, while Lloyd essentially retired, filming one ill-advised comeback in the forties. It was Keaton who took the hardest fall; plagued with alcoholism and bad business decisions, the thirties and forties found him reduced to working on Poverty Row pictures and writing gags for other filmmakers. But beginning in the late forties, something happened. By then in his fifties, Keaton was rediscovered, due to his highly visual brand of comedy, which perfectly suited the medium of television. A new audience, raised on his TV guest appearances and commercials, grew up in complete ignorance of his glorious past. Keaton amiably took work where he found it, using his unique sense of the absurd to star in many memorable TV ads, for, among others, Kodak and Ford vans. Perhaps the best known was the series of ads he filmed for Alka-Seltzer, back when it still made use of its mascot, Speedy—a red-haired little boy with a tablet on his head. One typical spot showed Keaton as a ship captain bedeviled by a cold symptoms as his ship approaches an iceberg. "Relief is just a swallow away," Speedy promises, echoing a sentiment often implied but seldom voiced in the real world.

5. SEÑOR WENCES FOR GUNTHER BEER

Unless you witnessed his act firsthand (so to speak), it is virtually impossible to convey to the uninitiated how *funny* Señor Wences was. Modern audiences might compare him to the kid's show *Oobi*, which likewise uses hands as puppets (and which doubtless drew inspiration from the Spanish entertainer). Wences was a ventriloquist, but not with the standard dummy on his lap. Affixing a pair of eyes to, and painting a mouth on, his left hand, he made a falsetto-talking character named "Johnny," rounded out with a long, blonde wig and a full torso and body, come to life. His standard comeback line to any put-down was (in a Spanish accent), "Deefeecult for you, easy for me!" And that wasn't all, folks. With his *right* hand, Wences supported a lidded box that held a talking head named Pedro (born of necessity early in his career when a railroad mishap crushed the body of his conventional dummy, sparing only the head). A gruff, bearded creature who preferred keeping the lid closed, Pedro never failed to elicit laughter with his signature exchange with Wences: "S'okay?" "S'awright!" Well, maybe you had to be there. But the act's surrealism was unmatched. In addition to the standard trick of drinking a glass of water, Wences smoked a cigarette while Johnny blew *perfect smoke rings!* Their act could be seen everywhere throughout their heyday, but it was especially well known to viewers of the *Ed Sullivan Show*. Their series of Gunther Beer ads featured variations of their shtick, including one where Pedro declared himself thirsty, compelling Wences to stick the neck of the bottle into the box for him to drink. For theater of the mind, you had to hand it to him. As for Gunther Beer, Hamm's bought the brewery in 1959 and immediately shut it down, thereby incurring the wrath of Gunther's loyal drinkers.

6. ERNIE KOVACS FOR DUTCH MASTER CIGARS

Proof that not all cigar smokers are pompous jerks could be gleaned from this television comedian's existence. A true pioneer of the medium, Kovacs was a master of the visual, with much of his act conveyed without words or to music. (His own opinion of the tube is worth mentioning: "It's appropriate that television is called a medium because rarely is it well done.") During his TV career, which spanned many years and many shows throughout the fifties and early sixties, Kovacs created a number of memorable characters and bits. One of the better known was an "act" called the Nairobi Trio. Picture a scene from *Waiting for Godot* as performed by simians, and you get the idea: three gorilla-masked "musicians," clad in topcoats and bowlers, pantomime to a catchy little song called, "Solfeggio," culminating with the "conductor" getting beaten on the head with mallets with every drum fill. (It has long been rumored that one of the apes was none other than Jack Lemmon.) Kovacs often included send-ups of other programs, and even advertisers, on his shows. It is therefore all the more remarkable that someone at Dutch Master trusted him as a spokesman, but on the other hand, he probably *was* the best-known cigar smoker in the land. (The fact that he *never* tasted a Dutch Master and invariably smoked foot-long Cubans mattered not.) True to form, the commercials he created were amusing and clever. The most memorable one showed Kovacs, fully dressed, *under water*, puffing on a (fake) cigar. At the appropriate moment, he lets out what looks like a billow of smoke (actually, it was some cream he had prepared beforehand). It is a matter of record that when Kovacs died in January 1962 behind the wheel of his Corvair, investigators found he'd lost control of the vehicle while attempting to light a cigar.

7. ADAM WEST FOR SUGAR FROSTED FLAKES

The former William West Anderson had been kicking around show business for several years in the late fifties, visible enough to be recognizable but not quite known. Between a stint in radio (putting his smooth delivery to good use) and finding work in TV westerns (for his six-foot two-inch frame as much as for his stage name), West was hired to plug this breakfast cereal at a time when that particular market was pretty cutthroat. Standard throughout much of the fifties and sixties were TV cast commercials. This required the ensemble of a given show, in character and on set, to deliver a plug for the show's sponsors (most often cereal or cigarettes, depending on the program), sometimes working up the ad insidiously as a presumed segment of the story. These were, of course, removed for rebroadcast, but seen today they are jarringly anachronistic, especially the cigarette plugs. (For instance, *I Love Lucy* was sponsored by Philip Morris; those spots evoke special hilarity, especially the ones that show the Ricardos puffing away in pajamas before crawling off to their separate beds.) Adam West, however, didn't have a regular TV gig in the fifties, which freed him up to appear as an actor in this spot. Playing a father at breakfast but coming on like a second-string Clark Kent, the pre-*Batman* West is seen interacting with a child. The audience sees the buttoned-down, no-nonsense professional transformed by his preschool-age daughter; when he tries to correct her table manners (and her inability to say "frosted flakes" without mixing up the consonants), he is instead seduced by the intoxicating mixture of sugars, frosting, and flakes, refilling his bowl and aping her primitive etiquette. A promising career in domestic comedies was thus thwarted when West instead followed the path that led to Gotham City.

8. MISS FRANCES FOR WHEATIES

Beginning in 1952, Dr. Frances Horwich, a specialist in children's education at Chicago's Roosevelt University, began broadcasting perhaps the best-known attempt to engage young minds through television. *Ding Dong School* (so named for the hand-rung school bell seen at the show's opening, not the quality of the students) was a direct forerunner of *Mr. Rogers' Neighborhood*, a gentle, low-key viewing experience devoid of loud, broad, slapstick entertainment. Instead, "Miss Frances," as she preferred to be known, engaged the audience at home as if she were actually in their living rooms, communicating with such stock dialogue as, "Wasn't that fun?" or "What did you think of that?" after every activity. Her activities included reading from Little Golden Books; demonstrating various arts and crafts, singing, and even cooking lessons ("How about a banana, peanut butter, and lettuce sandwich?"). The much-acclaimed show was supported by sponsors that met her approval. One that made the cut was Wheaties. (For a few brief years in the fifties, the "Breakfast of Champions" abandoned the sports motif in an effort to crack the kid's market. While sales among young'uns did go up, adult consumption dropped, leading to a reversal of this decision in 1958.) In a move that insured Horwich's hearty endorsement, the cereal maker offered a limited-time run of boxes that came with a black-board on the back—a specially coated surface conducive to chalk that could be wiped off. On the air, Horwich demonstrated the box's possibilities. Eventually, when the show went national out of New York, Horwich balked at the networks attempts to foist a BB gun sponsorship on her, leading to the program's cancellation in 1956. She continued to be active in environmental and kids' issues until her death at age 94 in 2001. (News editors faced the irresistible temptation to declare her passing by announcing "*Ding Dong* Horwich is dead.")

9.   JACK BENNY, WITH HUMPHREY BOGART, FOR LUCKY STRIKES

To generations of Americans, comedian Jack Benny was one of the greatest laugh-getters. Starting as a vaudeville violinist in the twenties, he honed his act alongside contemporaries George Burns and Gracie Allen, Ed Wynn, and Fred Allen, traveling the same path from stage to radio to movies to TV. Benny's persona as a vain, insufferable tightwad was well defined, as were those of his supporting cast of wife Mary Livingston, valet Rochester, announcer Don Wilson, and tenor Dennis Day. The ensemble's act translated effortlessly to the new medium, along with the tradition of working a word from the sponsor into the show. Lucky Strikes cigarettes became sponsors on radio in 1944, then on TV until 1959.

In October 1953, actor Humphrey Bogart appeared on Benny's show. In a spoof of *Dragnet*, Bogart displayed a heretofore little-suspected knack for vaudevillian slapstick. He played a suspect being interrogated by the hard-boiled Benny, during the course of which they managed to work in a plug for Lucky Strikes. One is unaccustomed to seeing Bogart acting with such deadpan hilarity, no less so when he belts out the Lucky Strike jingle without cracking a smile. The audience roared at the scene; one can sense that Benny is maintaining his composure but just barely. It is another of those sad ironies that Bogart was dead of throat cancer a little over three years later.

10. THE MARX BROTHERS FOR PROM

Of the three mainstays of the act, Groucho maintained the highest profile throughout the fifties, with his popular *You Bet Your Life* game show. As the eldest brother, Chico by rights should have retired long before, but his endless gambling habit and general financial mismanagement compelled him to keep going. (When mobster Bugsy Siegel was gunned down, in his pocket was an uncashed check from Chico Marx. This was some *serious* wagering.) One reliable source of income was his nightclub act, health permitting. Long accustomed to bailing out his errant elder, Harpo occasionally joined him. When Prom hair products signed on as sponsors of *You Bet Your Life*, the deal included starring Harpo and Chico in the ads that aired on Groucho's show—an ad hoc reunion of the act. So, in the most unlikely of backdrops—a home permanent commercial—Chico and Harpo made one of their final filmed appearances, but separately; Chico's role was on-camera narrator while his brother chased women around. Harpo repeated the shtick in spots for Labatt beer opposite a Bavarian marionette.

I Don't Remember *Mama*

Ponder this: future generations learning that people of our time were addicted to shows like *Survivor*, *The Osbournes*, and something called *American Idol*. Imagine a world where *Friends*, *Seinfeld*, and *Everybody Loves Raymond* don't exist in reruns, much less in memory. This may give you an idea of what you are about to read; a roll call of top-rated TV shows from barely a couple of generations back that consistently drew huge audiences, but are known today only to hard-core tube junkies. The lesson here: never underestimate the effect of reruns in bestowing immortality. Another observation: a quick glance at this list reveals that, at least in the 1950s, CBS (the "Tiffany" network) *ruled!* Add *I Love Lucy*, *The Ed Sullivan Show*, *The Jackie Gleason Show*, and *The Twilight Zone* into the mix, and there would be no reason for anyone to watch another network. Had NBC and ABC gotten savvy to the lure of "reality" TV, it would have been an entirely different story. Note: All times given are Eastern Standard Time.

1. *BIG TOWN* (OCT. 5, 1950–SEPT. 16, 1954), THURSDAY, 9:30 P.M., CBS

Based on a radio show starring Edward G. Robinson, this series centered on the exploits of crusading reporter Steve Wilson, who worked for the *Illustrated Press* newspaper. Patrick

McVey starred, with a succession of actresses portraying his love interest, Lorelei Kilbourne. Each week, Steve took on some worthy adversary, be it crooked politicians, organized crime, or social injustice.

Following its cancellation on CBS, the show was picked up and ran another two seasons on NBC. McVey went on to star for two seasons in the syndicated *Man Hunt* beginning in 1959, in a role that virtually reprised his character in *Big Town*.

2. *DECEMBER BRIDE* (OCT. 4, 1954–SEPT. 24, 1959), MONDAY, 9:30 P.M., CBS

This sitcom was based on efforts to match up widowed Lily Ruskin with a man. The socially attractive senior, as played by Spring Byington, lived with her daughter and son-in-law. Harry Morgan, as henpecked neighbor Pete Porter, was a frequent guest, eventually winning his own spin-off, *Pete and Gladys*.

3. *THE GEORGE GOBEL SHOW* (OCT. 2, 1954–MARCH 10, 1959), SATURDAY, 10 P.M., NBC

Originally running for 30 minutes, this comedy variety series later expanded to a full hour as the formula was tinkered with. Gobel was a folksy, flat-topped humorist, who began each show with a comic monologue and was prone to outbursts of, "Well, I'll be a dirty bird!" Years after his series ended, "Lonesome George," as he was known, became a regular on the original *Hollywood Squares*, replacing folksy comic Charlie Weaver.

4. *LIFE AND LEGEND OF WYATT EARP* (SEPT. 6, 1955–SEPT. 26, 1961), TUESDAY, 8:30 P.M., ABC

As a counterweight to CBS's *Gunsmoke*, this entry into the "adult" western niche more than held its own. The show was sandwiched between *Cheyenne* and *Broken Arrow*, making Tuesday evenings at ABC cowboy nirvana for like-minded viewers as well as something of a salvation to a network glutted with such dead weight as *It's Polka Time* and *Ozark Jubi-lee*. *Wyatt Earp* was unique in that it depicted events as they unfolded naturally, with all the continuity of a serial. "In-spired" rather than based on actual people, it nonetheless traced the famed lawman's career from city to city. (What no one seemed to notice was that Earp and Matt Dillon *both* held the position of town marshal in Dodge City simultane-ously. Parallel universe, perhaps?) The series concluded with events leading up to and including the famous gunfight at the OK Corral in Tombstone, Arizona. Mainstay through-out the show's run was Hugh O'Brian in the title role. Armed with a Buntline hand cannon, he enforced the peace without violence unless compelled. O'Brian reprised the part as a cameo in one of Kenny Rogers's made-for-TV *Gambler* mov-ies in 1991.

5. *THE LINEUP* (OCT. 1, 1954–JAN. 20, 1960), FRIDAY, 10 P.M., CBS

What *Dragnet* was to Los Angeles, this show was to San Francisco. True crimes were dramatized in each episode, cli-maxing with the title tableau being enacted. Former silent film child star Warner Anderson portrayed the series' lead, detective Ben Guthrie. He was abetted by inspectors Matt Grebb and Fred Asher during the show's initial four seasons, before the latter two retired and were replaced for the series finale. Such was *The Lineup*'s popularity that in 1958 it re-ceived feature film treatment. (In our own time, not even *Law and Order* has achieved that.)

6. *MAMA* (JULY 1, 1949–JULY 27, 1956), FRIDAY, 8 P.M., CBS

Based on a play and film, both entitled *I Remember Mama* (1948), this popular series was also set in San Francisco, circa 1917. The sentimental comedy told the story of the Hansen family, Norwegian immigrants Mama, Papa, and daughters Nels, Katrin, and Dagmar as well as assorted ex-tended family members. Stage actress Peggy Wood starred in the title role, at last gaining a measure of success that eluded her in film. For a series of such enormous popularity, the question is begged: why is it so forgotten? Shifts in taste aside, a partial answer lies in the fact that, unlike *I Love Lucy*, for instance, *Mama* was aired live, not filmed—therefore, no reruns. If any shows do exist, they would be on kinescopes (which consist of filming the broadcast off of a TV screen, with the accompanying distortion). Keep in mind that the burgeoning medium was not planned for an extended shelf life. Despite *Mama*'s consistently finishing in the top 25 for most of its run, CBS pulled the plug in the summer of 1956. A revival prompted by audience outcry only lasted 13 weeks before *Mama* retired for good.

7. *THE MILLIONAIRE* (JAN. 19, 1955–SEPT. 28, 1960), WEDNESDAY, 9 P.M., CBS

Things were a little different in the fifties. In this show, for instance, perfect strangers were given one million dollars, without having to answer arcane questions, or eating live insects and fecal matter, or endangering life and limb. No, the premise of this show was a little more intriguing—what would people do with their lives *after* being gifted thusly? The series featured the fictional John Beresford Tipton (whose identity was never revealed on camera), an eccentric millionaire. (Aren't they all?) Each show began with Tipton describing the proposed giftee to his secretary, who would then follow through on the assignment. The show was formatted as an anthology drama, so each week's episode starred nonrecurring guest actors and actresses. Marvin Miller (the only series regular) played the secretary. Once the show began getting noticed, Miller found himself on the receiving end of thousands of letters from people begging for his largesse, which he obliged by sending each correspondent a check for "one million dollars' worth of good luck." The richly baritoned actor later won a Grammy in the sixties for his work on Dr. Seuss recordings.

8. *PRIVATE SECRETARY* (FEB. 1, 1953–SEPT. 10, 1957), SUNDAY, 7:30 P.M., CBS

This durable sitcom starred brassy Ann Sothern as Susie Mc-Namara, who served in the title capacity to New York talent agent Peter Sands (played by Don Porter). The comedy played off of her penchant for meddling in ways that went beyond her job description. Though *Private Secretary* was a consistent top 25 performer, CBS showed Susie the door in 1957, only to welcome her back a year later as the star of the aptly named *Ann Sothern Show*. Some *Private Secretary* regulars ended up in the supporting cast of her second series, including Jesse White, known to millions as the original Maytag repair man. In 1965, Ms. Sothern provided her voice to the title 1928 Porter automobile in the famously execrable Jerry Van Dyke vehicle, *My Mother the Car*. *Private Secretary* sometimes turned up decades later in syndication under the title, *Susie*.

9. *YOUR HIT PARADE* (OCT. 7, 1950–JUNE 7, 1958), SATURDAY, 10:30 P.M., NBC

As one would imagine, this show's history went back to the days of radio, beginning in 1935 as the *Lucky Strike Hit Parade*. The format each week was to present a more or less accurate reading of the country's most popular seven songs, as rendered by the show's cast of singers. The ensemble was comprised of popular stars of the day, all but completely forgotten now. (Snooky Lanson, anyone?) Andre Baruch was the show's announcer, and in a shrewd bit of marketing, the audience had the choice of seeing or hearing each week's broadcast, as it was simulcast on radio. In the ballad-heavy pop music world of the early fifties, the show's group vocal framework supported the hit songs quite well. (The challenge came if a particular song *remained* popular for weeks at a time, necessitating creative staging of the performance to hold an audience's interest.) What ultimately led to the show's downfall was the arrival of rock & roll by 1955. Suddenly, a group of tuxedo-clad "grown-ups" uncomfortably finger-popping to "Sweet Little Sixteen" wasn't so cute. The kids tuned out in droves, and no amount of recasting could win them back. The boom was lowered and that was that. A wave of nostalgia in the early '70s saw an attempted revival hosted by Chuck Woolery, but it, too, faded.

10. *ZANE GREY THEATER* (OCT. 5, 1956–SEPT. 20, 1962), FRIDAY, 8:30 P.M., CBS

This western anthology series was hosted by movie actor Dick Powell, who occasionally starred in it as well. Powell gained fame in the thirties as a singing star in countless musicals at Warner Brothers. Chafing at the callow roles required of him, he reinvented himself in the forties as a film noir leading man, beginning with the role of Raymond Chandler detective Philip Marlowe in *Murder, My Sweet* (1944). Along the way Powell also found time to star as detective Richard Diamond on radio. As its title suggests, *Zane Grey Theater* was based on the western novels penned by the famed writer of *Riders of the Purple Sage* and other classics. As the series progressed, however, and the material ran thin, it began to include work by other writers covering the same ground. The entire last season of the show consisted of re-runs: NBC had lured Powell away to host a non-western anthology series structured exactly the same way, with the same ingredients, minus the horses.

I Coulda Been a Contender

Of special interest to TV-philes are the "might-have-beens"—shows that networks may have produced as far as the "pilot" stage before deciding against committing to a series. (A "pilot," as Jules would tell you, is a try-out filmed for the benefit of those who pick shows. If accepted, they are added to the programming schedule. If not, they become nothing.) The speculation here, because we all like to speculate, is: what if these shows *had* been picked up? In addition to an entirely different set of reruns that boomers would have grown up on, it's also possible that roles for which several actors became famous might never have happened had they been committed to another series already. For instance, had Alan Young's *Vernon Hathaway* series succeeded, *Mr. Ed* could have been owned by a completely different Wilber, if at all. Here now is a list of "nothings."

1. COMEDY: *THE SHRIMP* (CBS, 1953), STARRING RICHARD EYER AND SAMMY OGG

The blueprint for what ultimately became *Leave It to Beaver* was first sketched out in this never-was show. It concerned the efforts of a young boy (Ogg) to keep his younger sibling (Eyer) out of trouble. Ogg, who would later play Joe in *The Adventures of Spin and Marty*, was seen throughout the fifties in several episodes of *Dragnet* and guested in many TV westerns. Eyer, who had starred as Bobby in the TV version of *My Friend Irma*, made several films, notably *Friendly Persuasion* (1956) with Gary Cooper and Tony Perkins. He appeared in small TV roles until he gave up acting in the sixties to become a teacher.

2. COMEDY: *MR. BLANDINGS* (NBC, 1954), STARRING TOM EWELL

Kentucky-born Samuel Yewell Tompkins enjoyed a steady gig on Broadway beginning in the 1930s until Hollywood beckoned. His role as Judy Holliday's philandering husband in *Adam's Rib* (1949) won him some attention; a return to the stage in *The Seven Year Itch* won him a Tony. His put-upon, everyman persona made him a natural for the small screen, and NBC, casting about for the appropriate property, proposed a series based on the 1948 Cary Grant hit, *Mr. Blandings Builds His Dream House*. For whatever reason, the show failed to materialize, and Ewell went on to film *Seven Year Itch* opposite Marilyn Monroe. The *Blandings* concept was offered up again in 1959 with different casting, to no avail. Ewell, meanwhile, after starring in his second-best-known film, *The Girl Can't Help It* (1957), finally got a series in 1960, *The Tom Ewell Show*. It lasted one season. (*The Money Pit* in 1986 was a retooling of the original *Blandings* film.)

3. PANEL SHOW: *MEET THE HOBOES* (CBS, 1954)

That anyone ever seriously considered this concept for a network slot boggles the mind. It was to be composed of a panel of three genuine rail-riders and a *banker*, moderated by yet another Boxcar Willie; The exact premise has been lost to history, alas. But, if nothing else, it demonstrates CBS's predilection for putting the downtrodden to good entertainment use. Consider all of the so-called rural comedies offered up in the sixties: *The Beverly Hillbillies*, *Petticoat Junction*, *Green Acres*, *Hee-Haw*. (And these were just the hits!) The notion of implementing the poor for amusement lives on with CBS's efforts to revisit *The Beverly Hillbillies* as a reality show, with real-life rural residents being set up for sport. Howls of protest from at least one segment of the population before a show has even aired shows that there may be limits, at long last.

4. COMEDY: *THE LIFE OF VERNON HATHAWAY* (NBC, 1955), STARRING ALAN YOUNG

Though it only lasted one season, *Screen Directors Playhouse* was one of the better anthologies on television in a decade that saw many such efforts. The premise, as the title implies, was to offer famous filmmakers a shot at directing and casting their own half-hour program on any story of their choosing. One aspect of the show was to serve as a launching pad for other series. Such was the case with this comedy, centering on a Walter Mitty-esque character whose rich fantasy life enabled him to have many adventures. Cast in the lead was a Scottish actor by way of England and Canada, Alan Young. Something of a prodigy, as a teen he had had a hugely popular radio show in Canada that he scripted and starred in. He parlayed that success into his own half-hour sketch comedy show on CBS beginning in 1950, in a sort of throwback to earlier, more mannered humor. It vanished after three seasons, leaving Young free to work in films. His finest moment came in 1960's *The Time Machine*, as the father and son Filbys. A year later, he found himself finally accepting a role he'd turned down several years before: the owner of a talking horse. *Mr. Ed* assured his place in TV immortality.

5. DRAMA ANTHOLOGY: *THE ORSON WELLES SHOW* (NBC, 1956)

Hollywood's favorite enfant terrible had dabbled in the new medium from time to time with pretty fair success, but it was a love/hate relationship. He likened television to peanuts, which he hated, though he'd quickly point out, "but I can't stop eating them." Desi Arnaz approached Welles in 1955 to host and direct an anthology that entailed productions of classic works of his own choosing. Not about to turn his back on a blank check, he agreed, and the deal was struck. Being Orson Welles, however, he simply couldn't stop himself from turning the project into a nightmare for Desilu, what with his first opportunity for unfettered control since RKO green-lighted *Citizen Kane* back in 1941. Given 10 days to shoot a pilot, he took a month; given a six-figure budget, he spent a million, including hosting a spare-no-expense wrap party, which he billed to the studio. The story he chose to work his alchemy on was John Collier's *The Fountain of Youth*. To give the devil his due, the results were spectacular, innovative, and unlike anything seen on TV. But the series never had a chance, with the critics claiming (undoubtedly accurately) that it was too "arty" for American audiences. Though never again given such leeway, Welles had the last laugh when *Fountain of Youth* won a Peabody Award of Excellence.

6. COMEDY: *YOU KNOW ME, AL* (NBC, 1957), STARRING DICK YORK

Based on a series of Ring Lardner baseball stories, this show centered on a thick-skulled pitcher for the Pittsburgh Pirates. It was a role the young Dick York had some experience with, having played Wreck Loomis in *My Sister Eileen* (1955). York first appeared before the cameras in some educational short films, following a successful radio career that began in his teens. This led to some parts on Broadway, including *Tea and Sympathy* and *Bus Stop*. Between the film commitments that followed *Eileen*, York managed to squeeze in a steady stream of TV appearances, including several on *Alfred Hitchcock Presents*. One could speculate upon the impact that the failure of *You Know Me, Al* had on York's career—and life. While it's possible that had the show succeeded, he might never have been offered *Bewitched* in 1964 (he in fact was the second choice for Darrin—after Dick Sargent!), more significant is the likelihood that his commitment would have extricated him from film duties that resulted in an ultimately disabling injury. In 1959, York was shooting *They Came to Cordura*, set during the Spanish-American war. The film, with a cast that included Gary Cooper and Ava Gardner, was directed by Robert Rossen, a man York described as an alcoholic with little regard for the well-being of his actors. Numerous injuries occurred on the set, mostly involving horses. York's happened while he was operating a railroad handcar when one of the extras reacted unexpectedly to the call of "Cut!" The ensuing mishap tore the muscles in York's right back. The injury was treated improperly, resulting in years of ever-more-debilitating torture and dependence on painkillers. Eventually York's deterioration forced the end of his acting days, but not before he got in one last great cinematic moment, as the John Scopes character in Stanley Kramer's *Inherit the Wind* (1960). Two years later, he at last scored a regular role in a TV series, *Going My Way*, with Gene Kelly. The show lasted one season.

7. DRAMA: *COLLECTOR'S ITEM* (CBS, 1958), STARRING VINCENT PRICE AND PETER LORRE

To nonhorror film fans, Peter Lorre was best known to audiences for his roles in *The Maltese Falcon* (1941) and *Casablanca* (1942). The vaguely European actor (he was actually Hungarian) was also probably the most widely imitated personality of his day, with his creepy, sinister manner and readily identifiable voice. By the 1950s, casting Lorre in a project became cinematic shorthand for intrigue and danger. Covering similar ground idiom-wise was his friend, Vincent Price. Price's career in film went back to the thirties, but he didn't really develop a persona until cast in 1953's 3-D *House of Wax*. This film's success gave him an entrée into the world of mystery and horror, a genre he never left. Fresh off the heels of the original, superior film version of *The Fly* (1958), he and Lorre were offered starring roles in a series centering on an art dealer (Price) and his mysterious underworld friend, Mr. Munsey (Lorre). Adding to the dark atmosphere was direction by Buzz Kulik, a relative newcomer who nonetheless would make a name for himself for his work on *The Twilight Zone* and *CBS Playhouse 90*. Although the pilot didn't sell, Kulik had a hugely successful career directing in television, with credits that included *Brian's Song* (1971). Lorre and Price eventually starred together in a pair of Roger Corman horror spoofs, *Tales of Terror* (1962) and *The Raven* (1963), as well as 1964's *Comedy of Terrors* alongside Boris Karloff.

8. DRAMA: *JOHNNY RISK* (NBC, 1958), STARRING MICHAEL LANDON AND ALAN HALE, JR

Though born to parents "in the business," young Eugene Orowitz had no particular showbiz aspirations, channeling his energies instead into the school track team. That he ended up an actor at all was a bit of fluke; he accompanied a friend to an audition and won the part himself. A newly rechristened Michael Landon found an initial blush of success with the drive-in classic *I Was a Teenage Werewolf* (1957). This, along with a spate of TV guest shots primarily in westerns, led to his casting in this proposed series. The action concerned Landon as the title character, the owner of a gambling ship in 19th-century Alaskan territory. Odd choice, considering his youth, that he should have been picked at all. The ship aspect, at least, proved canny for the actor selected as his sidekick, future Skipper Alan Hale, Jr. The look-alike son of the famous Hollywood actor, Hale had worked steadily in B movies throughout the forties, mostly in supporting roles. With television his fortunes changed, and by the time of this pilot he had one starring role already come and go (in the adventure series, *Biff Baker, USA*). Following the failure of this project, he found work in syndication as *Casey Jones*, until answering the call of the longest three-hour tour in history.

9. COMEDY: *WHERE THERE'S SMOKEY* (ABC, 1959), STARRING GALE GORDON AND SOUPY SALES

A familiar face to TV viewers who came of age in the fifties and sixties was Gale Gordon. His dignified manner in the face of the disruption of order around him lasted only until he at last blew his top, the way the long-suffering do. His specialty was authority figures, usually with patrician-sounding names (Osgood Conklin, Theodore J. Mooney, Harrison Carter). Gordon was known for two particular traits: first, his precise elocution, the result of two surgeries to correct a cleft palate as a boy and subsequent speech therapy; and second, working with Lucille Ball. The pair's professional relationship went back to the forties on radio with *My Favorite Husband*, the precursor to *I Love Lucy*. This was followed in the sixties by *The Lucy Show* and *Here's Lucy*, and in the eighties by the disastrous *Life with Lucy*. Only his commitment to *Our Miss Brooks* kept him from being cast as Fred Mertz in *I Love Lucy*. When at last *Miss Brooks* ended, Gordon found work in a pair of back-to-back TV flops, *The Brothers* and *Sally*. Desilu then offered him this project, which centered on the sober, officious Gordon as a fire chief, and his clownish nephew and fellow firefighter, played by Soupy Sales, in the title role. The show's failure to get picked up enabled Gordon to sign up for the short-lived *Pete and Gladys* before stepping in to replace the deceased Joe Kearns on *Dennis the Menace*, as Mr. Wilson's brother. Sales, of course, found great success on his own throughout the next decade.

10. WESTERN: *THE FRONTIER WORLD OF DOC HOLLIDAY* (ABC, 1959), STARRING ADAM WEST

ABC was the network leader in westerns, the hit genre of the decade's last years. With *Wyatt Earp* a proven hit, a series for Earp's well-known sidekick seemed an obvious move. One year earlier, CBS came up with its own version of the Holliday story, scripted by Aaron Spelling and starring

Dewey Martin, but the effort did not pan out. Adam West came to Hollywood in the late fifties; his only prior showbiz experience was serving as a radio DJ after college and a stint on a children's show in Hawaii. Typecast for his looks (and also possibly his stage name), the lanky actor found much work guesting on a plethora of TV westerns beginning in 1958. Interestingly, he had already played Doc Holliday three separate times on as many shows (*Sugarfoot*, *Lawman*, and *Colt .45*) before this particular pilot was aired as an episode of *Cheyenne* titled "Birth of a Legend." The Holliday of historic record suffered from tuberculosis, not the most attractive of illnesses. Nevertheless, the intended series planned to play up the "terminal disease" aspect, to tell the story of a man who, while battling the bad guys, knows that his days are numbered. It's possible that the built in "yecch!" factor did the series in, or maybe just western redundancy. In any event, West continued to find TV work, chiefly in westerns, until he stumbled upon the Bat Cave in 1966.

Because We *Like* You

That lingering suspicion among boomers that the TV they enjoyed as children stood head and shoulders above today's fare (at least in terms of originality and creativity) is not merely wishful nostalgia. While it is true that the decade's offerings may have lacked the sophistication of the average Nick Jr. show today, an undeniable air of freshness (as the medium invented itself) and idealism went beyond mere time filling. Many if not all kids' shows found novel ways to instill learning as they entertained. Further, federal licensing requirements, in mandating x amount of airtime be set aside for children, paid strict attention to the content, ensuring that it be distinguishable from the advertising that supported it. A world where a kids' show wasn't merely a vehicle for moving spin-off product? Imagine! Here are some of the most notable programs from a less cynical time.

1. *HOWDY DOODY* (DEC. 27, 1947–SEPT. 24, 1960), NBC

Possibly the best remembered kids' TV show of the decade, Howdy Doody (the character) was actually spawned from radio. In the late forties, a children's show on NBC called *Triple B Ranch* featured a cast of characters that included a dimwitted ranch hand named Elmer. His signature opening line was, "Well, howdy doody!" Once the show moved to television, marionette versions of the newly rechristened cowpoke and his friends came into being. The initial likeness was considerably more grotesque-looking than the cheerful freckle face most people are familiar with. However, disagreements between its creator and the show's producers necessitated developing a new puppet when Howdy's maker left the show and took him along. It took a full three episodes to reveal the new Doody, whose altered appearance was explained away by "plastic surgery." No kidding.

Millions of boomers most certainly know the "It's Howdy Doody time" opening theme by heart. (It followed Buffalo Bob Smith's cry, "Hey kids—what time is it?") How many realize that the tune was actually a turn-of-the-century ditty entitled, "Ta-Ra-Ra-Boom De-Ay"? (Later perverted by labor leader Joe Hill into a song encouraging industrial sabotage.) Buckskin-clad Bob (named for his Buffalo, New York, origins, not western bison) was one of several human populants of Doodyville, a circus town presided over by Howdy's nemesis, Phineas T. Bluster. Additional humans included Chief Thunder Thud and Princess Summerfall Winterspring (the latter played by actress Judy Tyler, who later co-starred with Elvis in *Jailhouse Rock*). And what would a circus be without a clown? The prototypical seltzer-spraying mute was played initially by future Captain Kangaroo Bob Keeshan. His successor literally had the last word at the show's demise in 1960, when he broke character to say, "Good-bye, kids."

The bleacher-bound children who made up the studio audience were known as the Peanut Gallery. In addition to an assortment of puppet skits, they endured songs and silent shorts. Famously originating as part of the show's array of entertainment was the animated creature known to us as Gumby. (Judging by what he can do today, one wouldn't realize that he had once been a little green slab of clay.) In its day, the show's enormous popularity translated into a five-day-a-week run, a radio version, scores of eminently collectible spin-off products, and, for Buffalo Bob, a heart attack. After a year's recovery, the program's schedule was mercifully cut back to an hour every Saturday.

2. *KUKLA, FRAN, AND OLLIE* (NOV. 29, 1948–AUG. 31, 1957), NBC

This imaginative and at times sardonic series was closely tied to television's infancy. Unlike so many other shows that existed before TV, *KF&O* did *not* originate in radio. Creator Burr Tillstrom of Chicago brought his "kids" into being as part of a Depression-era Works Project Alliance project, leading to a gig at Marshall Field's department store. Soon after, Tillstrom and his cast of puppets, dubbed the Kukla-politan Players, served as representatives of RCA Victor at the New York World's Fair of 1939. Until regular network TV broadcasting began, they toured the country, demonstrating the new medium. Six weeks after the show's television run began, it became the first program to be broadcast live on NBC from coast to coast. Four years later, KF&O's production of "Saint George and the Dragon" inaugurated the network's foray into color broadcasting, raising the fortunes of peacocks everywhere. The cast of players was headed by Kukla (a Russian endearment for "doll"), a high-voiced, bald, arch-browed character whose dominant features were rosy cheeks and a big red nose. Oliver J. Dragon ("Ollie") was a single-toothed, fireless dragon who considered himself, somewhat matter of factly, to be a master thespian. Lending an air of calm to Kukla's high-strung nervousness and Ollie's childish impulsiveness was their human companion, Fran Allison. A veteran of radio, she provided the perfect foil to the cast—understanding, sweet-natured, and wise. Though commonplace now, a real person interacting with puppets was groundbreaking at the time. For the entire run, the show never left its proscenium arch stage. Entire worlds and situations were conveyed purely through their dialogue and a minimum of props. Amazingly, Tillstrom single-handedly enacted the entire puppet troupe, which included Beulah Witch, Madame Ooglepuss, Fletcher Rabbit, and Cecil Bill. With each character possessing a well-defined personality (and voice), the shows unfolded chiefly through improvisation—only a bare-bones plot might be sketched out in advance. For extra credibility in treating her castmates like real personas, Fran Allison never allowed herself to see the puppets backstage—only on the air, with Tillstrom's voice channeling through them. Thus, the fantasy of the premise was sustained with conversations carried on in a natural manner. Productions staged by the cast included *The Mikado*, *The Arabian Nights*, satires, and historical fare. (The aforementioned *Saint George and the Dragon* included musical support from Arthur Fiedler and the Boston Pops Orchestra. Pretty highbrow stuff for a kids' show.) Although its regular prime-time run ended in 1957, *KF&O* returned to the air for specials and guest shots. In the late sixties and early seventies, CBS booked the group to host the *Children's Film Festival*. Their long career eventually wound down after a stint on public television.

3. *MR. I. MAGINATION* (MAY 29, 1949–APRIL 13, 1952), CBS

Paul Tripp, a writer and composer of songs for children, struck gold in 1942 with a story illustrating how every different component of a larger group contributes to the whole with the deathless *Tubby the Tuba*. The success of that project brought him offers to work in television, and in 1949 his concept hit the air. He played a railroad engineer on a train that transported youngsters anywhere their imagination wanted to go. Through songs and skits, the show's cast encouraged the audience at home to "act out"—to enact whatever fancy their little minds could conceive. On the air, Tripp and ensemble did the same, through travel to places of the mind ("Ambition Town," "'I Wish I Were' Land," etc.), enacting historical events, or even bringing to life dreams and fantasies sent in by viewers. As a former entertainer at an urban settlement house, Tripp knew how to entertain kids on a limited budget. A washtub full of water doubling for the Atlantic Ocean was all in day's work. Key to the show's success was reaching kids on their own level. Often child actors were cast as real-life figures from history, while Paul's real-life wife played female characters on the show. Other semiregulars included Richard Boone and a young Walter Matthau. Some episodes were directed by future Siamese king Yul Brynner, who did much behind-the-scenes work in early television. *Mr. I. Magination* won a host of awards for general excellence and all-around value for inspiring children to think. Naturally, sponsors were mortified, and CBS canceled it after three seasons.

4. *THE BIG TOP* (JULY 1, 1950–SEPT. 21, 1957), CBS

One of several circus-theme shows to run throughout the fifties, this durable entry featured some of the biggest acts in the world. Filmed at the New Jersey locale where many circuses spent the winter, a bottomless pool of talent was always at hand. First choice for ringmaster was a young radio host from Philadelphia, Ed McMahon, but the role ultimately went to Jack Sterling. Instead, McMahon got the more desirable role: head clown.

5. *TOM CORBETT, SPACE CADET* (OCT. 2, 1950–JUNE 25, 1955), CBS

Space-theme shows were another popular avenue for children's entertainment. This extremely successful program came about from the desire to compete with DuMont's popular *Captain Video*. Unlike that network's offerings, *Tom Corbett* was not hamstrung by budget limitations. The producers could spring for far more convincing special effects and sets, all the better to simulate weightlessness and deep space travel. They hired on a real scientist as adviser, and meticulous attention was paid to factual accuracy in depicting the perils of the galaxy. Unlike in typical space entertainment, most of the dangers encountered on this show came from natural hazards such as asteroids and meteor showers. There was no need to create outlandish space enemies or stage intergalactic battles. Set in 2350, the series presented the exploits of a young group of aspiring Solar Guards aboard their ship *Polaris* and at their training academy. The title character was portrayed by Frankie Thomas, who seemed to have an affinity for such roles, having starred as Cadet Osborne in *The Major and The Minor* (1942) and in the film *Flying Cadets* (1941). As a direct precursor to *Star Trek*'s Spock, a Venusian named Astro was one of Corbett's sidekicks. Turning up as occasional nemesis was Eric, commander of the *Vulcan*, played by future *Gomer Pyle* Sergeant Carter, Frank Sutton. The show, originally based on a Robert Heinlein novel, was further propagated by comic books and a daily newspaper comic strip, as well as every imaginable toy. It is surprising that a big screen version never materialized. Now that the series has faded into memory, at least one artifact from the show has survived and entered common parlance: the opening began with a countdown that ended with "Blast off!"—a term coined by *Tom Corbett*'s writers.

6. *ROOTIE KAZOOTIE* (DEC. 9, 1950–MAY 7, 1954), NBC/ABC

Originating on the same network as *Howdy Doody*, this character might best be described as Howdy's peer rather than his competition. Rootie represented every boy, possessed by the dreams most small kids have: playing professional baseball, joining a circus, and so on. He invariably sported a rakishly pitched baseball cap and pinstripes. The puppet cast was rounded out by his dog, Gala Poochie; his best girl, Polka Dottie; El Squeako Mouse; and Rootie's rival, Poison Zoomack. Two humans appeared regularly: Todd Russell as Big Todd and John Vee as Deetle Dootle, a mute Keystone-looking cop who performed magic tricks. An element of the show that would have understandably drove parents nuts was the use of Rootie-Kazootie dialogue—like *Zoom*'s ubby-dubby, it was a variation of pig Latin that resulted in frequent use of words like "gosharootie" or "absotootie." Host Big Todd (whose head was of normal size), sang songs between the scenes. Many stories were contrived around villain Poison Zoomack, a Snidely Whiplash-like character, and his attempts to steal Rootie's "kazootie" (apparently something akin to his "mojo"). Dog Gala Poochie underwent revision during the show's run: originally, he was called Nipper and sported black spots. After RCA withdrew its sponsorship, the dots were removed and the dog's name was changed.

7. *MR. WIZARD* (MAR. 5, 1951–SEPT. 5, 1965), NBC

This long-running series probably did more to awaken kids to the possibilities of science and physics than any classroom lesson. Host Don Herbert made the abstract fun and easy to understand by illustrating scientific theory with countless experiments that anyone could replicate at home. In a decidedly Mr. Rogers-like manner, the soft-spoken Herbert directed an assistant, alternating boys and girls, through the steps, explaining the expected outcome and why. With live TV, sometimes the results didn't end up quite as anticipated, but Herbert would reason through them calmly and try again. Though the show endured for years, it must be noted that an entire generation of boys were disappointed as they waited in vain for the day Mr. Wizard explained how to make gunpowder.

8. *THE SOUPY SALES SHOW* (JULY 4, 1955–AUG. 26, 1955), ABC

Don't let the brief airtime fool you; this was merely the first *nationally* aired series from a man who'd worked steadily on the air since 1950 and would continue to be a presence well into the seventies. Born Milton Supman, Sales was an innately silly man-child who seemed much more comfortable lingering in a child's world than in "growing up." Hence, no heavy-handed lessons were learned on *his* show. Sporting a polka-dot bow tie, Sales was supported by a cast of puppets that included two dogs with opposing temperaments—White Fang and Black Tooth; Marilyn Monwolf; Herman the Flea; and Pookie the Lion. The show's fast pace matched the energy level of the kids it was aimed at, and the steady stream of puns, asides, and bad jokes made it irresistible to adults as well. Sales's stock-in-trade was the pie fight. Looking back at his long career, he once estimated that he had been hit by 14,000 cream pies. In 1959, *Lunch with Soupy Sales* began. The cast of puppets returned as well, and all the action took place on a set that included a door. A regular feature depicted someone's unexpected entrance, usually following some non sequitur sound effect. On one occasion, sounds of a woman screaming were heard, and Soupy went to respond, expecting something innocuous as scripted. What the cameras caught was his reaction to a stark naked young woman, dancing—as it were—to the strains of David Rose's "The Stripper." To compound matters, the same crew members responsible for the gag had arranged for all of the TV monitors to show what Soupy saw—leading him to believe that the sight before him was going out live to children everywhere. As his career flashed before his eyes, the momentarily speechless Sales was reduced to stunned laughter. Episodes like this may have led to persistent urban legends suggesting that his show was studded with sexual innuendo and double entendres. For example, some people still swear that they or someone they know witnessed a skit where Soupy was making a pie with a guest, saying in passing, "My wife sure can't make a cherry pie, but boy—can she make a banana cream!" To this day Sales denies all such charges.

9. *Captain Kangaroo* (OCT. 3, 1955–DEC. 1984), CBS/PBS

Sometimes a labor dispute yields unexpected dividends. When 25-year-old Bob Keeshan was terminated for a second time from the *Howdy Doody* show (minutes before airtime, as it happened, along with three other performers who were attempting to *organize!*), it merely marked the latest squabble between Clarabelle the clown and Buffalo Bob Smith. The two shared a particular animosity, although years later, after his own everlasting success, Keeshan generously acknowledged a debt of gratitude for all he'd learned on the show. After a brief stint at his father in-law's mortuary, Keeshan remarshaled his wits and began one of the most successful stints in children's television history. Until gutted by

CBS in the early eighties, the Captain (so-called because of the jacket with the huge pockets he always wore) and other regulars of Treasure House ruled kids' daily morning television. Keeshan's show was conspicuously low key and moved at a slower pace than most of its competition. Everything about the show seduced young senses—from the signature theme (entitled "Puffin' Billy," which millions even now can hum note for note) to the imaginative visuals found on the set (Grandfather Clock, for just one haunting example). One recurring piece of business involved a knock-knock joke concluding with an avalanche of Ping-Pong balls raining down on the hapless captain. (Like Charlie Brown and Lucy with the football, the trick became to avoid the inevitable.) As Clarabelle, Keeshan had been aggressive, mean-spirited, and petulant. A polar opposite in his new role, it was as if he were seeking atonement. Regulars included Mr. Green Jeans (played by "Lumpy" Brannum, a former bassist with Fred Waring's Pennsylvanians), the resident farmer who, when not inventing things, instilled a sense of animal appreciation among viewers with his stream of assorted farmyard visitors. Performing yeoman duty as a cast unto himself was Cosmo Allegretti, whose many roles included Dennis the Handyman, Mr. Moose, Mr. Bunny Rabbit, Dancing Bear, and Grandfather Clock. A recurring animation on the show was the Terrytoon *Tom Terrific*. *Captain Kangaroo* wielded tremendous influence in cultivating a sense of fair play, good manners, and sensitivity. That no worthy replacement has taken its place is our loss, as was Keeshan's death in early 2004.

10. *CIRCUS BOY* (SEPT. 23, 1956–SEPT. 1960), NBC/ABC/ NBC

Italian-born actor George Dolenz had carved out a niche for himself in Hollywood playing European nobleman types. In 1955, he landed his most lasting role, as the star of the TV series *The Count of Monte Cristo*. His only son, George Michael Jr. (known as Mickey), often visited the set. Possessing good looks and tons of personality, it wasn't long before Mickey was offered a series of his own. Lest a conflict between two Dolenzes working in television become an issue, the 10-year-old boy adopted the stage name Mickey Braddock, bleaching his brown locks blonde for good measure. His show concerned the adventures of a young boy adopted by a circus owner. Corky's parents, high-wire artists, had been killed in a mishap; the orphan found security in the only life he'd ever known and was given the job of water boy to the circus' baby elephant, Bimbo. The turn-of-the-century troupe moved from town to town each week, encountering transient troubles that required a 27-minute-long resolution. The circus owner, Big Tim Champion, was played by Robert Lowery, who, in addition to his many western roles, played Batman in the 1940s serial. Noah Beery, Jr., was on hand as Uncle Joey, a kindly old clown to whom Corky often turned when in trouble. The show proved to be quite popular, with a variety of spin-off toys, comics, and books. Its last season found it moved from prime time to Saturday mornings. Six years after the series's run, young Mickey got another shot at fame when NBC made a Monkee out of him.

Fun for a Girl and a Boy

And what was the younger set up to in this time of rampant paranoia and fear? Why, affixing facial features to raw vegetables, of course. What is impressive is that, try as one might, there is nothing in this roll call of vastly popular items that you can't go into a store and buy now. The fertile minds from which these inventions sprang could little imagine that five decades on, their work would continue to delight the cynical offspring of today (at least until they discover PlayStation). Here's a rundown of some of the most enduring.

1. SILLY PUTTY (1950)

The staggering success of this singular product was the result of several hands, each recognizing an "it" factor without quite grasping the whole potential. Scotsman James Wright, an engineer at the New Haven, Connecticutt, General Electric plant, was experimenting with ideas for a rubber substitute during World War II. Upon combining boric acid and silicone oil in a test tube, he saw the resulting compound polymer into a substance with many of rubber's qualities, but it wasn't exactly what he was looking for. He sent samples to his colleagues in the hope that someone somewhere could find a practical use for it, but to no avail. (He called it "Gupp," which couldn't have helped.) Ruth Fallgatter, privy to local science circles, became interested enough in the charming but useless substance to stock some in her toy shop. Unemployed advertising consultant Peter Hodgson came into contact with the Gupp while visiting Fallgatter's shop and foresaw the stuff's potential if properly marketed. Deeply in debt and desperate, Hodgson borrowed $147 and packaged the material, renamed "Silly Putty," into plastic eggs. (Being near Easter time, they were readily available and cheap.) Through sheer persistence and force of personality, he managed to talk some retailing chains into selling his product, after almost everyone in the toy world had taken a pass.

In August, his lucky break arrived when a writer visiting Doubleday's bookstore happened upon Silly Putty and did a piece on it for *New Yorker* magazine. Within three days, more than a quarter of a million orders poured in from across the country. A huge selling point became the substance's ability to reproduce any newsprint image it was applied to, allowing the user to stretch it and distort it any number of ways. That there was a demand for such capability had been little suspected, but we've always been an easily amused lot in this country. The substance also had a tremendous capacity for bouncing when thrown against a hard surface, providing hours of amusement for people with a compulsion to annoy others. A government embargo on silicone during the Korean War only helped to build the demand when the ban was lifted after a couple of years. The former Gupp reaped a fortune for Hodgson, with millions of little eggs sold every year since.

2. COLORFORMS (1951)

After five decades on the market, Colorforms remain inexplicably popular. They don't *do* anything—requires no batteries, make no noise, and aren't even particularly satisfying to destroy. Yet, they have survived and even thrived in a world very different from the one they were conceived in. Colorforms began with a discovery by two art students. Harry and

Patricia Kislevitz found that a certain vinyl used in making pocketbooks stuck to semigloss paint very well. It should have ended there, but it didn't. Being artistic types, the Kislevitzes cut out an assortment of shapes and decorated their bathroom walls with them. Further, they encouraged visitors to do the same by leaving out scissors and leftover material. Such is the stuff that fortunes are made of, for the intrepid pair decided that marketing what had been such fun for their friends and themselves might be enjoyed by all. Strangely enough, they were proven right.

The first Colorforms set was sold through F.A.O. Schwartz in New York. It came in an elegant black box (the Kislevitzes were nothing if not serious about their art), with a spiral-bound book containing some 350 colorful shapes in every size and configuration. With a tabula rasa included, purchasers were then encouraged to enact their most outlandish artistic impulses. Further enhancing the product's tremendous sales was canny television advertising geared to adults as well as children. Parents had to love a toy that not only engaged their kids, but also presented virtually no threat to house and home. Children's art need not result in crayon scribbles in all the wrong places; at worst, the voluminous pieces enclosed ended up as vacuum fodder. In 1957, the first outside characterization in Colorform came into being when its makers, University Games, licensed rights to Popeye and his pals. Forever after, no cartoon or kids' phenomenon had officially arrived until it was marketed as a Colorform.

3. MR. POTATO HEAD (1952)

Rhode Island's Hassenfeld Brothers had been manufacturing school supply boxes since the 1920s. Seeking to expand its line in the late forties, they began selling their boxes filled with doctor or nurse paraphernalia and paint sets. In 1951, one George Lerner approached the company with an idea for something to fill their boxes. During World War II, he conceived of manufacturing pushpins in the form of various facial features and body parts for kids to insert into any manner of vegetable. Because of wartime shortages and rationing, companies were loath to encourage anyone to play with food. The best Lerner had managed was to interest a cereal maker in giving away the pieces as a premium. But by the early fifties, the Hassenfelds found the idea intriguing. On April 30, 1952, Mr. Potato Head met the public. Due in no small part to the use of television to push the product (the first toy ever advertised on TV), sales skyrocketed, bringing in $4 million in the first year. Not bad for a toy that sold for less than a buck. The first edition contained 30 external parts, ranging from a full torso with limbs to a moustache. He could be accessorized with everything from a derby to a pipe. Only his actual head was not included—youngsters were expected to provide their own and need not limit themselves to spuds. The familiar plastic head/body did not arrive until 1964—10 years later, it doubled in size (a reversal of the usual trend of making something smaller—see G.I. Joe). Nineteen fifty-three saw the arrival of Mrs. Potato Head, and, eventually, a line of accessories like cars, boats, and pets arrived, Barbie-style. The manufacturer, now known as Hasbro, went on to even greater success with other product lines, including G.I. Joe, My Little Pony, and Transformers.

4. MATCHBOX CARS (1953)

As anyone familiar with these little vehicles may know, Matchbox cars originated in England. In the postwar recovery period, the two Mr. Smiths, Rodney and Leslie (no relation to each other), joined forces to manufacture *something*. Until they could discover what, they named their company Lesney Products. They began by supplying die-cast parts to industries rebuilding the country. As per tradition in England, all businesses conducted taxation inventories at the start of the new year, so orders for the last two months of year were slack. Rather than laying off workers at this time, Lesney decided to use their plant to knock off some inexpensive toys to sell during the holiday season. To their surprise, their array of products, which ranged from wheeled vehicles to mechanical animals, proved to be quite popular. In 1953 they created detailed miniature versions of some of their vehicle line, resulting in creations tiny enough to fit in a matchbox. The concept proved successful beyond their wildest dreams, and by the end of 1954, all of the company's other products were dropped. The first four in the Matchbox line were construction-type models: a cement mixer, dump truck, road roller, and tractor. As they grew in marketing savvy, the series expanded to include familiar items such as buses and trains. In 1956, the first "Models of Yesteryear" commenced, featuring notable vehicles ranging from horse-drawn transport to early Rolls-Royces to sporty 1920s cars. Things rolled merrily along until 1968, when Mattel's Hot Wheels hit the street. Built for speed, which Matchbox cars were not, and with a host of side products and track, Hot Wheels put the Lesney cars in serious trouble overnight. Their hand forced by direct competition, Lesney created a Super Fast series, which bought them some time until the mid-eighties, when financial woes brought ownership changes. By the time the dust settled in 1997, Matchbox *and* Hot Wheels were under the same roof at Mattel.

5. PLAY-DOH (1956)

Among the products manufactured by Kutol Chemicals of Cincinnati was a doughy substance used to clean wallpaper. It had been invented by Joe McVicker, son of the owner, Noah. During an offhand conversation with his sister-in-law, Joe heard her lament how impractical the modeling clay used at the preschool where she worked was. It got him to thinking about the qualities of the stuff he had developed, and he offered her some to test out on the kids. It proved to be an immediate success with not only the children but the teachers, who were excited about this nontoxic toy that nurtured creativity. Recognizing opportunity, Joe had the material patented as an educational modeling compound. Full-scale manufacturing of the substance, now dubbed

"Play-Doh," began in 1956. Initially, it was sold in $1\frac{1}{2}$-pound cans in an off-white shade. Its tremendous success led to the three-pack of blue, red, and yellow in 1957, and a four-pack (adding the original white) after that. By the age of 20, Joe was a millionaire. The product, whose exact formula remains a secret, has continued unchanged except for the addition of all sorts of accessories and a few other colors in the ensuing years. Perhaps its most lasting impression came in the form of "Mr. Bill," the late seventies staple of *Saturday Night Live.*

6. FRISBEE (1956)

Discovering that: 1), a Frisbie (or Frisbee) Baking Company once existed in the late 19th century in Connecticut; 2) that its pie pans bore the company imprint; and 3) that people were said to enjoy playing catch with them—well, frankly—this just sets off too many BS detectors. So does the story that tossing pie pans around was a popular fad on the Yale campus in (pick a decade) the twenties—the thirties—the forties. We will dispense with legend and move forward to the first practical application of the concept. Fresh off the heels of the Roswell story garnering widespread public interest, a California carpenter named Fred Morrison patented a toy disc he called a "Flying Saucer." Along with Walter Fransci-oni, the two marketed the invention through their company, Partners In Plastic. After initial interest dried up in the early fifties, Morrison retooled the product on his own and sold it as the "Pluto Platter." By 1956, novelty powerhouse Wham-O began to show an interest and bought him out, renaming the item "Frisbee" in 1958. Owners Rich Knerr and Spud Melin showed an unerring instinct for gauging public interest, and this particular one took off, so to speak, in a big way.

7. ANT FARMS (1956)

This tail sounds just as apocryphal as the Frisbee story, but Milton Levine swears it happened this way. In 1956, the 43-year-old novelties salesman was at a picnic when an epiphany hit—struck by the sight of parading ants, he recalled his childhood obsession with collecting ants in a jar and studying their activity. The idea of marketing a device that enabled kids to observe the insects as he once did hit him all at once, and Uncle Milton's Ant Farm was born. Once he ironed out the logistics of marketing live ants on store shelves without killing them, he was good to go. Children purchased his kit, which included a farm motif between two panes of glass, sand, ant food, and a booklet explaining ant behavior. A mail-in coupon was included that purchasers use to claim a contingent of live ants from the manufacturer's ant supplier that, presumably, would be fresher than if they'd been included with the start-up. Mustering all the marketing know-how he possessed, Levine advertised in kids' magazines and on TV, sometimes appearing on shows himself to demonstrate customized deluxe versions of his product. Ant farms were successfully pitched to educators as a learning tool, and through the years, both upscale and spartan versions of the original were marketed. (Levine wisely resisted demands that he include a magnifying glass for outdoor use.) The ant farm's success paved the way for marketing sea monkeys in the early sixties, and in the process made Milton Levine a very rich uncle.

8. HULA HOOPS (1958)

In yet another contribution to popular culture, Melin and Knerr of Wham-O adapted for Americans a novelty they'd discovered in Australia. The hula hoop, so named for the user's hip movement required to keep the thing in motion, was modeled after bamboo rings used as a fitness tool in gym classes down under. Their particular innovations were to make it in a variety of colors and to add those little beads inside to give the hoop the characteristic "whooshing" sound as it spun. After they gave hundreds away during initial demonstrations, the hoops caught on like gangbusters by word of mouth. Wisely marketing the product in late spring, Wham-O reaped a tremendous windfall by the time the craze spent itself in late fall. Though not a patentable concept (and other companies were quick to jump on the bandwagon with knock-offs), Wham-O nonetheless realized sales of over 100 million in a year's time. While certainly far from its peak of popularity in the fifties, the hula hoop continues to do well today—no small feat given this country's decline in physical fitness.

9.   FISHER-PRICE'S "LITTLE PEOPLE" (1959)

Those maddening little wooden figures of humanity, famously underfoot in any household where young children are present, got their start by degrees beginning in the fifties. To those unaware, Little People were those rounded, dowel-like figures with ball heads, roughly the size of an adult thumb. They came with a variety of clothes and faces painted on and were meant to be interchangeable with any number of Fisher-Price products (designed to be seated where a base hole is present). In typical use, however, they were immediately removed from the toy they arrived in, never to return. Usually they ended up being used as missiles. Although directly preceded by a primitive ancestor in 1932 (that we shall refer to as "Lucy"), the first modern LP came as the crew of 1950's Looky Fire Truck. Wisely, these figures were permanently affixed to the vehicle. Other toys followed, including 1952's Super-Jet and 1953's Racing Rowboats, all carrying prototypical Little People. Not until the 1959 introduction of the Safety School Bus were the passengers at last liberated from the permanency of their host vehicle. This school bus came with a driver figure as well as an assortment of students, now capable of moving about the bus (as students are wont to do). Strangely, these primordial Little People were not wooden but rolled cardboard (which made for interesting play when kids would stage bus crashes into water, wherein the little figures would bloat out like—oh, never mind). After 1960, the durable wooden play folk we all know arrived. Following safety concerns in the eighties (that is, the choke hazard they posed), a redesign effectively finished off the original race, paving the way for the hard rubber versions presently available.

10. BARBIE (1959)

The biggest success story of the fifties began with a product that nobody in the male-dominated toy world wanted anything to do with. Mattel's late-forties origins in a garage as a maker of picture frames had blossomed into its dominating the toy industry by the mid-fifties. A large part of Mattel's empire was supported through sponsorship of the *Mickey Mouse Club*, affording the company a tremendous platform from which to sell its goods (which at the time, boasted of something called a Burp Gun). For some time, Ruth Handler, wife of co-founder Eliot, had been urging him and his partner, Harold Matson, to begin marketing a concept she'd dreamed up while watching their daughter play with paper dolls. To her way of thinking, dolls weren't merely for playing mommy anymore—there was much fun to be had in dressing them up in an assortment of outfits. She conceived of a fashion doll, for which the real fortune was to be made in the clothes and accessories. It took years of persistent persuasion to sell her husband and his partner on the idea and a little more to research the production details, such as creating a head of hair that was realistic and would stand up to hours of rough treatment. Soon, Mattel was ready to debut its creation to retailers in New York City. The doll was named for the Handler's daughter, Barbie.

At the 1959 American Toy Fair, buyers representing retail chains were flabbergasted to behold a children's toy that sported long, slender legs, a small waist, and sizable, firm breasts. (It has been calculated that a human Barbie bearing the same proportions would stand 5 foot 6, with measurements of 39–18–33. It seems hardly coincidental that this toy did come not long after Hugh Hefner established an ideal "girl next door" with similar dimensions.) She came in a one-piece zebra striped swimsuit, painted eyes demurely averted down and away. There was no mistaking this doll for an ob-

ject to be nurtured; Barbie was unmistakably built for pleasure. Fifty percent of Mattel's regular customers took a pass,
but the others did not. Once the advertising kicked in, to the
amazement of everyone but Ruth, orders went through the
roof. (It would take *three* years to catch up, due to Mattel's
cutting production after the market's initial lukewarm response.) Barbie became an icon. She has been roundly con-
demned as the embodiment of materialism; she has been
pilloried for being unrealistically perfect and desirable. Support groups were formed to repair the damaged self-esteem
wrought upon a generation of girls unable to live up to Barbie's standards. (One attempt at righting Barbie's wrongs
came in the early nineties with the "Happy to Be Me" doll.
This big-bottomed, small-breasted creature met with universal apathy—perhaps a self-help treatise on the perils of looking to inanimate objects as role models would have helped.)
Barbie's defenders point to her many career paths as evidence of her self-empowerment. To the extent that an 11 and
a half-inch piece of polyvinylchloride may set an example
and inspire the impressionable, Barbie's supporters feel she
has made this world a better place.

now Here's Something We Hope you *Really* Like

F olks who grew up the sixties or after may take it for granted that cartoons on TV just sort of appeared one day, or that they'd been around always. Nope. While some animated series on the tube were recyclings of cartoons originally conceived for and run in theaters years earlier, several brand-spanking-new characters were specifically created for the burgeoning medium. The future dynasty of Hanna-Barbera, for example, was just getting started before hitting its stride in the sixties with *The Jetsons*, *The Flintstones*, and *Yogi Bear*, to name three examples. Here are some of television's earliest offerings.

1. *CRUSADER RABBIT* (1949–1951), nBC

Despite being the nephew of Terrytoons' Paul Terry (the studio responsible for Mighty Mouse, Heckle and Jeckle, and Deputy Dawg), Alexander Anderson could not drum up interest in his idea for bringing animation directly to television. (Until then, cartoons were considered purely a theatrical entity as warm-ups to kids' feature films.) Undeterred, he looked up Jay Ward, an old friend who'd been successful in real estate. Ward was looking for a career change, especially after having two legs broken when a bus with brake failure crashed through his storefront office and pinned him to a wall. (How very cartoon-like!) But rather than serve merely as cash cow, Ward became fired up with ideas and signed on as a full partner. Their initial collaboration resulted in three proposals: *Dudley Do-Right*, *Hamhock Jones* (a private eye whose nemesis was one half of a pair of Siamese twins), and *Crusader Rabbit*. The first two were passed on, but the third sold. *Crusader Rabbit* involved the title character, a Don Quixote-like creature, and his sidekick, Rags the Tiger. Part of Anderson's concept was to have personalities that played against type, that is, brave rabbit and dunce tiger. The story lines, as such, stretched out for weeks at a time with the show's episodic format. The animation was laughably low-tech even for its time, and it was in black and white besides, but Alexander asserted that the content would keep the kids hooked (a lesson not lost on the creators of *South Park*). Part of what made that content palatable was the input of Ward, whose trademark puns and wordplay made it into the mix. Upon the initial ending of the series, Ward and Alexander went their separate ways, but the show was revived in 1957, this time in color. As late as the early eighties, episodes still popped up in syndication, mostly on Fox stations.

2. *WINKY DINK AND YOU* (OCT. 10, 1953–APRIL 27, 1957), CBS

Co-creators Harry Pritchett and Ed Wyckoff were on a mission. They believed that television could be an invaluable tool to educate children, but not merely passively. They wanted kids to be actively engaged, so they conceived what became the first interactive show as well as an ingenious marketing ploy. *Winky Dink* was an animated little boy. With his trusty dog, Woofer, by his side, he would set out on some adventure, only to end up in need of help. Thereupon, viewers at home were asked to assist, with the *Winky Dink* kit they had sent away for. It consisted of a transparent plastic sheet to cover the TV screen and five crayons. Viewers were called upon to *draw upon the screen* the object that was needed to complete Winky's rescue. Brilliant concept, but do you see where this is going? Not everyone had a Winky kit; not everyone sprang for the magic crayons. With Winky and Woofer in need of rescue, what was a child to do? Use whatever was at hand, of course, which might be a magic marker. Can you see why this show might have been considered anathema to some parents? As an added incentive to buy the kit, each week's show included a "secret message" that required viewers to trace out segments of letters on the screen as they appeared on the show. ("Drink more Ovaltine" was not one of them.) Jack Berry hosted the live segments, assisted by *Howdy Doody*'s Dayton Allen as Mr. Bungle. A revival of the show came and went in the late sixties, and today someone is marketing a home video version, complete with kit. Though not perhaps exactly what its creators intended in practice, the show lives on through its interactive aspect in shows like *Dora the Explorer* and *Blue's Clues*—minus the onscreen doodling.

3.   *THE MIGHTY MOUSE PLAYHOUSE* (DEC. 10, 1955–SEPT. 2, 1967), CBS

For a show mostly remembered as inspiration for a bit by comic Andy Kaufman ("Here I am to save the day!"), this rodent proved to be nearly as durable as his cousin over in Anaheim. Initially called *Super Mouse* upon its creation in the early forties, "Mighty Mouse" was adopted in 1943 when Terrytoons became aware of an unrelated comic book character of the same name. The cartoon became a staple of kiddie matinees, even garnering an Academy Award nomination in 1945—no small achievement against the likes of Disney and Warner Brothers. Mighty Mouse proved to be the studio's biggest success, spinning off into a comic book in 1946. In 1955, Paul Terry sold his studio to CBS, which parlayed the acquisition into a Saturday morning television warhorse. Two other segments rounded out the show—Gandy Goose, an eminently forgettable creation, and Heckle and Jeckle, the two obnoxious magpies. The latter proved popular enough to warrant their own show the following year.

4. *THE GERALD MCBOING-BOING SHOW* (DEC. 16, 1956–OCT. 3, 1958), CBS

In 1950, United Productions of America commissioned Theodore Geisel (Dr. Seuss to you) to come up with an idea for a theatrical cartoon short, the sole criteria being that it was something *different!* His response was the creation of this character: a little boy who could not speak except through sound effects, many of which sounded like "boing boing." Being the master of abstraction, Seuss certainly gave the UPA its money's worth. The first of what became several film shorts won critical acclaim for defying animation clichés and was awarded an Oscar for best short subject. Its success spawned several sequels and, in 1956, a television series. In addition to the title character, the *McBoing* show presented educational segments and other UPA cartoons. The show consistently drew critical praise, a remarkable feat considering the low production values the studio was known for (*Mr. Magoo*, anyone?). That said, there were some quality hands behind the scenes: Bill Scott, who would move on to *Rocky and Bullwinkle*, and Bill Melendez, who gained immortality in the sixties for producing the *Charlie Brown* specials (as well as voicing Snoopy). Though the show had an imaginative concept, its short run and whimsical style seem to have worked against it. The *Gerald McBoing-Boing Show* remains sadly forgotten today.

5. *HECKLE AND JECKLE* (OCT. 14, 1956–SEPT. 8, 1957), CBS

Originally conceived as *The Talking Magpies* back in the forties, this durable pair of birds were Terrytoons' bad boys. Neither heroic nor particularly well-behaved, they went from situation to situation with a nonchalant violence and aggression, certain they would win out in the end. With one sporting a proper English accent and the other Brooklynese, the two chattered ceaselessly, attempting to think through a problem before choosing the worst option. It's a shame they are seen so rarely anymore, as their particular brand of humor

would likely wear very well today. Their first television showcase came during the prime-time *CBS Cartoon Theater*,
hosted by a presuperstar Dick Van Dyke in the summer of
1956.

6. *TOM TERRIFIC* (1957–1959, AIRED ON *CaPTaIN KaNGaROO*), CBS

This Terrytoon creation represented yet another low-tech bit
of kids' entertainment, though the content itself was palatable. As a regular competing for air time against Bunny Rabbit and Mr. Moose, *Tom Terrific* depicted the adventures of a
boy who could assume any shape he wanted to, as he battled
villains aided (but only barely) by sidekick Mighty Manfred
the Wonder Dog (the wonder being, how did he ever get the
gig?). Tom's main adversary was Crabby Appleton (who was
referred to as "rotten to the core.") The stories, constructed
in five-part segments, regularly featured cliffhangers and unfolded throughout the week before the inevitable resolution.
All the parts were voiced by Lionel Wilson, who would lend
his vocal talents in the sixties to Sidney the Elephant on the
Hector Heathcote Show.

7. *RUFF AND REDDY SHOW* (DEC. 14, 1957–SEPT. 26, 1964), NBC

In 1957, MGM shut down production of its animation studios,
leaving, among others, the creators of *Tom and Jerry* out
of work. Bill Hanna and Joe Barbera, quick to recognize an
opportunity, began laying the foundation for *the* cartoon
powerhouse of the sixties and beyond. It all began here, with
this primitive work about a dumb but lovable dog (Ruff, of
course) and his smart little pal, Reddy the cat. There was
nothing particularly fresh about the concept itself (*Crusader
Rabbit* being a direct antecedent). Rather, it was Hanna and
Barbera's method of creating engaging and lively cartoons
on the cheap, without the crudity of UPA or Terrytoons, that
helped win over the masses. (Ever notice how often the
backgrounds repeated?) The success that began here led to

Huckleberry Hound, *Top Cat*, *Yogi Bear*, *Quick Draw Mc-Graw*, *The Flintstones*, and a host of others.

8. *MATTY'S FUNDAY FUNNIES* (OCT. 11, 1959–DEC. 29, 1962), ABC

Mattel, the toy manufacturer, was responsible for this motley collection of B-list cartoons. Distributed by what became known as Harvey Funnies, they featured the likes of Casper (the wussy ghost), Little Audrey (a Little Lulu knock-off), Baby Huey (the insufferable overgrown duck), and Herman and Catnip (a rip-off of Tom and Jerry). Specially created for the show were the hosts: Mattel's logo, Matty (the crowned kid), and his sibling, Sisterbelle. The two were the public face for a vehicle designed to sell Mattel's product, at a time when toy commercials in general and Mattel's in particular were works of art. The show's real legacy was as the springboard for launching *Beany and Cecil* in 1962 as a cartoon show in its own right.

9. THE CHIPMUNKS (LATE 1958)

Though technically not a cartoon *show* until the sixties, these vermin were successful enough cartoon personas on record to include here. Ross Bagdasarian was quite a busy fellow in the fifties. (He also was a cousin of playwright William Saroyan, but don't hold it against him!) In addition to bit roles as an actor (*Stalag 17*, *Viva Zapata!*, *Rear Window*), he was a songwriter of note. Rosemary Clooney's recording of his 1939 composition, "Come on-a My House," was a smash in 1951. Under the moniker "David Seville," he began experimenting with speeded-up vocal tracks in the studio. The first result of his efforts was the novelty tune "Witch Doctor." To everyone's amazement, it reached number one for a three-week stay in April 1957. Its success led him to expand on the concept: if *one* speeded up vocal was amusing, how about *three*, singing in harmony? There was a Christmas tune he'd been fooling around with for some time that he felt lacked something. Once he'd decided to apply his newfound effects to it, he had to create personas to match the ridiculous vocals. Enter the Chipmunks: Simon, Theodore, and the errant Alvin. The names came from three execs at Liberty Records, who no doubt found reason to bless the project. Their faith was well founded; "The Chipmunk Song" hit number one in December 1958, and went on to sell four million copies. The Chipmunks became regular visitors to the Top 40 during the next four years. *The Alvin Show* premiered in 1961, the first cartoon spun off from a successful recording (to be followed through the years by the Beatles, Jackson Five, and Brady Kids cartoons). Even after Bagdasarian's death in 1972, his son successfully revived the project in 1980 with *Chipmunk Punk*, featuring a safety-pinned Alvin.

10. *ROCKY AND FRIENDS* (SEPT. 29, 1959–SEPT. 3, 1961), ABC

Jay Ward, *Crusader Rabbit*'s co-creator, made it to the big time with this creation and its cast of characters. In the years since *CR* had folded, Alexander Anderson had left the business while Ward dabbled in real estate just long enough to build up some funds. He found a new partner in Bill Scott, who'd come from *Mr. Magoo* and *Gerald McBoing-Boing*. Scott shared Ward's subversive sense of humor and desire to appeal to adults as well as children. Although as always the animation quality was little more than "illustrated radio," the superb vocal talent ensured the success of their witty scripts. June Foray, veteran of Looney Tunes (where she'd voiced Tweety's Granny) handled vocal chores for Rocket J. Squirrel, the feisty but responsible companion to the dim-witted Bullwinkle Moose, resident of Frostbite Falls, Minnesota. Together, the two attempted to thwart the designs of Mr. Big (a midget), as enacted by his agents, Boris Badenov and Natasha Fatale. (The former name is a play on Mussorgsky's opera *Boris Godunov*.) Scott himself voiced Bullwinkle (whose name was based on a Berkley car dealership Ward spotted one day). William Conrad, who had played Sheriff Matt Dillon in *Gunsmoke* on radio, supplied the narration.

The stories unfolded serial-style, with a cliffhanger resolved in the second half of each episode. Other bits included Bullwinkle's unsuccessful attempts at magic. Along with Rocky and Bullwinkle were several other equally memorable segments: *Fractured Fairy Tales*, featuring perversions of time-honored stories; *Aesop & Son*, likewise twisted; *Peabody's Improbable History*, historic events satirized through time travel; and *Dudley Do-Right of the Mounties*, the inept Canadian law enforcer. The various characters who populated the series amounted to a true ensemble—it's impossible to imagine any of them separated from the whole. When *Rocky and Friends* left ABC for NBC, it was renamed *The Bullwinkle Show* and ran another five years before living on in reruns. The Ward-Scott brain trust also extended to creating the Captain Crunch ads.

Ain't That a Shame

We've all heard stories of a certain kind—the ones passed around as fact, always based on someone's having heard them on the radio or from someone else who heard them on the radio, or saw them on TV, or read them in the paper, and so on. The kind of stories intended to provoke a "oh, wow—really?" from the listener, and boost the prestige of the teller as the possessor of some special inside knowledge. We delight in spreading such awe-inspiring tales, whether we believe them to be true or not, simply because everyone enjoys a good yarn. What's troublesome is when these myths become recorded as fact by some careless writer keen on coming up with colorful anecdotes. As a rule, if it sounds too good to be true, it usually is. Here are some oft-repeated stories unburdened by truth.

1. *RUMOR:* FRANK ZAPPA WAS THE SON OF MR. GREEN JEANS FROM *CAPTAIN KANGAROO*

It makes for a compelling story, but Hugh ("Lumpy") Brannum did *not* beget a son known to the world as Frank Zappa. Probably. Though he, too, was an accomplished musician, Brannum possessed no other commonality with Zappa that anyone will admit to.

2. *RUMOR:* FUTURE CUBAN PREMIER FIDEL CASTRO TRIED OUT FOR THE WASHINGTON SENATORS

This oft-repeated bit of folklore is usually told within the larger context of "If the guy had had a better arm, there never woulda been a Communist revolution in our own backyard, no Bay of Pigs, no missile crisis, or any of these other troubles, forcrissake." Some versions of the tale have the New York Yankees as the team that scouted him, but in any instance the irony of a future dictator and nemesis playing for either team tends to amplify the absurdity of the claim. About the only thing that is true is that Fidel loved the game and played it often. His enthusiasm, however, far outstripped his skills.

3. *RUMOR:* GROUCHO MARX'S RISQUÉ AD LIB TO A CONTESTANT

As fans of his quiz show *You Bet Your Life* know, Groucho would partake in some informal banter with his contestants before commencing with the quiz, affording the comedian an opportunity to hurl some humorous barbs at someone other than his announcer, George Fenniman. As the story goes, a woman appearing on his show was the mother of some 17 children. When asked to account for such a large family, she explained, "I love my husband." Without missing a beat, Groucho is said to have retorted, "Well, I love my cigar, but I take it out of my mouth every once in a while." The exchange was said to have provoked the longest sustained laughter from the audience in the show's history but, alas, was too ribald to air on TV.

While the remark sounds perfectly in character, the evidence that it happened is lacking. Groucho himself gave contradictory versions when asked about it. Others connected with the show believe the exchange occurred in 1947, during the show's *radio* run. Either way, anyone who says he or she *saw* it on TV is a liar.

4. *RUMOR:* TV'S SUPERMAN DIED AFTER ATTEMPTING TO FLY

As covered in the unnatural death chapter in this book, actor George Reeves did die under murky circumstances, but the fantasy that he somehow so identified with his character that he thought he really could leap tall buildings in a single bound is nonsense. (He also wasn't faster than a speeding bullet, evidently.) What the story sounds like is an attempt by adults to explain the death of their hero to children, as a sort of cautionary tale. Kids aren't stupid and would not very likely have missed completely the fact of Reeves's demise. It would have been plausible for grown-ups to mask the apparent reason for the actor's death behind something more easily explainable to children, lest they face the prospect of discussing the concept of suicide or murder.

5. *RUMOR:* TV'S BEAVER WAS KILLED IN VIETNAM

It's odd that there is anyone left who might still believe this one, considering that Jerry Mathers has hardly been the invisible man in recent decades. First, there was that revival of the show done in the eighties, *Still the Beaver.* (Given the show's morose themes, adult angst, and soapy slant, a more apt title might have been *Beaver-something.*) He also has since penned an autobiography and is trotted out periodically alongside other former child stars on TV talk shows (he even appeared as a contestant on *The Weakest Link*—the other kid stars gave him the business and voted him off first). As it happens, during the Vietnam era Mathers served in the Air National Guard, doing his duty stateside. He made a brief one-time TV appearance, in uniform and with full buzz cut. This may have planted the seed of his later casualty status.

Another tale connected with the show centered on Beaver's nemesis, Eddie Haskell. For a time, he was rumored to have grown up to become rocker Alice Cooper. Alas, actor Ken Osmond ended up a Los Angeles police officer. Years

after the show ended, he was shot four times while attempting an arrest but was saved from harm by his vest and belt
buckle. He has since left the law enforcement business. Alice
Cooper is in fact Detroit-born Vince Furnier, son of a minister
(not Mr. Rogers, either).

6.   *RUMOR:* AN ACTOR IN *BEN-HUR* WAS KILLED IN THE CHARIOT RACE SCENE

Viewers of the film's very impressive action sequences, especially the chariot races, can be forgiven if they're left with
the very convincing impression of an actual on-screen
death. There are several particular bits during these scenes
that, when watched naturally, give the impression of considerable violence being done. When viewed in slow motion and
freeze-frame, however, they are revealed to be clever cinematic effects achieved through the use of dummies and
sharp editing. That is not to say that these scenes are perfect;
a number of discernable continuity and anachronism problems crop up throughout the finished film. For example, a
trumpeter can be seen sporting a wristwatch in one scene. In
the chariot race, *tire tracks* from the vehicles used to carry
the cameras are clearly visible in the dirt.

These stories may have originated with a stuntman's
death that occurred 33 years earlier, during the Rome shooting of the silent version in 1926. A broken wheel on a chariot
caused its stunt driver to be pitched into the air, then landing
in a pile of lumber, which killed him. The accident resulted
in the production being finished back in California.

7.   *RUMOR:* TV'S CAPTAIN KANGAROO WAS A HERO AT IWO JIMA

This is an odd one. It has circulated on the Internet, but where
or why it started, other than someone making it up out of
whole cloth, is hard to determine. According to the story,
actor Lee Marvin was on the *Tonight Show*, then hosted by
Johnny Carson. A discussion of Marvin's military career as
a Marine during World War II ensued, with talk of his wound-

ing in a battle on Mt. Suribachi at Iwo Jima. Marvin then reportedly said, with a mixture of pride and awe, that he had served under the bravest man he ever knew, Bob Keeshan. "The world knows him as Captain Kangaroo" was the punch line. A great story, if it were true, but unfortunately, those pesky facts get in the way. Marvin was indeed a Marine who saw action in the Pacific theater, but he was actually wounded at Saipan, earning a Purple Heart in the process. Keeshan, on the other hand, was only a captain on TV. While he did enlist in the Marines two weeks before he turned 18, it was too late into the war to see any action.

8. *RUMOR:* BUDDY HOLLY'S FATAL PLANE WAS NAMED *AMERICAN PIE*

The chartered plane that took three rock & roll legends on their last flight was a Beechcraft A-35 Bonanza bearing the identification number N3794N. The legend that will not die is that "American Pie" was the name of the aircraft they died in, which is, of course, utterly laughable. "American Pancake," perhaps, or "American Turnover," possibly, but *Pie?*

9. *RUMOR:* JAMES DEAN'S PORSCHE WAS RESPONSIBLE FOR OTHER DEATHS LATER

With every aspect of the man's life rich in legend, it doesn't surprise that Dean's death should spawn several rumors, too. The most enduring is that, following his fatal accident (detailed in the unnatural death chapter), the remains of the Porsche Spyder he was driving were sold first to a man who charged the public admission to gawk. Later, Hollywood car designer George Barris took ownership; upon the car's delivery, it is said to have rolled and broken a mechanic's legs. The engine was then sold to a doctor who dabbled in racing. In his first race after the purchase, *his* Spyder crashed, killing him. A man who bought the drive train likewise ended up injured in a crash, though not fatally. As the story continues, a truck transporting the bulk of Dean's Spyder crashed, killing the driver; a New York man who purchased two of the tires was driving with them on his car when they blew out at the same time; and when last seen, the Spyder was being transported to a car safety exhibit when it just disappeared. The trouble with all of these stories is that, while some details appear to be correct (for instance, the doctor who purchased the engine *did* die in a crash on October 22, 1956), definitive ties to Dean's Spyder have not been proven, and there is a conspicuous absence of verified corroboration. Until something more solid is forthcoming, the stories must be regarded as just more hype.

10. *RUMOR:* FILM PRODUCER MIKE TODD WAS BURIED WITH EXPENSIVE JEWELRY

The late Mr. Elizabeth Taylor was known for his extravagances in life. His bride was equally well known for her love of expensive jewelry, and with both of these facts, stories circulated that the producer went to his grave after the 1958 plane crash in which he was killed with a particularly large and valuable ring. Most people would take this at face value and move on, but a would-be thief or thieves did not. In June 1977, workers at the Waldheim Jewish Cemetery in Forest Park, Illinois, discovered that the grave of Elizabeth Taylor's third husband (buried under his birth name of Avram Goldenbogen) was empty. Police scoured the boneyard and surrounding area, to no avail. Several days later, a private dick hired by Todd's widow ceremoniously led a camera crew to Todd's remains, hidden under some bushes 75 yards from the empty grave.

What the perpetrator couldn't have known was that what was recovered of Todd after the crash of the *Lucky Liz* (a truer name than he would ever know) was so badly burned it required dental records for a positive ID. His wedding ring, bent and charred, was discovered and returned to Liz, but what was left of her husband was quietly put into a body bag and buried in a closed casket. The whole 1977 affair had a smell to it, as police and detectives went over every inch of cemetery ground and found nothing. To them, the dramatic discovery, conveniently documented on film, seemed staged. None of this would have happened at all, had Mrs. Todd been granted her original wish back in 1958. Her plans to bury her husband under a nine-foot replica of "Oscar" were vetoed by both Mike Todd, Jr., and the Academy of Motion Picture Arts and Sciences.

You Can't Catch Me

For an era commonly recalled as calm and carefree, the fifties proved to be deceptively deadly. On the downside, crime ran the gamut from teenage serial killers to a cross-dressing grave robber. On the upside, several classic films were directly inspired by criminal events that took place in these years. Depending on which end of the criminal process one stood, there was never a dull moment. *Happy Days* indeed!

1. THE BRINKS JOB (JANUARY 18, 1950)

The chance discovery of lax security at Boston's Brink's terminal led journeyman thief Tony Pino to mastermind the biggest haul in history. The armored car company maintained a garage where the day's cash pickups were sent for counting and sorting. The former small-timer formulated a plan and handpicked 10 others to execute an operation resulting in a nearly $3 million score for Pino's 11. Specialists were chosen—safecrackers, drivers, alarm experts, and so forth. Strict discipline during nearly six years of preparation was miraculously maintained. On the evening of January 18, the team waited until the last drop-off was complete. Seven men sporting Halloween masks entered the building and headed straight to the counting room. There, six employees and one guard were subdued at gunpoint, after which the intruders removed the cash, bucket brigade-style. The entire operation took 30 minutes.

At the safe house, the booty was examined. After destroying $90,000 in certain-to-be-traceable, newly minted bills and discarding some security bonds, each man netted $100,000. The plan now called for the participants to go their separate ways, leaving the money untouched until the statute of limitations expired in six years. Literally days away from their payday, one of the 11, jailed on unrelated charges and certain that he would be cheated out of his cut, ratted out the others. An unsuccessful hit ordered on him by Pino assured his cooperation with the authorities. One by one the gang members were arrested and tried. Two of the original 11 had died, but the remaining eight received life sentences, much to the disgust of the public, who had come to see them as folk heroes. The money was never recovered.

2. WILLIE SUTTON ARRESTED (MARCH 1952)

Setting out on his chosen career path in the late 1920s, Sutton was known as "the actor." A certain panache set him apart from others who robbed banks during the Depression: this flair included a fondness for costumes, false mustaches, and beards as well as a gift for disguising his voice or affecting a limp or other physical trait. He also had a talent for escape—three times in 10 years. Never part of any gang, Sutton operated as a lone wolf. While in custody, when asked why he robbed banks, he shrugged, "Because that's where the money is." All told, he'd netted over $1 million from some 20-odd bank jobs.

Brought to justice in 1942, he "paroled" himself by 1947. For the next five years, he moved about freely in plain sight on the streets of New York City, but in early 1952 his luck ran out. On February 16, he was spotted and recognized on a subway by 24-year-old Arnold Schuster, who tipped off the police. Sutton was picked up, marking the end of his hold-up days. But the story didn't end there. Schuster unwisely milked his 15 minutes of fame, repeating his story all to the papers, over the airwaves, and to anyone who would listen. One man watching was mobster Albert Anastasia. Seeing Schuster on television one night, he flew into a rage. "I hate squealers! Somebody hit that guy!" Though Anastasia didn't know Sutton, the gloating offended him.

On the evening of March 8, 1952, Schuster was brutally gunned down and killed in the street, shot twice in the groin and once in each eye. Though still in custody, the authorities threw the book at the blameless Sutton, who wouldn't see freedom again for more than 20 years. (As for Anastasia, he met his own end in 1957, the victim of a hit himself.) Upon his release, Sutton penned his memoirs, calling the book *Where the Money Was*. He died in 1981.

3. BOBBY GREENLEASE KIDNAPPED (SEPT. 28, 1953)

The Bobby Greenlease case echoed the Bobby Franks murder in Chicago 30 years earlier in several respects. In both instances, the young son of a rich entrepreneur was kidnapped for ransom. Both crimes were committed by a pair who attempted in partnership what each could not do alone. Both had no intention of releasing their captive alive after collecting the money. And both crimes displayed an absolute senselessness that defied rational explanation. Robert Greenlease was a wealthy Kansas City car dealer. A son from his first marriage who attended military school as a teen made the acquaintance of one Carl Hall, the son of a judge. Hail became obsessed with the fortune he believed his classmate was heir to. Following graduation, he spent his time drifting aimlessly. The senior Greenlease remarried and in 1946 fathered a son. Meanwhile, Hail eventually hooked up with a bar slut named Bonnie Heady. In Leopold and Loeb-like fashion, the two formed a symbiotic partnership that led to crime, but unlike the earlier killers, there was no particular moral philosophy or iota of intellect behind their madness. A plan to kidnap Robert Greenlease's younger son was hastily thrown together and set into motion with the purchase of quicklime, a shovel, and a .38 caliber revolver. Lastly, Carl

Hail dug a grave. Having studied their quarry, Hail and Heady were familiar with young Bobby's movements. Arriving at the boy's school one September afternoon, Bonnie identified herself at the office as his aunt, telling school authorities that Bobby's mother had had a heart attack and that he must leave with her at once. The bewildered boy was whisked into a waiting taxi and driven away. Meeting up with Carl, they shot the seven-year-old in a field and buried him in the quicklime. Then they sent a ransom note demanding $600,000 for his safe return.

The community reacted with shock. How could anyone be brazen enough to snatch a child in broad daylight? How was it that just anyone could show up at a school and walk away so easily with someone else's child? Parents were aghast and demanded answers. Meanwhile, the money was dropped one week later. The next day, October 6, the two were arrested following a drunken spending spree during which they all but advertised what they had done. Justice was refreshingly swift: following a confession and a guilty plea, Hail and Heady were executed on December 16, 1953.

4. MARILYN SHEPPARD MURDERED (JULY 4, 1954)

The brutal murder of Dr. Sam Sheppard's wife made headlines across the country, no less for its viciousness than for the fact that the accused was a highly respected pillar of the community. On its face, the story Sheppard told strained credulity, but subsequent investigations have favored his version of events: asleep on a downstairs sofa, he was awakened by screams from his wife. Rushing upstairs to investigate, he was attacked from behind by at least one, possibly two, intruders. He evidently passed out, and when he came to, he first checked his son's room. Confirming his safety, Dr. Sheppard entered his own bedroom in time to find a stranger standing over his wife's battered body on the bed. He chased the attacker outside, where he was again attacked and fell unconscious, bleeding from a nonfatal wound. Eventually he sought help from neighbors who called the police.

When word of an affair with a co-worker leaked out, this, coupled with the unlikeness of Sheppard's story, led to a murder charge. For weeks, newspaper trial coverage hysterically proclaimed his guilt. Sheppard was convicted in December after four days of jury deliberation. Sentenced to life, he sought and won an appeal on the basis of the blatantly unfair trial he had received. F. Lee Bailey defended him for the second go-round and won him an acquittal in 1966. It was then, at the height of renewed interest in the case, that a television series based loosely on the real-life event first aired. *The Fugitive* starred David Janssen as an accused doctor pursuing the "one-armed man" who murdered his wife as he himself is chased by the authorities.

In real life, Dr. Sheppard's victory was short-lived. He died of liver failure four years after his acquittal, having battled the bottle throughout his final years of freedom. Bizarrely, he spent part of that time working as a professional wrestler under the billing "Killer Sheppard." His son continues in the effort to remove all taint from his father's name. New investigations and two books naming names provide credible evidence of Sheppard's innocence. Proof that the police actively suppressed materials favorable to the accused has emerged, including the fact that blood found near the crime scene matched neither the victim nor the accused. In 2000, a third attempt to reach justice went before a jury. The doctor's son marshaled a group of experts and new evidence, but these failed to sway the panel to reopen the case. Nonetheless, young Sheppard has vowed to continue the fight.

5. SCHUESSLER-PETERSON MURDERS (OCT. 16, 1955)

One rainy Sunday evening, the households of Malcolm Peterson and Anton Schuessler, Sr., realized every parent's nightmare. Alarmed at their sons' failure to return from an afternoon movie outing, and after their own unsuccessful search of likely routes home, the two fathers notified the Chicago police. Two days later, a salesman eating lunch in a parking lot near a wooded area spotted something white lying in a nearby ditch. Upon closer inspection what he first thought were discarded mannequins turned out to be humans. Police identified the naked bodies of Bobby Peterson, 14, and the two Schuessler boys, John, 13, and Anton, 11, piled atop each other. Though all three had been choked to death, there was no evidence of sexual abuse, public belief notwithstanding. Telltale matter found on their feet led to police conjecture that their clothing was removed to obscure evidence revealing where they'd been killed. Also, an odd imprint found on two of the boys was later matched to the floor mats of a certain Packard automobile model.

Reconstructing the boys' movements proved to be of little help. The movie had ended downtown between 5:00 and 5:30 p.m., but by 7:30 p.m., the trio was seen back on the northwest side. A friend spotted them at a bowling alley, where they discussed the film and the fact that they'd exhausted their bankroll on public transportation. They soon ventured out into the sporadic rain. It was believed that they met their killer while attempting to hitchhike the final distance home. Police pursued every lead without result. The agony of the loss took its toll on the families, with the elder Schuessler suffering a fatal heart attack three weeks after the death of his sons. The story eventually faded from city newspapers, all but forgotten.

The ensuing years saw new speculation. Crime researchers noted that mass murderer John Wayne Gacy, then 13 years old, lived near the Schuesslers' home, and that his father owned a Packard. The intriguing suggestion that young Gacy was somehow involved seemed somewhat fanciful, however. Then in 1994, a bombshell: prosecutors announced charges against an associate of convicted murderer Silas Jayne for the killings. Kenneth Hansen, 21 years old in 1955, allegedly revealed his guilt to four acquaintances through the years, each one keeping it to himself until 1993. Their dubious veracity convicted Hansen—twice. (The first verdict was overturned, but the 2002 retrial produced the

same result.) Meanwhile, a woman surfaced who told authorities that her husband had confessed to the killings years before, after which she'd left him. The man had since died, but
researchers discovered that he did own a Packard that he
had sold shortly after the crime. So who killed these boys?
While Hansen is no angel, credible evidence against him is
lacking. In light of these circumstances, this brutal crime
must be considered unsolved.

6. THE UNITED AIRLINES BOMBING (NOV. 1, 1955)

Jack Gilbert Graham was a moody ne'er-do-well whose ha-
bitual larceny was enabled by his mother Daisy King's largesse. Financially set through her second marriage, she'd
bailed him out of least one scrape by repaying funds he'd
embezzled in Denver. Seemingly having learned his lesson,
he married and started a family. With his mother's backing,
Graham opened a fast-food drive-in in Denver but quickly
grew weary of repaying her from the store's meager profits.
Forced to rethink his approach to business, Graham soon fell
back on old habits.

One evening, the restaurant mysteriously burned. Graham readily recouped the loss with an insurance claim.
Later, a truck he owned was destroyed by a train while
caught on a set of railroad tracks, and he was likewise com-
pensated. Graham must have felt he was on to something,
for with his next plan he grew even bolder. He took out insurance policies totaling $62,000 on his mother. Before she left
on a trip to visit her daughter in Alaska, Graham gave her
a gift-wrapped package to take along, telling her it was a
Christmas present. She packed the parcel in her suitcase,
and along with 43 others, including an infant, Mrs. King
boarded United Airlines Flight 629 to Seattle. Eleven minutes into the flight, over Longmont, Colorado, the aircraft
was shattered by a tremendous explosion, killing all aboard.
Investigators examining the wreckage discovered evidence
of detonation in the luggage hold on the plane. Remnants of

a battery, blasting wire, and a timer were also uncovered. Only Daisy King's baggage was obliterated.

An apparently distraught Graham was brought in for questioning. While he was in custody, his story kept changing. Though he had joked earlier about boxes of shotgun shells in his mother's suitcase going off, he now said that the gift he brought her was in fact a craft kit. His confidence getting the better of him, he challenged the police to search his home. They did and uncovered more of the copper wire used to trigger the charges. When confronted with this and other evidence, he finally cracked. He told police that he'd rigged 26 sticks of dynamite to a timer device set to go off while the plane was in flight. Later he recanted, saying the story was a lie he'd concocted after seeing a picture of FBI men capturing Nazi saboteurs during World War II. No one bought this, and after a drawn-out legal process involving sanity hearings, he was judged fit to be tried, convicted, and executed. He died at age 25 on January 11, 1957.

7. ED GEIN ARRESTED (NOV. 16, 1957)

Frank Worden, a deputy sheriff in Plainfield, Wisconsin, returned from hunting deer to find his mother missing. The hardware store Bernice ran was unexpectedly locked up that afternoon; after breaking in, Frank found blood on the floor and the cash register gone. On the counter was a handwritten receipt for a half-gallon of antifreeze. He then remembered an encounter with a familiar customer the night before; local resident Ed Gein, 51, had stopped by at closing time to buy some antifreeze. After learning that Worden planned to go hunting on Saturday, Gein indicated that he would return in the morning to complete his purchase. His suspicions aroused, Worden headed out to one of Gein's known hangouts. After a cryptic exchange, the deputy was certain he had his man.

His hunch paid off when some colleagues entered Gein's darkened farmhouse about seven miles outside Plainfield. The house lacked electricity, so the search was conducted

PDImages.com

Amateur anatomist Ed Gein solicits menu suggestions.

by flashlight and gas lantern. Entering an unlocked side shed in the back, the men were startled at first by a large shape looming above them in the darkness. Supposing it was merely a gutted deer, they shined their lights upon it and met the shock of their lives: an armless, decapitated woman, suspended from an overhead beam. A head found nearby, bearing a gunshot wound, confirmed its identity as Mrs. Worden. Further horror awaited inside the house. In a pan on the kitchen stove was a freshly harvested human heart. An unspeakable array of human body parts, all female, was uncovered scattered about the premises. A partial inventory included four noses in a cup; nine peeled faces likened to "death masks"; a tom-tom made from human skin stretched over both ends of a coffee can; a vest and pair of leggings made of human flesh; and a stockpile of human organs in the icebox. All told, the pieces came from at least 15 different women, including a barmaid who had disappeared three years before.

In custody, Gein spilled his *own* guts. Alone on the farm since the death of his domineering mother in 1945 and in no particular financial need, Ed had taken it upon himself to launch a study of the human female. With the company of women taboo while his mother was alive, Gein was eager to make up for lost time. He spent his days poring over medical texts and books on anatomy as well as accounts of Nazi atrocities. At some point in his madness, his curiosity to investigate the female experience firsthand got the best of him. Enlisting the help of an elderly but similarly addled neighbor named Gus, Ed scanned the papers for burial notices. At night, the two harvested the fresh corpses, which Ed would then spirit away to his house for further exam and study. After Gus was committed to a home, Ed carried out his research alone.

Ed told the officers how he shot Bernice Worden with a rifle from the store, supplying the fatal bullet himself. (The cash register he took with the intention of studying its workings before returning it. Warped, depraved, and twisted he may have been, but Gein informed his inquisitors that he was no thief.) They learned of his desire to become a woman, inspired perhaps by the saga of George/Christine Jorgensen. A do-it-yourselfer at heart, Gein had no use for surgeons. Following examination by the state's best shrinks, he was declared insane and institutionalized. He lived out his days as a model inmate at the Mendota Mental Health Institute, dying from natural causes in 1984. Of course, Hollywood couldn't ignore a story so rich in horror. First, writer Robert Bloch used Gein's story for the basis of mother-obsessed taxidermist Norman Bates in *Psycho*. Spiritual kinfolk included Leatherface in *The Texas Chainsaw Massacre* and Buffalo Bill from *The Silence of the Lambs*.

8. NATHAN LEOPOLD PAROLED (MARCH 13, 1958)

Rich in psychodrama, the story of the 1924 murder of Bobby Franks in Chicago continues to captivate. The list of works directly inspired by the crime includes books, plays, and films: Meyer Levin's *Compulsion*; Alfred Hitchcock's *Rope*; the play *Never the Sinner*; and, more recently, the 1992 homoerotic art film *Swoon* and 2002's *Murder by Numbers*. The unlikely enactors were academic prodigies, sons of millionaires both (as was the victim). Their genius IQs (Leopold was a world-class bird authority) belied the inept execution of what became the first "thrill killing" to enter public consciousness. Not for material gain or to avenge a wrong—this murder was committed simply as an attempt to carry out "the perfect crime." That two bright, charismatic, rich young men could throw away all that life had given them so recklessly fascinated the public then as now.

Like so many others before and since, Leopold, 18, along with best friend Richard Loeb, 19, was enthralled with the ideas of German philosopher Friedrich Nietzsche. Of particular interest was his so-called superman theory, which held that a select few in society are destined to rule over the others and, therefore, are not bound by any moral code or laws. To test this thesis, the two began an escalating series of crimes, ranging from cheating at bridge to burglary, auto theft, and arson. This left murder untried—their successes thus far made the perfect crime seem eminently within reach. Ostentatious planning of every conceivable detail lacked one essential x: the victim. Fate dictated that their 14-year-old neighbor was the one lured into their car, killed, and dumped. A pair of glasses traceable to Leopold found near the body sealed their fate, thoroughly discrediting their "superman" delusions.

A crime generating the sensation of this one, now solved, could end only one way: with the hanging of the two teenage killers. But the prosecution didn't count on the most famous attorney in the country, Clarence Darrow, weighing in for the defense. Jumping at the chance to strike a blow against capital punishment, he succeeded in getting the pair sentenced to life in prison. (Richard Loeb would end up murdered in a fight at Stateville in January 1936.) For years afterward, Leopold actively lobbied for parole at every opportunity, scoring points for his good works behind bars. An accumulation of press over his "rehabilitation" made his release an increasing likelihood, with writers like Erle Stanley Gardner and Carl Sandburg rallying public support. The drive was aided further with the publication of Leopold's memoirs, the self-serving *Life Plus 99 Years*. In the face of such unprecedented goodwill, Leopold was granted parole. He settled in San Juan, Puerto Rico, where he found employment in a hospital. In time he married a widow, resumed his study of birds, and devoted his remaining years to atonement for his crime. Following his 1971 death, his widow destroyed the photograph of Richard Loeb Leopold had kept in their home.

9. STARKWEATHER KILLING SPREE BEGINS (JAN. 28, 1958)

Nineteen-year old Charles Starkweather, a short, red-headed high school dropout, fancied himself a rebel in the mold of his idol, the late James Dean. As he worked collecting garbage, he dreamed of one day likewise going out in a blaze of glory. One late January day, he went to the home of his 14-year-old girlfriend, Caril Ann Fugate, to await her return from school. Her mother had never abided him, and on this occasion, her suggestion that he leave was followed by a slap to the face. He responded in kind, and when Caril's stepfather tried to intervene, Starkweather shot him with the .22 rifle he carried with him. He then settled his business with Caril's mother in similar fashion. When Caril arrived, she found her boyfriend choking her baby sister to death by shoving the rifle barrel down her throat. Her less than panicked response may have stemmed from something she knew: he had killed before. Two months earlier he had robbed and killed a 21-year-old service station attendant but somehow had escaped suspicion for that crime. Caril helped him dispose of the bodies, then sat on the couch in front of the television while he made sandwiches in the kitchen. Lest the two be disturbed by any nosy relatives, Caril put up a sign on the outside that read: "Stay Away. Every Body is sick with the Flue."

The ruse worked for a couple of days before Caril's grandmother, turned away by Caril, decided something was fishy and went to the sheriff. By the time they entered the premises with the sheriff and discovered the crimes, Charlie and Caril were gone. Lacking any direction or purpose other than general mayhem, the couple set out on a bloody odyssey, leaving seven more corpses in their wake. Finally, their luck ran out. With pursuers hot on their trail, they attempted a carjacking that ended with their intended victim turning the tables and disarming Charlie. He took off alone and surrendered only after being cut by flying glass shattered by police bullets. Believing himself badly injured, he staggered out of the car, shouting, "You lousy bastards shot me!" His initial chivalry evaporated once Caril turned on him, declaring herself an unwilling hostage. At the trial, he detailed her role in the killings, as both accessory and hands-on murderer. In the end, he got his moment of glory: before he was executed on June 24, 1959, he boasted of the group of young girls who hung around the Nebraska State Prison to support him. As for Caril, she received a life sentence. After protesting her innocence for years, she eventually won parole in 1977, four years after *Badlands*, a fictional account of her tale starring Martin Sheen and Sissy Spacek as the doomed couple, was released.

10. THE *IN COLD BLOOD* MURDERS (NOV. 15, 1959)

Richard Hickock was doing time for robbery when his cell-mate, an inmate named Floyd Wells, told him about a farmer he had once worked for named Herb Clutter. Clutter, he told Hickock, kept great sums of money in a safe in his house in Holcomb, Kansas. Intrigued by the prospect of "the perfect score," Hickock sought a partner to pull the job with him. Convinced the key to the plan's success was to leave no living witnesses, he needed someone to do his killing for him, coldly and remorselessly, something that was beyond his own meager talents. He found his man in fellow prisoner Perry Smith. Upon their respective releases, the two men set out for Holcomb. They arrived after midnight on Saturday night. Entering the home through an unlocked side door, they roused Herb Clutter from his sleep and demanded that he open his safe. An incredulous Clutter protested that he didn't have a safe and that the only money on hand was the $30 in his wallet. After fruitlessly tapping the walls for telltale sounds, the pair of cons bound and gagged Herb; his invalid wife, Bonnie; and the couple's youngest two children, Nancy 16, and Kenyon, 15. Hickock was dissuaded from raping the terrified girl by Smith, who then proceeded to cut the elder Clutter's throat. Angered and out of control at the prospect of a "score" that consisted of $38 and a transistor radio, the two left after shooting all four family members with the shot-gun they'd brought along.

Hearing of the brutal crime, a still-imprisoned Floyd Wells told the authorities whom they should look for. The pair were eventually picked up in Las Vegas, their dreams of settling in South America on the spoils of their deed long soured. After going through a lengthy legal process, the two were hanged on April 14, 1965. Writer Truman Capote, long known for his fiction work, became fascinated with the crime. As the case played out, he gained access to Smith and Hickock and began work on what he called a "nonfiction novel." *In Cold Blood* became a bestseller and came to the big screen in 1967. In it, the underrated Scott Wilson played Dick Hickock and former *Our Gang* member Robert Blake took on Perry Smith. In the performance of his life, Blake was mesmerizing.

Fasten Your Seatbelts—It's Going to Be a Bumpy Night

T hen as now, catastrophes make for compelling human interest stories. It's not that people draw pleasure from the suffering of others as such, but the fascination value of horrifying events is undeniable. Here are 10 calamities from the fifties, most long forgotten except perhaps by those whose lives were affected. Not too many readers might readily admit their fascination with others' misfortunes, but just try to skip over this chapter.

1. MINING DISASTER IN WEST FRANKFORT, ILLINOIS (DECEMBER 21, 1951)

A 1947 coal mine explosion in Centralia, Illinois, resulted in 111 casualties. Inquiries were launched and federal recommendations made, but heavy lobbying by the operators ensured that the new laws lacked any real teeth. This was evident in July 1951 when federal inspectors visited the New Orient Mine #2 and cited 21 violations uncorrected since the previous inspection. Warnings that the unused workings at the site needed to be sealed went unheeded, with devastating results. On Friday, December 21, men arrived for the 4 p.m. start of the second shift. This was to have been the last working day before Christmas break, and no doubt the men, ranging in age from 19 to early 60s, discussed their plans for the holiday. That night, a high school basketball game was taking place in the nearby gym. More than a few of the workers with sons or brothers in the game would have expressed regret at having to miss out.

At around 7:40 p.m., a tremendous explosion rocked the mine. Explosive coal dust from an unused area had spread into the working mine and was ignited, possibly by a spark. Huge supporting timbers were snapped, and rail cars laden with coal weighing several tons were thrown off their tracks. Employees away from the center of the blast found the power was cut off when they attempted to call for help. Within minutes, the shafts and tunnels were swept by an eerie wind of death roaring through, carrying dust and lethal gases. Those away from the affected areas scrambled for help, and soon rescue teams were on the scene. Struggling frantically against falling debris, noxious fumes, and the trail of corpses in near-zero visibility, they discovered that those not immediately incinerated by the blast died from inhaling lethal carbon monoxide. Eventually, four survivors were found, one of whom later died. Meanwhile, the basketball game was stopped and the gym was turned into a morgue. Shocked families staggered in looking for loved ones, and the death toll eventually reached 119. As they buried their dead in the days to come, it would forever after be remembered as Black Christmas.

2. DESTROYER *HOBSON* COLLIDES WITH AIRCRAFT CARRIER *WASP* (APRIL 26, 1952)

The outbreak of fighting in Korea meant pressing many vessels into service for naval training. Among them was a minesweeper, the USS *Hobson*. Engaged in battle simulations, the ship was part of a convoy that included the USS *Rodman* and the aircraft carrier USS *Wasp*. All three ships had seen extensive action in World War II, with the *Hobson* receiving a presidential citation. On the night in question, the two smaller ships acted as rear guard to the *Wasp* for any returning aircraft needing to ditch into the sea. As the trio sailed toward the Azores in the north Atlantic, the already dark night turned choppy with a sudden wind shift. By just past 10:30 p.m., skeleton crews manned the ships as the bulk of the sailors bunked down for the night. The *Wasp*, in the midst of recovering aircraft, adjusted to the change in wind by altering course to better accommodate the landing planes. The crew aboard the *Rodman* acknowledged the maneuver and adjusted accordingly, but the *Hobson*, sailing to the rear and starboard of the *Wasp*, did not. Instead, the skipper, Lt. Commander W. J. Tierney, ordered a right turn, then "left rudder" twice. Instead of pulling away from the mammoth carrier's path, the *Hobson* went directly into it.

Meanwhile, the *Wasp* was experiencing a radar failure, leaving the difficult task of spotting the *Hobson* to crewmen armed with binoculars. Challenging conditions magnified the danger. Only when the *Wasp* was nearly on top of the smaller ship did the crewmen spot the *Hobson*'s red track lights. As the carrier bore down upon the minesweeper, Captain Mc-Caffree gave the emergency braking command, "all engines back," but it was too late. The bow of the *Wasp* struck the *Hobson* amidships, slicing the destroyer in two. Without warning, the 236-man crew, most of them sleeping, found themselves pitched into the bone-chilling sea. In less than four minutes, the waves swept over the two halves of the ship, claiming 175 lives. The *Wasp*, needing to maintain its course for the sake of the returning planes, did not stop but instead rained life preservers down into the sea. All 61 survivors were recovered by the *Rodman*. A naval inquiry found Captain Tierney responsible for the disaster, committing a "grave error" that led to so many deaths, including his own.

3.   LONDON'S KILLING FOG (DEC. 3–7, 1952)

It was the most insidious killer the city had ever witnessed. There was no single event or sudden trauma, but instead a situational condition that reached into homes and businesses and struck people going about their business. So thick was the fog at the peak of its invasion that people couldn't see their own feet in daytime; trains came to a halt while on bridges because they couldn't tell where they were; traffic was at a standstill; and theaters closed because people couldn't see the stage. Some victims succumbed to asphyxiation in their beds. Others simply drowned by falling into the Thames. As the body count climbed, undertakers ran out of caskets. In the initial week, authorities would place the death count at 4,000, but further studies placed it as high as 12,000, counting all the sick who died from the fog's effects. Though it was commonly believed that the dead were mostly elderly and those with respiratory ailments, the doubling of the infant mortality rate during the crisis was downplayed, for obvious morale reasons. Adults age 45 to 60 took a hit, mostly due to smoking, which compromised their lungs' capacity to handle the lethal air.

The deadly force behind the fatalities was a lethal mix of sulphur dioxide and coal smoke, combined with vehicle emissions and industrial pollutants. More than a century's worth of industrialization had led to the expelling of all the waste into the air. When this foul byproduct suddenly had nowhere to go and became earthbound, the population instantly became aware of the price of progress. A mass of cold air from the continent had stagnated over London, trapping the pollutants close to the ground. It was as if the whole of the city were under a giant lid. With the cold snap, millions of residents and businesses reliant on coal-burning stoves for their heating fired them up. Due to the depressed British economy at the time, the best-burning, least-polluting grade of coal was reserved for overseas sales, leaving the lower-grade, more sulphurous variety for the populace. In reaction to the catastrophic event, Parliament passed the Clean Air Act of 1956, but even that wasn't enough to prevent a recurrence during the 10th anniversary week of the killer fog in 1962, which claimed 136 more lives.

4. HURRICANE ALICE AND THE RIO GRANDE FLOODS (JUNE 24–30, 1954)

Nineteen fifty-one marked the beginning of what would be almost six years of uninterrupted drought in south Texas.

London Fog outerwear proved disastrously
ineffective against the killer fog.

The "almost" came in the last week of June 1954, when the remains of Hurricane Alice hit landfall 20 miles south of Brownsville, bringing with it 27 inches of rain in a little over 24 hours. Moving northwest along the Lower Rio Grande Valley, the rains exceeded 35 inches. Never in its recorded history had the Rio Grande so overrun its banks. From Laredo to Del Rio, rail and traffic bridges alike were swept away with never-before-seen violent tides. US Highway 90 was under 30 feet of water, and vehicles were carried miles downstream. The border bridge at Laredo was rendered useless when the causeway on the U.S. side was torn apart.

As the waters engulfed towns along the river's path, a Southern Pacific passenger train became marooned upon a high bed of track near Langtree, Texas. While awaiting rescue, the desperate passengers watched the rising waters; the sight of arriving U.S. Army helicopters, specifically dispatched to evacuate the trapped people, allowed the passengers to sigh with relief. The twin towns of Eagle Pass, Texas, and Piedras Negras, Mexico, were hit especially hard. The river between them had spread to three miles wide; downtown Eagle Pass was flooded past parking meter height, while on the Mexican side, a delay in public warnings led to numerous drownings. One minor bright spot in the entire calamity was the newly built Falcon Dam reservoir. Nearly dry before the rains came and expected to take three or four years to reach conservation level, the dam attained that level within three days of the flood. When it was all over, 55 American and more than 130 Mexican lives were lost. Drought relief arriving all at once rather than over time exacted a terrible cost.

5. GRAND PRIX CRASH AT LE MANS, FRANCE (JUNE 11, 1955)

A quarter of a million people turned out to witness the internationally famous auto racing spectacle begun in Le Mans, France, in 1923. Amid a carnival-like atmosphere of music and rides, crowds pressed as close to the action as possible to see the cars whizzing by at speeds between 125 and 160 mph. At about 6:30 p.m., two and a half hours into the race, leader Mike Hawthorne inadvertently blew by a signal to re-fuel. Because of his delayed response, Hawthorne was forced to jerk rather suddenly to the right. In the process, he cut off racer Lance Macklin, who had to veer to the left to avoid rear-ending the Jaguar. This put him in the path of Pierre Levegh, who was driving a Mercedes. Levegh managed to put up his arm to signal to his teammate behind to slow down, but he was himself unable to avoid hitting Macklin's Austin-Healy. The two speeding vehicles fused together and screeched down the narrow straightaway before separating. Macklin continued his skid before safely escaping his burning vehicle; Levegh's car hitting an earthen wall before catapulting into the crowd.

The flying vehicle spread mayhem in all directions as its pieces separated. The hood spun through the air and into the crowd like a buzz saw, mowing down everything in its path, while car's rear axle tumbled like a log into the clutch of spectators. The engine block, made of ultralight magnesium, shattered and burned. Levegh, thrown from the wreckage and killed instantly, lay beside the track as the race continued. Reporters and photographers on the scene likened what they saw to a war zone, with decapitated bodies, human parts, and dead children strewn everywhere. In all, 83 were killed outright and more than 100 were injured. A snap decision not to cancel the race may have been made in the interest of not spreading panic among the throngs who in any event were not about to leave. The juxtaposition of people continuing to drink and make merry while rescue workers surveyed the horror did not go unnoticed. As it happened, Mike Hawthorne won the event. Four years later he, too, died in a motor accident.

6. TWA CONSTELLATION COLLIDES WITH UA DC-7 OVER GRAND CANYON (JUNE 30, 1956)

In the last pre-jet days of air travel, passengers traveling coast to coast were often treated to the sight of the Grand

Canyon as they crossed the American southwest. With the lower-altitude flights, airlines happily accommodated the crowd-pleasing custom of allowing a little sightseeing. With air traffic controllers overtaxed then as now, however, pilots were expected to use their own resources (that is, their eyes) to maintain a safe altitude. The public remained blissfully unaware of the very real dangers until they were graphically illustrated one fine summer day in 1956. That morning, a Kansas City–bound Lockheed Super-Constellation (TWA Flight 2) left Los Angeles 30 minutes late, carrying 70 passengers and crew members. Several minutes later, a Douglas DC-7 (United Airlines Flight 718) took off for Chicago, with a total of 58 aboard. Once airborne, the two planes were separated by 2,000 feet of altitude. But Flight 2, experiencing some turbulence, asked controllers for permission to fly above the clouds, which would put it at 21,000 feet, the same altitude as the DC-7. Salt Lake City controllers pointed this out to Los Angeles, which told the TWA flight to maintain its current altitude of 19,000 feet. Rephrasing the request, this time asking for "1,000 on top," permission was inexplicably granted. The two planes were set on a path of convergence. It was just about 10:30 a.m.

As each pilot, in complete ignorance of the other's proximity, positioned himself to best display the scenery to the passengers, the planes drew dangerously close. Suddenly the DC-7 radioed control: "Salt Lake! United 718! We're going in!" Another voice was heard shouting, "Up! Up!" then nothing. Without warning, the UA plane's left wingtip had struck the center tail fin of the Constellation and proceeded to slice into the fuselage from just forward of the tail to the main cabin entrance. The TWA plane, effectively broken in two, spilled its contents into the canyon. The DC-7, left wing now partly detached, dropped helplessly from the sky. It is believed that all of the 128 dead were killed instantly. No single body was found intact, and the debris was so widely scattered that tourists were still recovering pieces for more than a year afterward.

7. *STOCKHOLM* COLLIDES WITH *andrea doria* in ATLANTIC (JULY 25, 1956)

In last decade of great transatlantic luxury liner service, the *Andrea Doria* was Italy's crown jewel. Named for the country's *second* favorite admiral, she began service in January 1953. Though not the fastest or biggest liner afloat at the time, she was arguably the most luxurious; few who sailed her could dispute that claim. Beyond the usual crowd of monied aristocracy among the 1,706 passengers and crew aboard, a few celebrities could be found, including rock & roll songwriter Mike Stoller, one half of the team responsible for many classics. The *Stockholm* made no such boast. She was strictly business, a sort of Scandinavian Southwest Airlines. The steerage trade was her bread and butter as she conveyed the less well-to-do to a better life and good fortune in America. One-third the size of *Andrea Doria*, the *Stockholm* had one extravagance—a specially reinforced bow for navigating the dangerous, ice-laden sea lanes of the north Atlantic. On this evening that bow would prove deadly.

A mid-summer fog had settled off the notoriously difficult to navigate sea near Nantucket. Though the ships were armed with radar, seamen trusted their own eyes more and kept a vigilant lookout. The *Andrea Doria* slowed as it entered the fog bank, blasting its warning horn to signal its blindness. Steaming east from New York, the *Stockholm* was having trouble staying on course, with a heavy current pushing it to the north, far from its prescribed route. The two ships first became aware of each other's presence at about 10:40 p.m. What ensued was a series of misreadings and bad judgment that couldn't have set a better course for disaster if it had been planned. Following several ill-conceived maneuvers by both ships, the *Stockholm* rammed into the starboard side of the *Andrea Doria*, creating a 30-foot, V-shaped hole. As she backed away, the *Andrea Doria* immediately took on a steep list with water pouring into the gash, rendering most of the lifeboats unlaunchable. Although the ship was mortally stricken, its death throes unfolded slowly enough to allow evacuation of all of the now wide-awake passengers. Almost all of the resulting 52 deaths were a result of the collision itself.

The charge was leveled, not without reason, that the crew onboard the *Andrea Doria* looked after themselves first, with the passengers' needs being a mere afterthought. No general alarm was sounded, and at the first sign of trouble, the crew essentially abandoned ship, leaving the passengers to their own devices. The first rescue boats picked up by the *Stockholm* were filled with—you guessed it—uniformed crew members. The subsequent inquiry found both parties equally responsible for the accident, although the court of public opinion judged the Italian crew harshly. Recovered passengers were greeted by friends and relatives in New York, among them Mike Stoller's partner Jerry Leiber. Each had good news for the other: Stoller, that he was alive, and Leiber, that Elvis's recording of their song "Hound Dog" was burning up the charts. *Andrea Doria* survivors found that their status gave them a leg up in securing New York City apartments (in most instances) as recently as the nineties.

8. DYNAMITE BLAST LEVELS TOWN OF CALI, COLOMBIA (AUG. 7, 1956)

A freighter ship was unloading at the port of Buenaventura, Colombia, in early August 1956. Twenty trucks carrying munitions and dynamite disembarked—13 bound for the capital city, Bogotá, and the rest for other destinations. Arriving at Cali on August 6, the seven remaining trucks were parked for the night near the town's railroad station. Nearby, a garrison of troops and MPs kept watch on the convoy. Just past midnight, a tremendous explosion rocked the city. The entire fleet of trucks exploded with the force of a megabomb, virtually redrawing the entire downtown. Two thousand buildings and structures were gone, including the offices of two American automakers and Abbott Labs. Windows were shattered for more than three miles in every direction. Killed outright were more than 1,200 people, including some 500 soldiers asleep in their barracks, and thousands more were injured. The ruling dictator, General Gustavo Pinilla, blamed an anti-government conspiracy, but the true cause of the blast was never uncovered.

9. HURRICANE *AUDREY* STRIKES CAMERON, LOUISIANA (JUNE 27, 1957)

Hurricane season doesn't usually start until August. Not only did Audrey arrive early, but its force proved exceptional as well. Audrey formed as a tropical storm in the Gulf of Mexico, off the Bay of Campeche. As it began its deadly course toward land, the speeding storm claimed its first victims by taking out some fishing vessels and offshore oil platforms before reaching the hurricane-battered city of Galveston, Texas. Causing relatively moderate damage, Audrey was just warming up, marshaling its forces for a full-scale assault on the low-lying coastal cities of Louisiana. Winds reaching nearly 100 mph slammed into the town of Cameron. The residents, for the most part unaccustomed to such ungodly storms, did not pay as much heed to the warnings as they might have. By the time many were prepared to evacuate, the menace was upon them. Cars were lifted and smashed by surging torrents of water, pushed by category 4 winds. As houses crumbled and trees snapped, means of escape quickly vanished for many. Those not already washed away by the current fled to the rooftops. Stories were told later of desperate attempts to hold onto loved ones until the pull of the water won out.

For many who survived the initial onslaught, the brightening skies and sudden calm were an unexpected relief. With everything familiar gone or under water, the reassuring presence of sunshine was cause for celebration. That joy was tragically misplaced, however; unfamiliar with storms of this magnitude, the population was unaware that the "eye of the storm" was but a temporary lull. By the time the storm left town for good, the body count from Hurricane Audrey reached 534. Cameron was leveled, but the storm continued on farther north and east, pummeling Ohio and Pennsylvania with 80 mph winds until it at last spent itself.

10. OUR LADY OF THE ANGELS SCHOOL FIRE IN CHICAGO, ILLINOIS (DEC. 1, 1958)

Anyone who ever attended a school equipped with sprinklers or fire doors has some angels to thank—93 of them, to be exact. The outrage and anguish in the wake of this all too appropriately named Chicago school spurred legislation and new safety codes like nothing else had. Students were only moments away from dismissal that Monday afternoon when the unmistakable odor of smoke began wafting its way upward from the point of origin, a trash barrel beneath a stairwell in the basement. The fire had been burning for at least 20 minutes before a janitor spotted the blaze and notified the school housekeeper, who then called the fire department. It didn't occur to anyone at this juncture to sound a general alarm, inform the second-story classes, or evacuate the building. As the fire consumed the stairwell and spread upward, the first floor was spared by heavy wooden doors that the flames couldn't breach. Instead, it rose to the second floor, where no such doors existed. Superheated gases ignited in the attic, bringing death from above as well as from the fire-engulfed hallways. The deadly smoke quickly doomed any children not yet out of the building.

Those trapped on the second floor were left with little choice: they could attempt an escape out the windows, a 25-foot drop, or simply pray and wait for firemen to rescue them. The more proactive students seized the initiative, amassing at the window sills and battling for survival alongside their peers. By the time firemen finally arrived and set their ladders in place, for far too many children it no longer mattered. The would-be rescuers were anguished at the cries for help that suddenly died out just as aid was within reach. In a *Titanic*-like series of events, everything that could go wrong did. The first arriving firemen had been misdirected to the rectory around the corner, wasting valuable minutes. The school's antiquated design ensured that all building materials save the outer walls were extremely flammable, quickly turning the school into a roaring inferno. The area below the second-story windows where panic-stricken children attempted to save themselves by jumping was composed of crushed rock and concrete, causing further injury and some deaths. Though the fire was under control in an hour, help arrived too late to save the 90 students and three nuns who perished. The fire was officially ruled "of unknown origin," although the Archdiocese and city officials were content to pillory the building's head maintenance man for supposedly creating the conditions that allowed the fire to happen. A former student with a history of pyromania later confessed, agreeing to sit for a polygraph exam that bolstered his claim. Ten years old at the time, he told investigators he simply didn't want to have to go to school the next day.

The Whole Town's Talking

The years following the trauma of World War II found Americans looking forward to settling back and enjoying some good old salacious gossip to replace the real-life horrors they'd become accustomed to reading about. Hollywood, television, even politics all did their part to feed what fed this country's insatiable appetite for sordid doings. Here's a sampling.

1. CHARLIE CHAPLIN'S VISA IS REVOKED (SEPTEMBER 19, 1952)

Beloved film comedian Charlie Chaplin had won a worldwide audience during his decades-long film career, but he also made some powerful enemies along the way. Leftist-leaning in times of political volatility, he had an air of condescension and taste for just-legal babes that rubbed many the wrong way. A 1943 paternity claim by starlet Joan Barry provided ammunition to those longing to ruin him. Though a blood test in court cleared him, he was ordered to pay child support anyway. The bruising of his public image coupled with the rising wave of paranoia made for a volatile mix of mutual resentment. Opportunistic politicians casting about for victims correctly pegged Chaplin as damaged goods in the public eye. As the witch hunt began in earnest, his name topped the list of potential "undesirable" aliens the country would do well to cast aside. The Immigration and Naturalization Service began looking into that possibility, while the FBI launched a three-year investigation into allegations that Chaplin had been a member of the Communist Party. The irony lost on everyone was that the truly subversive elements in this country had no use for Chaplin, seeing him as an out-of-touch capitalist who, despite owning a studio and production company, failed to aid any of the blacklisted writers or actors in Hollywood.

When word got out that Chaplin's next film, *Limelight*, was to be released within two weeks of the national elections in 1952, suspicion that the event might be used for some anti-American editorializing heightened. One day after Chaplin and his family set sail on an extended European holiday, the INS lowered the boom. Word that his visa had been revoked, barring his reentry, reached him at sea. Angry and hurt at the shabby treatment he'd been given, Chaplin vowed never to return that "fascist" country. Twenty years passed before all was forgiven on both sides, and the film legend returned to America to accept a special Oscar for his brilliant film work. He died five years later.

2. NIXON DELIVERS HIS "CHECKERS" SPEECH (SEPTEMBER 23, 1952)

By 1952, California senator Richard Nixon had managed to parlay his red-baiting persona into the number two spot on the GOP presidential ticket, providing balance to the moderate Dwight Eisenhower. Ideological differences aside, Nixon's performances in previous campaigns repulsed Ike. He was not alone; the young senator had seemingly made a career of cultivating enemies, including Harry Truman, who called him a "shifty eyed, goddamned liar." Saddled with a running mate he had little use for, Eisenhower and his advisers were delighted by allegations of impropriety raised against Nixon. The story, that a group of rich California businessmen had passed the hat and collected a "secret" fund for Nixon's personal use, could provide a reason for dropping the perceived dead weight. While the fund certainly did exist (in fact, most politicians had similar pots for day-to-day expenses), the implication was that Nixon was being lavishly bankrolled above his means. The candidate responded with typical vitriol, swinging wildly at his enemies' attempts to smear him. Ike's refusal to come to his aid enraged him further. Emboldened with ire, he told the general by phone, "There comes a time when a man must shit or get off the pot!" Unmoved, Ike left it up to Nixon to clear himself.

Interests sympathetic to the candidate suggested that he address the nation on television and plead his case directly before "the people." Seeing an opportunity to bypass the press, the ex-thespian jumped at the chance. With wife Pat in support, he soberly outlined his means, detailing the struggles faced in raising two children. He pointed out that his wife did not have a mink coat. "But she does have a perfectly respectable Republican cloth coat. And I always tell her she'd look good in anything." For her part, Pat Nixon was mortified at her husband's shameless use of his family and upset in particular that he chose to invite the entire country to inspect their bank book. Lest he lose his audience before he reached his exit, Nixon then decided to play the dog card.

"There is one other thing I should mention," he began in summation. He went on to tell the audience of another contribution he'd received from a supporter: a black-and-white, spotted cocker spaniel his daughters had named Checkers. Indignation rising in his throat, he announced: "I just want to say this right now—regardless of what they say about it, we're going to keep it!" With that, his allotted time ran out. Nixon felt that he'd blown his chance and wept. But the press recognized the human interest value of this maudlin, self-pitying performance. An enthralled public rallied to Nixon's side, leaving Ike no choice but to embrace his "boy." The ticket went on to victory, but the episode was never mentioned again by the Republicans, who thought the stunt cheap and sentimental (values they would embrace in the years to come). Democrats, on the other hand, instinctively

PDImages.com

Vice President and Mrs. Nixon price cloth coats.

grasped the camp potential and forever after hounded Nixon (so to speak) on the campaign trail with taunts of, "Tell us a dog story, Dick!" The publicity-shy Checkers died in 1964.

3.   THE PRINCESS MARGARET-PETER TOWNSEND AFFAIR (1953–1955)

The newly crowned Elizabeth II was literally *minutes* into her reign when observant bystanders at the coronation spotted trouble. Her sister, Princess Margaret, was seen affectionately brushing a loose strand of hair off the uniform of Group Captain Peter Townsend, newly appointed Comptroller to the Household of the Queen Mother. Such public display of familiarity could mean only one thing: something was going on between the two. At 38, Townsend was a favorite of the family, the late king especially. He and Margaret saw a lot of each other, and a closeness grew, despite their 15-year difference in age. When Margaret's father died, it was Townsend who consoled her and her mother, distracting Margaret from the sudden change her sister's ascension meant.

Two weeks before the coronation, Margaret revealed her intent to marry Townsend, forcing a confrontation with serious implications. The age difference may have been one issue and his coming from the position of royal servitude another; but the primary obstacle was Townsend's earlier marriage and recent divorce. This put the Queen in an awkward position, for though she loved her sister and was very fond of the group captain, as head of the Church of England she couldn't allow such a pairing. As grown adults, they could certainly marry, but that meant that Margaret had to renounce her title and her inheritance. The matter might have been resolved quietly by keeping such private matters in house, but Margaret's public action had not escaped the notice of the press. Now the pressure was on.

A firestorm was ignited within the church and government as well the press and the Queen's subjects. Everyone had an adamant view, with traditional institutions dead set against the union and suggesting that Margaret would create an ugly precedent by flouting Church law. The tabloid press, predictably, championed the couple's right to happiness, tradition be damned. Elizabeth was likewise torn, ever conscious of the eyes of the world upon her. Desiring to wash her hands of the matter, she chose an easy out—simply to wait two years until Margaret turned 25, whereupon she could do as she wished while the Crown would not be held accountable. A separation was contrived, with Townsend accepting a post in Brussels. At the end of the two years, however, neither party had budged. Elizabeth was at last forced to act, privately advising Margaret that she was powerless to fight the will of the Cabinet in this matter. Margaret was ultimately compelled by loyalty and respect for the Crown to put duty ahead of her own happiness. On October 31, 1955, the palace announced that there would be no marriage. In 1960, Margaret married the eminently acceptable Antony Armstrong-Jones. They divorced in 1978.

4. ARTHUR GODFREY VS. JULIUS LA ROSA (OCTOBER 19, 1953)

It's hard to imagine now that any one figure in show business could be popular enough to appear in *three* separate series at the same time *and* do a radio show besides. Such a person was Arthur Godfrey in 1953—a genuine cornball in a time bereft of irony. It's even harder to conceive of so much airtime being given to someone so—modestly talented, shall we say. A barely passable singer and a marginal ukulele player at best, Godfrey was gifted with a presence as predictable and stale as day-old Wonder bread. The fact was, advertisers loved him. He could move product like no one else, mostly on the strength of his folksy, plainspoken charm. He also was shrewd enough to stock his show with talent much more sparkling than his own. Such was the basis of the long-running *Arthur Godfrey's Talent Scouts*, a show that "discovered" the unsung from many walks of life.

In December 1951, Godfrey featured a young Navy enlistee he'd uncovered in Florida, Julius La Rosa. Blessed with an exceptional tenor voice and an earnest stage presence, La Rosa proved popular enough to be added as a series regular following his discharge in 1952. Godfrey functioned as paterfamilias on his show, supported by a cast of mostly callow, fresh-faced kids he referred to as "the little Godfreys." In addition to unquestioned obedience, Godfrey demanded complete loyalty. What he never banked on was one of the kid's stars outshining his own.

In early 1953, La Rosa scored with his first hit record, "Anywhere I Wander." By the end of summer, his fan mail surpassed Godfrey's. Returning for a new season that fall following surgery, Godfrey was in no mood for nonsense. Learning that La Rosa had hired an outside agent rubbed him the wrong way. On Monday, October 19, Godfrey slated La Rosa for the show's final minutes. After bringing La Rosa out with the rhetorical query, "Is being on the show a pain in the neck?" he let him do his song. As the applause faded away after the number's finish, Godfrey told the audience, "That, folks, was Julie's swan song." The naïve La Rosa didn't know what a swan song was and had to ask, "Was I just fired?" The country's reaction was swift and furious: people were shocked and dismayed at Uncle Arthur's heavy-handed public discipline. An unrepentant Godfrey told reporters that La Rosa "lacked humility." Following the incident, Godfrey's ratings went into a decline from which they never recovered. As for La Rosa, he enjoyed several more hit records and minor roles in film and television before fading away.

5. FORMER NEW JERSEY GOV. HOFFMAN DIES (JUNE 4, 1954)

While it is common enough for political figures to be branded as crooks and thieves, it's rare that such accusations turn out to be an understatement. When Harold Hoffman died of a heart attack that Friday morning in June, what had been a suspicion became a full-blown shocker. A note left to his daughter revealed an unparalleled, systematic career of embezzlement and theft. For decades, the former banker and one-time Republican governor of New Jersey had been looting inactive bank accounts, submitting inflated expense reports, and shifting public money to his own personal use on a grand scale. That he got away with it for so long and to the tune of so much money was stunning. As much as half a million dollars in state money had vanished, and when he died, Hoffman took many secrets to his grave. As a former banker, Hoffman knew how to manipulate the system without arousing any undo suspicion. His career in theft began while he was still in banking, when he happened to notice unclaimed funds in his bank. By moving the money around from account to account, he was able to access the cash and still hoodwink any auditors who might happen along. The deposits he siphoned off became seed money for his start in politics. He began as mayor of South Amboy before winning a seat in the U.S. Congress in 1927. After his reelection, it must have occurred to him that living in Washington left him too far away to keep proper tabs on his chicanery. In 1930, he returned to New Jersey to head the state's commission of motor vehicles, an odd career move. But his popularity with voters took on a life of its own, and in 1937 he was elected governor. A colorful, larger-than-life figure, Hoffman (at five feet seven inches and 210 pounds) was known for his garrulous manner, his free spending, and his bottomless repertoire of off-color jokes. Barely in control of himself at the best of times, he once flattened a reporter he outweighed by 90 pounds with a single punch.

His public suggestion that the state's case against convicted Lindbergh kidnapper Richard Hauptmann was less than solid ended the public's infatuation with him. He then took a job with the New Jersey unemployment commission, positioning himself to become even wealthier. By 1954, however, then-Governor Robert Meyner, suspicious of possible malfeasance, began looking into state financial irregularities. Hoffman was suspended while matters were being investigated. As the stress of a long overdue comeuppance took over, his health failed. Perhaps feeling that his clock was ticking, he unburdened himself on paper, detailing his array of sins. Only in death did the full extent of his handiwork become evident, by which time he was beyond the reach of any earthly court.

6. JERRY LEE LEWIS TAKES A WIFE (DECEMBER 12, 1957)

Before his great balls of fire landed him in hot water with the public, Jerry Lee Lewis was on a roll. From the start he proved a talent to be reckoned with, with songs like "Whole Lotta Shaking Goin' On," "Breathless," and "High School Confidential" to his credit. The success of those Sun singles posed Elvis his first serious threat—a white man who rocked as convincingly as he did. Lewis, known as the Killer, had a stage show that was literally incendiary, ending on at least one occasion with his baby grand set aflame. While the King had the swivel hips and a palsied demeanor, Lewis was a wild man, pounding the piano with hands and feet, and kicking the stool away, overgrown forelocks dangling over his face—in short, talent coupled with charisma and more than a whiff of danger. His overtaking of Elvis in popularity seemed assured when, suddenly, word of his recent marriage leaked out. This unto itself shouldn't have stopped his career in its tracks, but for the fact that 1) he was five months into his marriage with wife number three before he bothered to divorce wife number two; 2) the bride was 13 years old; and 3) she was his third cousin. The resulting furor made people quickly forget any of Elvis's excesses. Exacerbating matters was Lewis's arrogant, defiant response to the public outcry. Contrition just wasn't in him—instead, the resulting heat made him all the more antagonistic. The timing couldn't have been any worse for a tour of the UK, coming so fast on the heels of the breaking story. Upon arriving in England so publicly with his child bride, the petite, gum-snapping Myra, Lewis faced the hostility of the British press and an incensed public. After only four shows promoters canceled Lewis's remaining dates. Getting the boot from his hotel, the unrepentant pianist returned home to find his career in ashes. In time, he resuscitated his career by exploring the more forgiving niche of country music, a market where his troubles seemed unremarkable. The entire compelling saga was laid out in the biopic, *Great Balls of Fire*, starring Dennis Quaid as Jerry Lee. As Myra, Wynona Ryder is true to form, stealing every scene she is in.

7. LANA TURNER'S BOYFRIEND MURDERED BY HER DAUGHTER (APRIL 4, 1958)

Born Julia Turner, Lana's "discovery" was the stuff of legend—at 15, someone spotted her good looks while she downed a soda at the famous Schwab's drugstore. Her capacity for filling out a sweater was parlayed into a film career. Though capable of turning in the occasional inspired performance, by and large Lana's body of work was fairly pedestrian. Her personal life wasn't faring much better. By 1958, she'd been married four times, including twice to the man with whom she'd had a daughter, Cheryl, in 1943. Following the breakdown of her marriage to Lex Barker in 1957, she began making time with a beefy ex-Marine named Johnny Stompanato. Unbeknown to her, Stompanato was a small-time hood and protégé to mobster Mickey Cohen. He was also a bully with a short fuse and given to jealous rages. But Lana was smitten, writing him lurid love letters when the two were apart. These separations became increasingly rare as the relationship deepened, with Johnny demanding to accompany her on location shoots. While Lana was filming *Another Time, Another Place* in England, he became enraged at what he saw as her male co-star's extravagant attentions and picked a fight with him. Unperturbed, young Sean Connery knocked Stompanato unconscious. By early 1958, Lana had tired of his abuse and decided to end the affair.

On Good Friday evening, she informed Stompanato of her intent, and a violent argument ensued. The intensity of this one surpassed any before it, with Johnny threatening to ruin her looks permanently. "I'll cut you up!," he raged. Hearing all of this from the next room was 14-year-old

Cheryl. Grabbing an eight-inch kitchen knife, she hastened to her mother's defense. Stompanato rushed her as she held out the blade, driving it into his belly and severing his aorta. He was dead within minutes. The evening's melodrama attracted enormous public interest, much of it stirred up by Mickey Cohen, who leaked Lana's torrid letters to the press. At the coroner's inquest, Lana gave the performance of her life, tearfully detailing the horror of that night. Cheryl herself did not take the stand, submitting instead a written account of her actions. After weighing all evidence, the court ruled that the killing was justifiable homicide. An investigation into Turner's fitness as a mother followed, resulting in Cheryl's banishment to her grandmother's until she was 18. Lana Turner's film career didn't suffer any; in fact, her next project, centered on a mother's neglect of her daughter, did quite well, bearing the exquisitely appropriate title *Imitation of Life*.

8. QUIZ SHOWS BUSTED (1958–1959)

Striving to stay fresh, CBS stumbled onto an idea that took hold with viewers: making ordinary people rich overnight for possessing specialized knowledge. In June 1955, *The $64,000 Question* went on the air and quickly became TV's top-rated show. It didn't take long for the other networks to take notice—by 1958, there were no less than *24* quiz shows on the tube. The spectacle of ordinary folks sweating out the pressure of choosing between increased prizes versus greater risks made for addictive viewing. Producers also came to realize that viewers chose favorites among the contestants, so they tried to anticipate which ones would be popular to ensure an audience-pleasing outcome. While not exactly kosher in a fair play sense, the networks saw themselves primarily as entertainers. Advertisers needed viewers; to keep them happy and tuning in, the networks needed to give them what they wanted. So the status quo was maintained, until a contestant named Herb Stempel was picked to appear on *Twenty-One*. This show had gotten off to a rough start since it demanded a broader range of knowledge than, say, *The $64,000 Question*, which booked contestants with deep expertise in select fields. After initial broadcasts resulted in embarrassingly flat scores, Stempel, an apparent brainiac, was brought on to jump-start the failing series. Hedging his bets, producer Dan Enright visited Stempel at his home, running by him the questions to be used on the actual broadcast. A shocked Stempel accepted this as standard procedure, along with cues from the director: his reactions, how long to take before answering, and other bits of stage craft. As he began to win big, the audience grew.

Emboldened by their success, the show's producers decided after eight weeks to fine-tune the formula by ditching the unstoppable Stempel for someone more charismatic. That someone was Charles Van Doren, a handsome academic from Columbia University. Instructions to, in essence, "take a dive" did not sit well with Stempel. Though he did what he was told, he remained resentful and complained loudly to anyone who would listen. Finally, he went to the New York City district attorney with the complaint that TV quiz shows were a fraud. Though vigorously denied by the participants, Stempel's charges led Congress to opening hearings into the matter. Van Doren, as the most visible symbol of the deception, was pursued until he cracked. Networks canceled their entire quiz show lineups overnight, but truth be told, very few viewers were upset by the revelations.

9. ROCK & ROLL PAYOLA (1959)

Fresh on the heels of the quiz show scandals, the House Oversight Committee set its sights on investigating whether rock & roll radio disc jockeys accepted bribes to favor certain records over others for airplay. (The word, "payola," was derived from pay—as in cash or goods—and "Victrola" as in record player.) The practice of cozying up to DJs with gratuities was as old as radio; only when this particular genre came along did anyone decide that the country's moral fabric was at risk. At the top of the target list was New York City disc jockey Alan Freed. His resume as the biggest booster of rock roll (as well as having popularized the term, if not actually inventing it) was unmatched. The yang to Freed's yin was Philadelphia DJ Dick Clark. By then the host of *American Bandstand*, Clark was similarly coming under examination. It was noticed that an inordinate amount of airtime was given to records that Clark had a financial stake in, through his pressing plant interests as well as copyright ownership. With the writing being on the wall, his bosses at ABC ordered him to divest himself of his tainted interests in October 1959. Clark complied, further 'fessing up to having accepted a fur stole and jewelry, for which his wrists were duly slapped. The recalcitrant Freed, however, remained defiant. "What they call payola in the disc jockey business they call lobbying in Washington," he declared before Congress. Had he accepted gifts and cash from record companies attempting to curry favor? Sure he had—they were paying him consulting fees for his expertise and judgment. Other DJs owned up to the standard practice of accepting "auditing" fees. With hundreds of new releases flooding radio stations every week, "listening fees" were accepted to help select what records made it on to the air. At last, investigators had heard enough. An antipayola bill was enacted, mandating $10,000 fines or one year's imprisonment for violations. Scores of disc jockeys lost their employment, and Freed, facing 29 separate charges, was finished as a rock impresario.

10. LIZ TAYLOR AND EDDIE FISHER (1958–1959)

The Taylor-Fisher saga requires some background. Two days after an Acapulco divorce from second husband Michael Wilding, the 26-year-old actress wed Hollywood producer Mike Todd. Exuberant, brash, and impolite, the self-made millionaire swept Taylor off her feet, despite being old enough to be her father. Todd's best friend was singer Eddie Fisher. In fact, he and wife Debbie Reynolds named their son Todd when he arrived in February 1958. One month later, Mike Todd was scheduled to fly to New York to attend an awards ceremony. He intended to bring Elizabeth, but ill with a bronchial infection, she stayed behind. On the night of March 22, he took off from Burbank Airport. Within the hour, the plane crashed into a New Mexico mountain, killing all aboard. Elizabeth, then filming *Cat on a Hot Tin Roof,* was shattered.

Beside herself with grief, Elizabeth was able to fully share her despondency only with Eddie. The two commiserated over their loss together, leaving Debbie home to babysit both sets of kids. Over time the inevitable occurred; comfort crossed the line into socializing and then something more. Rumors began swirling, and the situation reached a climax when a suspicious Debbie phoned Elizabeth's hotel room late one night and Eddie answered. *Busted!* When gossip columnist Louella Parsons broke the news, Taylor was incredulous at the uproar. "Mike's dead and I'm not," she told her. "What do you expect me to do—sleep alone?"

The two married in Las Vegas on May 12, 1959, hours after Eddie's divorce became final. Though the public did not know that the Fishers' marriage had been in trouble for some time, someone had to pay for this indecent spectacle, and that someone was Eddie. Following a deluge of hate mail, Coca-Cola, which sponsored his television show, abruptly canceled it. Meanwhile, Taylor's career rolled right along. Her role as a call girl in the forgettable potboiler *Butterfield 8* garnered her an Oscar in 1960, though even then it seemed to be a sympathy vote for a woman who had nearly died of pneumonia that year.

By the time Elizabeth had signed on with 20th Century-Fox to play the title role in *Cleopatra,* Fisher's role in her life had become increasingly marginalized. His hours were spent babysitting while she worked, playing the occasional supper club gig, or just being one more bystander on the sidelines at her film sets. (Writer Truman Capote referred to him as "the busboy.") By the time co-star Richard Burton (husband number 5 and 6), a married man himself, was boasting to the crew of how he'd "nailed" Taylor in his car, Fisher was ready to cash out. Their divorce became final in early 1964, two years into the Taylor-Burton romance.

Once I Had a Secret Love

In virtually every public arena of the 1950s, to be recognizably "queer" was the kiss of death. In Hollywood, studios often went to extravagant lengths to keep a bankable star's private predilections buried. Rock Hudson, for instance, though unambiguously gay, went along with the studio's efforts to have him seen publicly with any number of attractive women before marrying him off to a secretary for a brief time. Those in the know were not fooled by the ruse, but the general public remained blissfully unaware. Unless provoked, the press usually backed off, allowing celebrities to go about their lives secure in the knowledge that their personal indulgences would remain off-limits. You may well ask: what business is it of ours then to read about the private matters of others? Why should we be privy to other people's means of orgasm attainment? The answer is: you shouldn't. Shame on you for even browsing this chapter. Those of you not already going to hell may skip ahead—the rest of you, read on.

1. LEONARD BERNSTEIN (AUGUST 25, 1918–OCTOBER 14, 1990), COMPOSER AND CONDUCTOR

Pretty, witty, and gay, Leonard (born Louis) Bernstein epitomized a sort of urbane cool that made highbrow worth aspiring to. His ubiquitous presence in the country's consciousness came from his many facets: conductor of the New York Phil-harmonic; composer of several hit shows, including *Candide* and *West Side Story*, and host of the *Young People's Concerts* on television in the fifties and sixties. Bernstein was to classi-cal music in this country what Michael Jordan would one day be to basketball: an individual who defined the genre, whose charisma coupled with exceptional talent made his field of achievement accessible and exciting even to nonbelievers.

A large part of what made Bernstein a star was his unbri-dled passion for living. Anything worth pursuing he threw himself into completely, whether it be conducting *or* scoring. He received quite an education in both at the knee of his early mentor, Aaron Copland (composer of "Hoedown" and "Fanfare for the Common Man"). A certain amount of "when in Rome" informed the secret promiscuity that began in Bernstein's 20s as he joined New York's cultural inner circle. Though he dated women and married, he never abandoned his pursuit of intimate male companionship. Close friends said that it was a part of himself that he despised; an at-tempted "cure" through psychotherapy proved fruitless. (That is to say, he did *not* succeed. Which is to say, it didn't take. Whew!)

His marriage produced three children. Through the years, wife Felicia maintained an almost superhuman denial of her husband's ways, until he finally forced the issue by allowing her to catch him red-handed (or something). The two sepa-rated for a brief time before reconciling, and remained to-gether until her death from cancer in 1977. Following her loss, Bernstein's long in-check self-destructive drives mani-fested themselves—drink, drugs, and dissipation. In October 1990, at age 72, he announced his retirement from live per-formance. One week later he was dead.

2. ROY COHN (FEBRUARY 20, 1927–AUGUST 2, 1986), NEW YORK ATTORNEY

This red-baiting lawyer's reputation as not a nice guy is richly deserved, learning the art of the smear, innuendo, and

ruthless tenacity as he did at the elbow of Senator Joe Mc-
Carthy. Cohn has been the subject of both a movie (*Citizen
Cohn,* starring James Woods) and two plays (*Angels in
America* by Tony Kushner and *Roy* by Joel Ensana). He first
garnered public notice for his role in the conviction of Julius
and Ethel Rosenberg. As a member of the prosecution team,
Cohn helped to broker a deal with the judge that ensured
death for Ethel Rosenberg. He next appeared before the public during the Army-McCarthy hearings. Through these and
other controversial activities, he created a name (as well as a
considerable fortune) for himself as a no-holds-barred street
fighter unburdened by conscience.

His singular notions of strength and weakness pro-
foundly shaped his personal outlook. It would not be inaccu-
rate to characterize Cohn as an anti-Semitic Jew as well as
a pathologically closeted homosexual. Literally to his dying
day, he publicly denied his gayness, even after he was
stricken with AIDS. Only after his death at age 59 did his
closest acquaintances confirm what had been long suspected. By then, few were left to mourn him.

3. RICHARD DEACON (MAY 14, 1921—AUGUST 8, 1984), TELEVISION ACTOR

An actor whose face is known to millions, if not his name,
Deacon began his career in films, usually as an inflexible officious type. His notable appearances include the films
Them! (1954), *Blackboard Jungle* (1955), and *Invasion of
the Body-Snatchers* (1956). But it was television that gave
him his enduring recognition upon him, beginning with
Leave It to Beaver in 1957. Deacon played Fred Rutherford,
Ward Cleaver's insufferable boss and father of Clarence
"Lumpy" Rutherford. Further heightening his profile was the
role of Mel Cooley on *The Dick Van Dyke Show,* beginning
in 1962. As Mel, his duties consisted of sucking up to
brother-in-law Allen Brady (Carl Reiner) while enduring the
insults of Buddy Sorrell (Morey Amsterdam). Later in the sixties, he stepped into the role of Roger Buell in *The Mothers-*

in-Law, Desi Arnaz's final sitcom production, after the first season's actor was fired (ironically for violating his morality clause). As his career wound down in the seventies, Deacon became a regular panelist on *Match Game PM*.

Bald, bespeckled, and baritone, his button-down image kept his private peccadilloes unsuspected. Early on Deacon committed to pursuing character roles, a choice that ensured his longevity. His desire to work continuously compelled him to keep his personal business to himself. A heart attack claimed him at age 63.

4. RONNIE GILBERT (B. SEPTEMBER 7, 1926), FOLK SINGER

The Weavers were at the very vanguard of the folk music craze that peaked in America in the early sixties. The lone female among the quartet was contralto Ronnie Gilbert. Though the group had quite an impressive string of hits, their leftist ways in times of zero tolerance of anything remotely freethinking sealed their doom. It's hard to imagine what the public reaction to Gilbert's sexuality might have been in the early fifties; at the very least, it would have cast "Goodnight Irene" in a different light.

Following the group's demise, Gilbert continued as a solo performer, often in musical theater. Her retirement from things musical ended in 1983 when folk singer Holly Near lured her out, and the two recorded and performed together for several years. Today, Ronnie Gilbert devotes her energies to peace activism and women's issues.

5. TAB HUNTER (B. JULY 7, 1931), ACTOR

Would it be surprising to learn that Hunter's humble origins began with his discovery while working as a stable boy? Rock Hudson's agent, Henry Willson, recognized a good thing when he saw it: a blonde to go with his brunette. He renamed Arthur Gelien (allegedly because he had to "tab" him *something*!) and took the young man under his wing. Blessed with Aryan good looks, a buff physique, and a presence the camera loved (but precious little else), Hunter became a star with the 1955 film *Battle Cry*. That same year, his fledgling career nearly derailed when police raided a boys-only "pajama party" he hosted. *Confidential* magazine, a celebrity-busting tabloid, ran the story of Hunter's arrest on vice charges, but a funny thing happened. Rather than offer him up as a sacrificial lamb to protect Rock Hudson, the far bigger star, the studios simply ignored the report as though it had never happened. So large was the public's evident need for wish fulfillment ("Big, strong Tab Hunter couldn't be one of *those*") that the story simply blew over, leaving Tab unscathed.

Perhaps feeling invincible after having dodged that bullet, the young star next took on the world of pop music. At the suggestion of a record producer, Hunter recorded his version of the recently released single, "Young Love," by country singer Sonny James. To everyone's astonishment, Hunter's inferior remake outsold James's, scoring a number one. (History has a way of rectifying its errors; nowadays, you are more likely to hear the original by Sonny James on oldies radio.) Several more record releases followed, and in 1957 he starred as pitcher Joe Hardy in the film version of the Broadway musical *Damn Yankees*. He even had sitcom of his own, *The Tab Hunter Show* (1960–61), in which he played a cartoonist. Younger audiences may know him from *Grease 2*; he also co-starred three times with female impersonator Divine: in *Polyester* (1981), *Lust in the Dust* (1985), and *Out of the Dark* (1989).

6. SHEILA JAMES KUEHL (B. FEBRUARY 9, 1941), ACTRESS, LAWYER, STATE SENATOR

This child actress got her start as Stu Erwin's tomboy daughter in his eponymous, five-year-long sitcom. But the role for which she was best remembered came in 1959, in *The Many Loves of Dobie Gillis*. In the series, Sheila (Sheila James then) played Zelda Gilroy, whose unrequited pursuit of the title character was equaled only by Dobie's delusional fixation on Thalia Menninger (played by Tuesday Weld). Though

Zelda was something of an anomaly as the only intelligent girl on the show (or on TV at the time, for that matter), Dobie managed to elude her designs. Following the end of the series, producers decided to spin Zelda's character off onto her own show. But after four episodes were filmed, the network canceled the project, fearing that rumors of Sheila's personal life had begun to spook would-be sponsors.

Sheila fully lived up to her brainy persona, graduating from the Harvard University School of Law and becoming an activist for feminist issues. In between her nonstop good works, she managed to trot out Zelda one last time in the made-for-TV movie *Bring Me the Head of Dobie Gillis* (1988). In the years that followed, she became more and more politically active, culminating with her election to the California Assembly in 1994 and the State Senate in 2000. As the first openly gay woman to win the seat, she has tirelessly championed the causes of women, children, and minorities.

7.   JACK LARSON (B. FEBRUARY 8, 1933), TELEVISION ACTOR, PLAYWRIGHT

While in school, young Jack discovered a talent for writing that led to much theater work. In creating roles for himself, he quickly transitioned into acting. It wasn't long before a Hollywood agent spotted him and signed him to a contract at Warner Brothers, where in 1948, he starred alongside newcomer Rock Hudson in *Fighter Squadron*. Around this time, a romantic interlude occurred with actor Montgomery Clift, busy shooting Alfred Hitchcock's *I Confess* at the same studio.

By age 18, Larson's dream of establishing a foothold in legitimate theater on Broadway seemed assured, but a funny thing happened. His agent fielded an offer for a role in a syndicated TV show, *The Adventures of Superman*, as cub reporter Jimmy Olsen. Larson resisted signing on for such a ridiculous part on a low-budget kids' show, but he was persuaded by the lure of "no one will ever see it—take the money and run." Much to his dismay, the show proved to be huge when it hit the air in fall 1952, and as the callow, bow tie-wearing youth, he found himself regularly spouting such inanities as, "Gee, whiz!" and "Jeepers!" From one week to the next, the hapless Olson existed solely to be caught in every manner of indignity at the hands of the bad guys, necessitating rescue by the title character ad nauseam. This did nothing to promote him as a serious actor.

Thus pegged, by Larson's early 20s his acting career was as good as over. When denied decent parts due to the indelible impression he'd made after five years as Jimmy Olsen, he returned to his first love, writing plays. Along the way he hooked up with writer/director James Bridges (*The China Syndrome, Urban Cowboy*). While Larson and Bridges didn't go out of their way to remain in the closet, the first most people knew of their long relationship was when Bridges died of cancer in 1993. A collection of poems that Larson had written for his longtime love were set to music and released as a CD by singer Brian Asawa titled *More Than a Day*. With years of success in the theater, producing, and with screenplays behind him, Larson apparently felt secure enough to revisit the role that defined him in the minds of millions to play an older Jimmy Olsen in 1996 on *Lois and Clark: The New Adventures of Superman*.

8.   JOHNNY MATHIS (B. SEPTEMBER 30, 1935), POP SINGER

When *US* magazine revealed in 1982 the closely held secret of Johnny Mathis's sexuality, millions of fans were left to wonder: what would his Mary say? In fact, Mathis had always been something of a gender-neutral phenomenon. A crooner going against the rising tide of rock & roll, he preferred laid-back, marshmallow-soft tunes that likely found more favor with the average teen's parents than the teens themselves. His plaintive wail, often heavily echoed, gave listeners an eerie, otherworldly listening experience. Still, one can't fault his choice of material: from his debut single, "Wonderful, Wonderful," in 1957 through 1960's "Starbright," he was a regular visitor to the Top 40. As late as 1978, he could still pull off the odd number one by adding his voice of reason to Deniece Williams's caterwauling on "Too Much, Too Little, Too Late." And in between, he gave the world a holiday classic, his *Merry Christmas* LP, the first of half a dozen such works he released over the years. Two years after he signed his first recording contract, he'd racked up enough smashes for his record label, Columbia, to issue the very first "greatest hits" album by anyone. Furthermore, its unheard-of success (490 straight weeks on the album charts—nearly nine years!) warranted a mention in the *Guinness Book of World Records*.

John Royce Mathis was born in Texas but moved to San Francisco while yet young. Beginning singing lessons at the age of 13, he was something of an athletic prodigy as well, specializing in the high jump. At 19, he found himself at a crossroads: a record label scout had spotted him and offered him a contract, while at the same time he was busy qualifying for a spot on the American team for the 1956 Olympics. He had to choose, and the rest is history.

9. RODDY MCDOWALL (SEPTEMBER 17, 1928–OCTOBER 3, 1998), ACTOR

Odd to reckon that a talent as demonstrable as his would be bookended by animals—playing opposite them in his early roles (*Lassie Come Home* and *My Friend Flicka*, both 1943) before actually *becoming* one as Cornelius in the *Planet of the Apes* series (beginning in 1968). English-born Roderick Andrew Anthony Jude McDowall was the very definition of a discreet, erudite gentleman. When not before the camera as an actor, he sometimes worked behind the scenes, providing vocal talent ("Mr. Soil" in *A Bug's Life* [1998], as one example).

His career included dozens of pictures during his child acting heyday of the 1940s. As he grew into adolescence and adulthood, he answered the call of stage dramatics, shining as one of the killers in a dramatization of *Compulsion* and scoring a supporting actor Tony for his role in (ahem), *The Fighting Cock*. During this lull in making films, he was linked romantically for a time with Tab Hunter. The sixties and seventies saw his return to the screen, running the gamut from historical epics (*The Longest Day* [1962] and *The Greatest Story Ever Told* [1965] to children's fare (*That Darn Cat!* [1965] and *Bedknobs and Broomsticks* [1971]). He narrowly missed an Oscar nomination for 1963's *Cleopatra* due to, of all things, a clerical error.

His love affair with Hollywood was deep and mutual. A world-class amateur photographer, he filled four published volumes with personal photos of his star friends. In a cut-throat industry, McDowall was a rarity—a man much loved and completely devoid of enemies. Only after his death was he officially "outed," by professional celebrity brownnoser Dominick Dunne.

10. ANTHONY PERKINS (APRIL 4, 1932–SEPTEMBER 9, 1992), ACTOR

Oh, Mother! If ever a role returned to haunt an actor, it would surely be Perkins's portrayal of the psychopathic Norman Bates in Alfred Hitchcock's *Psycho* (1960). Decades after the first and best, he succumbed to financial pressures and reprised the character three times too many, cheapening it in the process. Luckily, his many other roles leave his legacy as a sensitive, gifted actor intact. For many, his best work was among several films he made in the fifties: as a conflicted Quaker alongside Gary Cooper in *Friendly Persuasion* (1956); as conflicted ballplayer Jimmy Piersall in *Fear Strikes Out* (1957); and as a conflicted Naval officer in Stanley Kramer's postnuclear *On The Beach* (1959).

In 1990, Perkins was diagnosed with AIDS. For his remaining two years of his life he and wife Berry Berenson kept the diagnosis a secret, fearing for his employability. Upon his death, his posthumous statement was released, reading in part: "I chose not to go public about this, because, to misquote *Casablanca*, I'm not much at being noble, but it doesn't take too much to see that the problems of an old actor don't amount to a hill of beans in this crazy old world." He stated further that he had learned more about selflessness and love since contracting the disease than he ever did in the industry he'd long been a part of. His widow was at a complete loss to explain how he could have become infected; it took the publication of Charles Wynecoff's *Split Image* to detail the secret gay life Perkins led long before he'd been married, sharing a boy toy with Leonard Bernstein back in the day. Despite his past, theirs was by all accounts strong love. She supported him through the ravages of the disease, and he died holding her hand. Just after the ninth anniversary of his passing, on September 11, 2001, Berry was a passenger on American Airlines Flight 11 out of Boston, bound for Los Angeles. She never made it.

Vaya con Dios

L et's face it—there aren't many of us who will manage to summon the resources to put together one last coherent thought, much less a sentence, as we prepare to draw our final breath. (And if we do, it's usually some variation of "Mama! Mama! Mama!") Then there are those exceptional souls who somehow marshal their forces and utter one final departing line that is so them (typically those whose end is already penciled in, whether by their own hand or the state's). Still others, without the benefit of foresight, may happen to come out with something that ends up resoundingly apropos or moving. ("It's not loaded" doesn't count. "It's not loaded, but I am," maybe.) Finally, there are those who just blurt out anything, leaving those whose purpose it is to pick at bones and sift ashes to ponder and attach some significance. Here are some parting shots from across the social spectrum, whose wisdom we all may reflect upon.

1. GEORGE BERNARD SHAW, PLAYWRIGHT (D. NOVEMBER 2, 1950)

"Sister, you're trying to keep me alive as an old curiosity, but I'm done, I'm finished, I'm going to die." *To his attending nurse.*

The Irish-born writer and critic was 94 and had been, for nearly as many years, a vegetarian, teetotaler, and celibate (though married). The only man ever to win both a Nobel Prize (for his play *Saint Joan* in 1925) *and* an Oscar (for *Pygmalion* in 1938), he died of injuries incurred from falling when pruning apple trees. His final wish was for his cremated remains to be mixed with those of the wife who had died before him seven years earlier.

2.   MARTHA BECK, MURDERER (D. MARCH 8, 1951)

"My story is a love story, but only those who are tortured by love can understand what I mean. I was pictured as a fat, unfeeling woman. True, I am fat, but if that is a crime, how many of my sex are guilty. I am not unfeeling, stupid, or moronic. My last words and my last thoughts are: Let him who is without sin cast the first stone." *From the statement handed out just after her execution.*

Morbidly obese from an early age, Martha could naturally expect a lifetime of social difficulties. (One paramour attempted suicide rather than marry her when she was with child.) By 1947, burdened with two children as well as more than 200 pounds, she placed a lonely hearts ad. Professional conman Raymond Fernandez responded, and rather than fleece her as he had so many others, the two fell in love. Now he had a partner whose domineering personality and pathological jealousy made for a volatile mix. From mere theft, the two embarked on a multistate career of murder. The authorities caught up with the two by the time the body count had reached 19. Following a widely publicized trial, the two were electrocuted at Sing Sing in New York.

3.   ROBERT WALKER, ACTOR (D. AUGUST 28, 1951)

"I feel terrible, doc. Do something quick!" *To his attending physician, who administered a sodium amytal injection that put him into a coma from which he never recovered.*

After a few rough years of seeking a foothold in the business, Walker and his actress wife at last found success in Hollywood in 1943. Robert was cast in a series of light comedies, and his wife, renamed Jennifer Jones, was gaining notice in *The Song of Bernadette*, especially from the film's producer, David O. Selznick. In short order, she split from her husband and married the powerful mogul, a man twice her age. It was a blow from which Walker never recovered. Though his own career gathered steam, peaking with his penultimate performance in Alfred Hitchcock's *Strangers on a Train*, depression and drinking kept a firm hold on him. Seeking medical help in battling his demons, an agitated Walker was brought to the hospital by a close friend, who held him down as the doctor administered what turned out to be a lethal overdose of the antidepressant. He was 32.

4. DYLAN THOMAS, WRITER/POET (D. NOVEMBER 9, 1953)

"I've had eighteen straight whiskies. I think that's the record." *His last recorded words before his collapse.*

The writer of such classic works as *Under Milk Wood*, *Portrait of the Artist as a Young Dog*, and "A Child's Christmas in Wales" had another favorite avocation: drinking to excess. Few who knew him in the course of his 39 years could recall ever seeing him without a bottle nearby. Though Thomas's fame and literary reputation were hailed around the globe, a discernible self-destructiveness marked his behavior. Financial responsibility was never his forte, and he continually needed to accept offers of money to support his family. It was on his third lecture tour of America in the autumn of 1953 that his habits finally did him in. An exact reckoning is unclear, but following a drinking binge in New York City, he succumbed to pneumonia, alcohol poisoning, or their combined effects with the morphine given to him at St. Vincent's Hospital. Slipping away while in a coma, he went "gentle into that good night."

5. EUGENE O'NEILL, PLAYWRIGHT (D. NOVEMBER 27, 1953)

"I knew it! I knew it! Born in a hotel room and—God damn it—died in a hotel room!" *A dramatic declaration worthy of any of his plays.*

One of America's foremost playwrights, O'Neill was born in 1888, the son of an actor then working on Broadway. At age 24, O'Neill became infected with tuberculosis and spent six months in a sanitarium. It was there that he threw himself into an intense study of drama, culminating with his own steady output of plays and poetry. Many of his better-known works were made into films, including *Anna Christie*, *Ah! Wilderness*, *Mourning Becomes Electra*, and *The Iceman Cometh*. Three years after his death came the staging of his last great work, *A Long Day's Journey Into Night*.

By the 1940s, O'Neill's glory days were largely behind him. Furious at his teenage daughter Oona's taking up with Charlie Chaplin, and believing himself to be crippled by an impenetrable case of writer's block, he fell into despair. Many around him blamed his current woes on his hard-drinking past, and he shared that view, shunning alcohol. In fact, newly examined evidence points to a rare neurological malady as the cause of his physical decline: cortical cerebellar atrophy, an undiagnosed and little understood disorder. Frustrated by his inability to work, O'Neill lived out his final days in a hotel room, largely in solitude and awaiting death. Only his third wife, Carlotta, and his attending nurse and physician were allowed to witness his final curtain.

6. SAM "SHEMP" HOWARD, COMIC ACTOR (D. NOVEMBER 23, 1955)

"Taxi!" *His last recorded utterance.*

Though branded at birth with the Hebrew name Schmool, the eldest of the Three Howard (né Horwitz) Stooges gained his deathless moniker from his Lithuanian mother's attempts to shout the anglicized, "Sam!" which came out sounding more like "Sham!" Young Sam displayed a talent for pranks and shirking physical work at an early age. Saddled with phobias of nearly everything—water, automobiles, flying, confinement, you name it—he masked his fears behind hyperactive bluster and double-talk, which eventually led him into show business. Contrary to public perception, Shemp was no mere second-rate also-ran when called to take his ailing brother Curly's place in the act in the late forties. It was in fact a return to the fold; he'd been one of the original Stooges on the vaudeville stage while the trio was still bound to top banana Ted Healy in the twenties and early thirties. But Shemp's distaste for Healy's alcohol-fueled abuse compelled him to strike out on his own, giving younger brother Jerome his big break. Shemp enjoyed a successful career in Hollywood as Knobby Walsh in the *Joe Palooka* film series as well as in movies opposite W. C. Fields and Abbott and Costello.

After rejoining brother Moe in 1946, he worked steadily due to public demand until his death. Shemp spent his last afternoon at the racetrack and his last evening at the fights. After the bout, he stood with friends at the curb and hailed a cab. Once inside, he characteristically began to light up a cigar when he was suddenly felled by a massive stroke. He went, friends said, with a smile on his face. He was 60.

7. JAMES WHALE, DIRECTOR (D. MAY 29, 1957)

> "The future is just old age and illness and pain. . . . I must have peace and this is the only way. . . ." *From his suicide note.*

A stage director by trade but an artist by inclination, Whale achieved cinematic immortality in 1931 with his third filmed outing, *Frankenstein.* His signature uses of detailed sets, lighting, and unusual but pitch-perfect casting were taken to the next level with his acknowledged masterpiece, *The Bride of Frankenstein* (1935). Between those two classics, his other memorable efforts include *The Old Dark House* (1932) and *The Invisible Man* (1933) for Universal. Though Whale was commonly regarded as a horror director, an undercurrent of black humor also informed his best work. Two departures from the genre that made him famous include the elaborate costume pictures *Show Boat* (1936) and *The Man in the Iron Mask* (1939). As an openly gay man in a mostly closeted community, Whale's eventual distaste for studio politics led to his retirement in the early forties, whereupon he concentrated on his painting.

The effects of declining physical and emotional health led him to choosing death on his own terms rather than waiting for it passively. He threw himself headlong into the shallow end of a little-used swimming pool at his home, taking care to leave a note and a book at his bedside entitled *Don't Go Near the Water*. The exact circumstance of his passing as well as the fact that he was drunk at the time of his drowning went unreported for decades. A fictionalized treatment of his last days was the basis of the 1998 film *Gods and Monsters*, starring Sir Ian McKellan and Brendan Fraser.

8. LOU COSTELLO, COMEDIAN (D. MARCH 3, 1959)

"That was the best ice cream soda I ever tasted." *Spoken just before his second and fatal heart attack.*

The former studio carpenter and journeyman comic at last struck gold in the late thirties when he was paired with straight man Bud Abbott. Appearing together on radio and on the vaudeville stage, Abbott and Costello performed the immortal "Who's on First?" routine, building a name for themselves. The two went on to cut quite a successful swath through Hollywood in the forties, starring in such films as *Buck Privates* (1941), *Hit the Ice!* (1943), and *Abbott and Costello Meet Frankenstein* (1948). They eventually added television success to their credits, beginning in 1952 with their eponymous comedy program. But as the men aged, their act seemed even older. After being superceded by Martin and Lewis for the public's affections, the two split up in 1957. Costello managed to finish work as a solo act in one film, *The Sixty Foot Bride of Candy Rock* (1959), before being stricken by a heart attack on February 26. For a while he seemed to be on the mend. Within the week, his agent Eddie Sherman thought to cheer him by bringing him a strawberry ice cream soda. No sooner had he finished it when a second attack claimed him, three days shy of his 53rd birthday.

9. EDMUND GWENN, ACTOR (D. SEPTEMBER 6, 1959)

"Yes, it's tough, but not as tough as doing farce." *His response when asked if he thought dying was tough.*

The theatrical career of this Welsh-born actor was jump-started in the early 1900s in London's West End by George Bernard Shaw himself. It wasn't until the 1940s that Hollywood began to take notice of the distinguished, grandfatherly gentleman in its midst; when it did, two best supporting actor nominations (in 1947 and 1950) followed. The first resulted in a win for the role for which he is best known, Kris Kringle in *Miracle on 34th Street*. Gwenn also managed to squeeze in performances in two Alfred Hitchcock films, *Foreign Correspondent* (1940) and *The Trouble with Harry* (1955), the latter pairing him with future Beaver Jerry Mathers. Adept at comedy as well as drama, one of his final roles was in the sci-fi classic *Them!* (1954) opposite some plutonium-enhanced insects. Droll to the end, he died at 83.

10. ROGER TOUHY, GANGSTER (D. DECEMBER 17, 1959)

"I've been expecting it. The bastards never forget." *Spoken as he lay mortally wounded after being ambushed by fellow mobsters.*

Nicknamed "The Terrible" in a wild overreach of hyperbole by the press, Touhy was a highly successful bootlegger during Prohibition. Headquartered in the Chicago suburbs, Touhy and his brothers found themselves challenged by the encroaching ambitions of Al Capone, and a turf war ensued. Wishing to be rid of his rival once and for all, Capone orchestrated a kidnapping frame-up of con man John "Jake the Barber" Factor (brother of movie makeup mogul Max).

Touhy took the fall and was sentenced in 1934 to 99 years in Joliet State Prison. Eight years later, he and several others made a daring daylight escape that grabbed headlines, prompting the production of the B-movie *Roger Touhy, Gangster* in 1944. Recaptured and with his sentenced doubled, Touhy cooled his heels until his lawyer was able to demonstrate the chicanery behind his earlier conviction. In November 1959, Touhy was released from prison. The Chicago mob, with Tony Accardo calling the shots (literally), recognized the nuisance a free and vocal Touhy posed to their interests and made plans to silence him. Though broke and sickly, Touhy had recently filed a suit for damages against all those responsible for his incarceration.

After a meeting with his lawyers on the evening of December 16, he returned to his sister's home accompanied by his bodyguard. His killers were waiting and fired numerous shotgun blasts wildly as the two men neared the front porch. Touhy's legs were nearly amputated by the pellets, and though conscious he died from blood loss within hours. At 61, his freedom had ended after 23 days.

See You Later, Alligator

Here lies a roll call of folks ranging in age from 24 to 76, each in his or her own way a star. Some expected brighter days ahead; others were in decline, living well past their days of glory. Though long gone, most of these 10 are still remembered today. Even the lesser-knowns made an impression in their time, and when their end came, the public mourned.

1. JEROME "CURLY" HOWARD (D. JAN. 18, 1952)

The youngest of the Horwitz brothers was known to intimates as "Babe." The last to join the act, but arguably the most naturally gifted, Curly was the Stooge to whom fans were most devoted. The "Three Stooges" ensemble was originally conceived by vaudevillian Ted Healy and "Shemp" Howard, the oldest of the acting brothers. (Second-youngest Harry, known as "Moe," became part of the team when it began in 1923, with middle-man Larry Fine joining five years later.) Creative animosity and a desire to strike out on his own led Shemp to leave in 1932, paving the way for Curly's big break. Over Moe and Larry's objections and Ted's skepticism, Shemp orchestrated his baby brother's entrance into the big time. With his shaved head, rotund physique, and high-voiced, man-child persona (he came on, Moe said, like "a fat fairy"), Curly quickly developed his own comic identity. The Stooges broke with Healy for good in 1934, and their ensuing popularity turned Columbia Pictures into a major player. The price for their success was the toll their violent brand of slapstick exacted on their bodies. As the team's star, Curly received most of the abuse. Although the trio was trained to pull their punches and break their falls, the damage caused by countless smacks and blows to the head was more severe than anyone knew at the time. It is now believed that Curly suffered a series of undetected small strokes before the big one came. In reexamining the Stooges films, it's clear that past a certain point his speech became slightly slurred, his body movements sluggish, and his energy diminished. In addition, Curly drank heavily, seeking relief from the trauma of three broken marriages and the pressures of carrying an extremely physical act.

In 1946, while on the set of *Half Wit's Holiday*, Curly failed to respond to his cue. Moe found him slumped in a chair, unable to speak, tears streaming down his face. He had suffered a massive stroke; an early prognosis that, with a bit of rest, he'd soon be able to rejoin the act turned out to be tragic nonsense. Time away from stooging proved to be beneficial in the short term. His thick head of wavy hair grew back, and his weight dropped down to a healthier level. He married a fourth time, this time happily, and the couple produced a daughter. In 1947, Curly visited the set one last time, for a cameo as a snoring train passenger in *Hold That Lion!* But as his health deteriorated, studio hopes for his eventual return slipped away. Wheelchair-bound and barely able to speak (much less declare himself a "victim of circumstance"), the 48-year-old comic actor lived out his remaining weeks at the fittingly named Baldy View Sanitarium, until he suffered a final, fatal stroke.

2. HANK WILLIAMS (D. JAN. 1, 1953)

Without a doubt, the first *modern* star of country music was this man—a musician whose talent, struggles, and downfall had all the makings of legend. That he should meet his end so young and under such murky circumstances only enhances the myth. On December 13, 1952, Williams finished his latest drying-out stint at a sanitarium. It was no more successful than any of his earlier attempts as he struggled with the twin demons of alcohol and drug abuse. A chronically aggravated back condition led to a painkiller addiction, while personal issues fueled a fondness for drink. Newly remarried, Williams played what would be his last show in Montgomery, Alabama, his hometown, on December 28. Sleeping only fitfully the following night, he told his new bride, "I think I see God coming down the road." Though God's travel plans are not known, Hank's included a trip to Charleston, West Virginia. He hired 18-year-old, part-time cabby Charles Carr to power his brand-new powder blue Cadillac on the grueling winter journey. After hours of hard driving, the pair attempted unsuccessfully to contract a plane in Knoxville to speed them on their way. Some time after 6 p.m., they checked into the Andrew Johnson Hotel. Within hours, a doctor hastened over to treat Williams (described as "very drunk"), who apparently was having convulsions. He administered a shot of B-12 and morphine. Before 11 p.m., Carr checked out, using porters to load the moribund Williams into the back seat. He drove on through the night, apparently undisturbed by the backseat passenger's decided lifelessness. Not until dawn, in West Virginia, would the suddenly alert Carr notice his boss's rather stiff demeanor. At the Oak Hill Hospital, Williams was declared dead on arrival. Though the autopsy confirmed the presence of alcohol, no test was done for narcotics, and the death certificate blandly concluded that his condition was due to an "insufficiency" of the right ventricle. One attending physician further concluded that the subject had been recently "beat up." Whatever befell the much older-looking 29-year-old that night probably will never be known. One can only marvel at the prescience of his last single, "I'll Never Get Out of This World Alive."

3. CHARLIE PARKER (D. MAR. 12, 1955)

This celebrated jazz saxophonist was a man of excess in physique as well as talent. (In his autobiography Miles Davis describes an occasion when, as the two shared a cab, he watched in disbelief as Parker devoured a whole chicken while simultaneously being serviced by a prostitute.) Once Parker's legend became established, his oversized appetite turned to drink and drugs. He embodied the "tortured artist" archetype, pushing his creativity as well as his body to the limit and creating a mythology that long outlived him. Fortunately, romanticizing addiction is not his only legacy. The Bird lives on with a peerless body of work, which includes his recordings of "Lady Be Good," "Ko Ko" (a record that virtually invented bebop), and "Ornithology."

The late forties marked the beginning of his decline. Erratic behavior, fueled by heroin and drinking binges, managed to get Parker banned from his own club, New York City's *Birdland*. The first of several nervous breakdowns and suicide attempts occurred, resulting in stints at Bellevue and other psychiatric hospitals. He reached his breaking point in 1954 when, while on tour in California, he learned of the death of his two-year-old daughter from pneumonia. In the early months of 1955 he was subsisting on cheap red wine, aggravating an already ulcerous stomach. On Saturday, March 5, he played his final gig; by some accounts, it was a disaster, with musicians storming off the stage. Within days he complained of not feeling well. One week after that last performance, while Parker was visiting a friend, he collapsed and died. The coroner attributed his death to pneumonia, with cirrhosis of the liver a contributing factor. Not recognizing the dead giant before him, he estimated the deceased to be 55 or 60, but Charlie Parker only was 34.

4. ALBERT EINSTEIN (D. APRIL 18, 1955)

To the public at large, Albert Einstein remains at the pinnacle of human knowledge. Naturally, upon his death, many were anxious to uncover his secret, because surely there had to be *some* logical explanation for why he was so brilliant and the rest of us . . . aren't. To backtrack a little: during surgery for a stomach ailment in 1948, doctors discovered an aneurysm of the main cardiac artery. There was little doubt that the condition would prove fatal, but all attempts to persuade the most brilliant physicist in history to slow down went unheeded. Dietary restrictions were usually observed, though he railed against them. While forbidden by his doctors to buy tobacco, he saw no reason not to "steal" it when he could, frequently attempting to cadge some off of his peers if given half a chance. Though he declined an invitation from the newly established State of Israel to become its leader, he did work with renewed energy to discover a basis for his unified field theory. But with his depleted physical resources beginning to run dry, he began to plan for his death. He was adamant about having no funeral or service of any kind, not even a grave. He wanted to have his remains cremated and scattered secretly—his brain, however, he allowed to be preserved for study. Just past midnight on the 18th of April, his nurse found him muttering something in German, a language she did not understand. At the age of 76, Albert Einstein passed into legend.

Autopsist Dr. Thomas Harvey seized the opportunity to remove the physicist's brain and spirit it away. For years, he crisscrossed the country, the famous organ preserved in two cookie jars traveling in the trunk of his Buick Skylark. Harvey parceled out small samples for study before deciding to return it to Princeton Medical Center, where it is today. A recent study revealed that the inferior parietal region, thought to govern mathematical thought, was 15 percent larger than normal, but since the people studying his brain possessed an inferior parietal region 15 percent smaller than Einstein's, no further conclusion could be drawn. Also, it was found that the groove running from front to rear in the brain did not extend all the way. Hence, if Albert had gotten his groove back, he'd be no better off than the rest of us.

5. JAMES DEAN (D. SEPT. 30, 1955)

After Dean finished work on *Giant*, the 24-year-old was eager to resume his auto-racing hobby. (Insurance carriers had banned him from indulging while the film was in production.) On September 21, 1955, he accepted delivery of his dream car, the new Porsche Spyder 550, the hottest race car on the circuit. Anticipating an October 1 race in Salinas, California, Dean was eager to put the vehicle through its paces and get acquainted with its abilities. He drove the car everywhere, the moniker "Little Bastard" emblazoned on the tail. On race day's eve, Dean elected to cover the distance to Salinas by driving the Spyder himself, accompanied by his mechanic, Rolf Weutherich. Not long after leaving Los Angeles, Dean was ticketed for doing 65 in a 55 mph zone. (The irony of it coming two weeks after he filmed a public service ad for safe driving did not go unnoticed.)

After a brief stop for a Coke, the two set out again. Opening up the throttle, Dean attempted to pass a slower-moving car containing a family of four, only to find a Pontiac in the oncoming lane headed right for him. Trapped, he opted to run the family off the road. Shaking off the close call, he now stayed closer to the speed limit as he neared the town of Paso Robles. Although it was now twilight, Dean had yet to turn on his headlights. Up ahead lay a crossing shaped like an inverted Y. Approaching Dean in a 1950 Ford was 23-year-old engineering student Donald Turnipseed, who needed to turn left across Dean's path to continue his journey. Looking ahead, he would have found it difficult to spot the silver, low-slung Porsche hurtling toward him in the early autumn sunset. Noting the peril, Dean remarked to Weutherlich, "That guy's gotta see us. He *has* to stop!" But Turnipseed did not and, instead, began his turn. Suddenly aware of the danger, he panic-braked, his car serving as a metallic speed bump for the hapless Dean. Turnipseed later described seeing both passengers raise their arms in a protective gesture as the Spyder attempted to veer right, colliding with full force on the driver's side. Weutherich was thrown free, but Dean was pinned, impaled on the steering column. His chest and forehead were flattened, but a broken neck would be listed as cause of death. Thus in a blaze of screeching tires and shattering glass did Dean pass into immortality. It is not known if Turnipseed watched much TV, but the actor's words in that final public service ad rang fittingly apropos: "The life you save might be *mine!*"

6. JACKSON POLLACK (D. AUG. 11, 1956)

Whether your art taste leans more toward Pablo Picasso or Thomas Kinkade, most everyone can agree that Pollack was an original. A first-rate provocateur if only a second-rate human being, Pollock electrified the world in the 1940s with his "action" paintings—large canvases apparently crisscrossed at random with drips and spatters of paint. His art, he told critics, represented an expression of his subconscious mind—not unreasonably, considering his bouts of depression and alcoholism. Pollock enjoyed ascension to notoriety when *Life* magazine ran a spread on him in 1949, ensuring his status as a household name, even for those who didn't follow events in the art world (which was most of America). By the mid-fifties, however, his personal vagaries were catching up with him at the expense of his artistic output, which in his last year had nearly ceased.

Beyond the 44-year-old painter's diminished capacity, his marriage to fellow abstract artist Lee Krasner had likewise fallen on hard times. Although they were not formally separated, Pollock's violence toward Krasner was reason enough to absent herself to Europe for an exhibition of her work. Wasting no time, Pollock set up house with his young mistress, an art groupie named Ruth Kligman. Soon enough, she became a target of his abuse, but his hold on her was strong enough to coax her back even after she decided she'd had enough. When she did return, she brought along her friend, Edith Metzger. On that fateful day, Pollock began drinking especially early. By the time the trio set out that evening for a concert, he was beyond reach. After a dinner stop, Metzger refused to get back into the car with him, but the combined forces of Ruth's pleas and Pollock's rage wore her down. He immediately gunned the Oldsmobile convertible, his fury increased by her screams. Barreling down a dangerously curved and uneven road, he lost control, causing the heavy vehicle to spin and then cartwheel. Both he and Ruth were thrown, she to land relatively unharmed, he to have what brains he still possessed dashed into a tree. With the Olds landing on top of Edith and crushing her, Pollock contributed one final bit of ugliness to the world.

7. JUDY TYLER (D. JULY 4, 1957)

To the generation of boys who reached adolescence between 1951 and 1954, this little hottie would have caused the first vague stirrings south of the equator. No, not in any Carmen Miranda sense—this girl rose to fame for her portrayal of the American Indian maiden on *Howdy Doody*, Princess Summerfall Winterspring. For all the attention sent her way, she responded in kind, for Judy liked men. A lot. In the parlance of the times, she got around. How shocking it would have been for parents familiar with her TV persona to learn that in her off hours, she enjoyed a successful nightclub career as a sultry saloon singer, along with her pianist *husband* (she was 17 at the time). That, along with a nicotine habit and the vocabulary of a longshoreman, made her, in short, a typical New York career girl. By the time this driven young starlet auditioned for the show that put her on the map, she was a seasoned pro.

After three years as the Princess, she was ready to cash in on her obvious star quality. She headed west and screen-tested, landing the lead in a quickie exploitation flick for United Artists entitled *Bop Girl Goes Calypso*. Then came the opportunity any ingénue would have killed for: female lead

opposite Elvis in *Jailhouse Rock*. Strings were pulled to ex-
tricate her from other commitments, and filming began in
late spring. By now divorced, she wed actor Greg Lafayette
during a break in production. Three days after filming
wrapped, she and her husband, accompanied by a cat and
dog she'd bought for her agent, headed back to New York by
car. It had been a long drive, and no doubt a certain amount
of fatigue had set in. Near Rock River, Wyoming, a vehicle
suddenly pulled onto the road in front of them. Greg swerved
into the oncoming lane to avoid it, only to smash head-on
into another car. That driver was killed instantly, as were the
pets. Judy and Greg were rushed to a hospital in Laramie but
died within hours. Meanwhile, their wrecked car was looted
of cash, furs, and jewelry. Both Elvis and Judy's former
Howdy co-stars were devastated by the news. The former
could never bring himself to watch what would ultimately be
one of his best films. As for Judy, her death at 23 deprived
her of the lead role in *Marjorie Morningstar*, the story of an
aspiring actress. Instead, the part went to another doomed
actress, Natalie Wood.

8. BELA LUGOSI (D. AUG. 16, 1956)

A handful of performers in the annals of cinema became so
strongly identified with a single role that it proved to be an
albatross, preventing them from being considered for other
worthy parts. Among them was the Hungarian stage actor
born Béla Blasko. His 1927 portrayal of Bram Stoker's *Dracula* on Broadway made him a sensation. Though Lugosi
was not initially considered for the screen adaptation, the
cancer death of Lon Chaney made him the obvious second
choice. Greatly assisted by his own Slavic accent and compelling features, there could never again be such a definitive
portrayal of the Transylvanian count. (Public perception to
the contrary, Lugosi only played Dracula twice, the second
time in a comedy.)Though one can see how such a vivid depiction might lead to typecasting, Lugosi didn't help himself
with his remarkably indiscriminate career choices thereafter.

He first damaged himself by taking a pass on the equally high-profile role of the monster in Universal's production of *Frankenstein* in 1931, asserting that the heavy makeup and lack of dialogue would waste his stage-honed abilities. Instead, English journeyman actor Boris Karloff got the part and enjoyed stardom ever after. (Ironically, Lugosi finally portrayed the monster in 1943's *Frankenstein Meets the Wolf Man*, when he was no longer in a position to be so choosy.) Within three years of establishing himself as an A-list star in Hollywood, Lugosi accepted employment in a string of low-budget "Poverty Row" pictures and serials that did nothing to enhance his reputation. Major studios offered him an occasional supporting role but nothing more.

By the early fifties, Lugosi's addiction to painkillers had debilitated him nearly to the point of unemployability. (Chronic discomfort from a leg injury incurred during World War I led to his dependency.) Just when his prospects couldn't get much lower, aspiring cinema wunderkind Ed Wood, Jr., entered his life. The two struck up an odd symbiotic friendship—Ed wanted the cachet Lugosi's name could bring to his projects, and Lugosi wanted to work. *Glen or Glenda?* (1953) must qualify as one of the least explicable films of any era, while *Bride of the Monster* (1955) marked a return to the sort of mad scientist role Lugosi had specialized in at Monogram Studios. That same year, he checked himself into a rehab center for treatment of his morphine addiction. Upon his release in August, he married for the fifth time. His final year was marked by future plans and bad health. On August 16, the 73-year-old succumbed to a heart attack at his home. Per his final wishes, he was buried in full Dracula regalia. As fellow actors Vincent Price and Peter Lorre paid their final respects before his open casket, Lorre wondered aloud if they should drive a stake into him, just in case.

9. CARL "ALFALFA" SWITZER (D. JAN. 21, 1959)

Rascal revisionism has it that young Carl was a petulant terror, regularly tormenting his *Our Gang* co-stars. It makes for entertaining gossip, but even if any of it is true, his shabby end is no less tragic. Conventional wisdom paints him as a washed-up has-been who met a predictable bad end, but a further look warrants a less severe judgment. First, he actually worked steadily during the transition from juvenile to adult roles, despite enduring some humiliation along the way. ("Come on, Alfalfa! Sing off-key for us!" was a taunt he endured more than once.) Though sometimes reduced to unbilled support (for example, see *It's a Wonderful Life*—the school dance scene), his last job promised bigger things to come—a bit part in Stanley Kramer's high-profile *The Defiant Ones*. As a child of the outdoors, Carl loved to hunt and fish, which led him to do quite well for himself as a guide in northern California, supplemented with the occasional bartending gig. His son, the product of a brief marriage in the early fifties, was godfathered by none other than Roy Rogers. Hard to square this reality with the troubled ne'er-do-well of tabloid infamy. The story handed down is that Carl was in partnership with a rough character named Bud Stiltz, training Stiltz's dogs for hunting. On one occasion, a dog he borrowed from Stiltz ran off. Carl posted reward notices for the dog's recovery, and eventually a rancher found him, demanding the promised $50 bounty. This he paid, and as the story goes, Carl stormed into Stiltz's house one evening, demanding reimbursement. Unsatisfied with Stiltz's response, he pulled a knife, whereupon Stiltz drew a gun and shot Carl in the stomach, killing him. Stiltz claimed that he only shot after Carl threw a knife at him first. A folded penknife was indeed found near the body—Stiltz said that Carl closed it as he went down (!). Police ruled the death self-defense, and no charges were ever filed.

In fact, Carl was not alone when he arrived at the Stiltz's house; he had brought along a friend named Jack Piott. *His* story was that Carl was unarmed, and that Stiltz flew into a rage and got off two shots, the first of which blew a big hole in the drywall. After shooting Carl, he came within seconds of killing Piott before police sirens scared him off. Another witness was 14-year-old Tom Corrigan, Stiltz's stepson. Years after the event, he told a newspaper that a fight erupted after Stiltz pulled his gun, and that the two men fought for control. Never, he said, did Carl either pull a knife or threaten to kill Stiltz. He said that while he did see a *folded* knife near Carl's body, he believes it fell from his pocket as he slumped to the floor. Further investigation was brushed aside, despite the fact of Carl's wounding by a bullet fired at him the year before. Kenneth Anger's *Hollywood Babylon*, a book rife with hyperbole, matter-of-factly reported that the death came as the result of a "drug burn." So what exactly happened? Was the dog story a red herring concocted by vested interests? The Switzer family never came to terms with Stiltz's escaping justice. Each year at Christmas, they sent him a holiday card emblazoned with Carl's picture and signed, "See you soon! Alfie." Carl was buried beneath a slab depicting, of all things, a hunting dog. In the final indignity inflicted on this man, karmatically bad timing had it that his murder fell during the same news cycle as Hollywood producer Cecil B. DeMille's death. Guess whose passing got more ink the next day?

10. GEORGE REEVES (D. JUNE 16, 1959—GUNSHOT WOUND; RULED A SUICIDE)

The 1959 death of TV's Superman has warranted much attention through the years, including two books (*Hollywood Kryptonite* and *Speeding Bullet*), as well as coverage in segments on *20/20* and *Unsolved Mysteries*. The controversy stems from the ruling of suicide that for many, rings false. Investigation into the events of that night paints a picture of a deadly love triangle covered up, rather than a supposedly despondent actor unable to handle type-casting. As reported, Reeves, scheduled to wed two days hence, was hosting some friends for a celebration at his home. At some point, the party broke up and everyone retired to bed. After 1 a.m., however, persistent knocking roused the Man of Steel's fiancée, Lenore Lemmon, who admitted a couple of friends.

Reeves himself was reportedly agitated by the latecomers' arrival, but he did join them long enough for a nightcap before retreating upstairs once again. As the guests continued to make merry, a single gunshot rang out; the startled partiers ran upstairs to find the nude Reeves bloodied and dead. He was depressed over the end of his career, stories said. After a highly successful run, *Superman* had been canceled in 1957, and roles beyond that of superhero were impossible to find.

Rubbish, said those who knew Reeves. The man was engaged to be married to a pretty New York socialite; *Superman* was about to be revived, with Reeves getting a pay increase and a chance to direct; and just before the scheduled nuptials, the former boxer was slated to take on fighter Archie Moore in a televised exhibition match, an event he described to reporters as the "highlight of his career." Why should he impulsively decide to end his life? Examination of the evidence suggests a contrary conclusion. Reeves left no note; friends felt it unlikely that the modest man would choose to be found in a state of undress; ballistics suggested an awkward, unnatural trajectory for a self-inflicted head wound; and the absence of powder burns proved that there was too much distance between the gun barrel and the body for Reeves to have shot himself.

Despite this mass of contrary evidence, a verdict of "likely suicide" was reached. While the exact shooting circumstance remains unknowable, looking into Reeves's personal life leads to some compelling conclusions. Divorced since the forties, Reeves had been involved in a seven-year relationship with Toni Mannix, wife of a powerful industry exec. An open secret known to many, the affair ended—abruptly—when Reeves became engaged to Lenore. Toni did not take it well, and her persistent barrage of calls led Reeves to seek a restraining order. Later it was uncovered that threats were made via phone to both Reeves *and* Mrs. Mannix. Further, Reeves was involved in three separate near-disastrous vehicular incidents in the preceding months. The last came when, after Reeves hit a brick wall, he discovered that his car's brake lines had been drained. All of this suggests anything *but* suicide. To this day, some continue to work the case, hoping to unearth a solution to this superhero's end.

The Signpost
Up Ahead

Here's a roll call of 10 notables whose chief fame or infamy is associated with another time: the sixties, seventies, eighties, or beyond. Most were out of high school—some (like number one) had already experienced what for most would have been their shining moment, only to reach their zenith later in life. Before the immortality grenade landed at their feet, here were some early clues to the new direction.

1. RONALD REAGAN, ACTOR, FUTURE PRESIDENT

The early fifties saw this B-movie actor's transformation from minor celebrity to political figure in the making. In 1947, he was first elected president—of the Screen Actors Guild, Hollywood's biggest and most important union. During his 12-year reign, two things characterized his tenure: fanatical zeal in rooting out (and ratting out) perceived "un-American" types, and a singular record for selling out his union members' interests in favor of studio management. One of the "friendly" witnesses to testify before HUAC, he secretly supplied the FBI with names of those whose activities—labor or political—displeased him. While head of SAG, Reagan ruled that no residuals would be paid for use of filmed work predating 1960, effectively robbing older actors of retirement income while providing a cash cow for his handlers at MCA. (For those whose work became ubiquitous on TV, like the Three Stooges or the Little Rascals, the decision literally cost them a fortune.)

As for Reagan's own career, it had peaked back in 1941 with the release of *King's Row*. Nothing he ever did on a soundstage again garnered the same acclaim as that particular role. Embarrassments like 1951's *Bedtime for Bonzo* (which cast him opposite a chimp) reinforced his obsolescence. Divorced since 1948 from actress Jane Wyman, he remarried in March 1952 to with-child contract player Nancy Davis. Reagan and wife made only one film together, 1957's *Hellcats of the Navy*, a routine potboiler involving submarines and a love triangle. Mediocre as it is, it represented a step up from what surely was Reagan's professional nadir, as a Las Vegas song and dance man in February 1954. With no film work and owing a fortune in back taxes, Reagan had his manager call in some favors and get him a two-week stint at the mob-owned Last Frontier Hotel. His duties included introducing the hack singers and third-rate comic acts, engaging in a bit of stand-up, and taking some pratfalls. All that was missing was the seltzer bottles. The freak show indeed packed 'em in, but performing for drunks left a bad taste in Reagan's mouth. After signing on as host of *General Electric Theater* on TV shortly thereafter, he vowed never to sell himself so cheaply again. History records a high price paid for Ronald Reagan in the years to come.

2. LIZ SHERIDAN, DANCER, FUTURE TV ACTRESS

When watching *Seinfeld* reruns, it probably doesn't occur to anyone to reflect back on what Jerry's parents, or at least the actors playing them, might have been like in their younger days. Witnessing the matronly, sharp-tongued, overly protective Sheridan in action, it strains the imagination to ever see her as a young, wild, Bohemian dancer in 1950s New York City. But that's what Dizzy Sheridan, as she was then known was up to, when on a rainy afternoon in the autumn of 1951, a chance encounter brought her into contact with an equally struggling young actor. The two clicked immediately, bonding as friends, then lovers. Though 22 at the time, she evidently had never had a boyfriend before (though he had). Their intense, passionate affair lasted over a year, until the young man was cast in a Broadway play that put him on the path to Hollywood. Unwilling to subjugate her ambitions, and not interested in riding his coattails, Dizzy went to the Caribbean, where between the Virgin Islands and Puerto Rico, she found steady employment. On return visits to her see her mother, she sometimes saw her friend. They kept in touch through letters, but she was in the islands when news came of his death in late September 1955. She called him Dudley—he was James Dean to you. Upon the shock of hearing about his death, Sheridan got drunk and burned all of his letters to her. Time healed her heart, but his memory never fully left her. She returned to America in the sixties, worked on Broadway for all of the seventies, and then went to Hollywood, picking up some small film roles before hitting it big in television. Her role as Mrs. Ochmanek on *Alf* led her to TV immortality as Helen Seinfeld in 1989. Since then, she has penned a tome on her fifties memories entitled *Dizzy and Jimmy—My Life with James Dean*.

3. MEL BROOKS. TV WRITER, FUTURE DIRECTOR

That we didn't lose the former Melvin Kaminsky before we ever got to know him is a minor miracle. During World War II, Brooks's Army duties included disarming land mines in North Africa before the infantry came in. Having survived that scrape, Brooks put himself in the line of fire further by doing stand-up at Catskills resorts after the war. The circuit known as the Borscht Belt was a proving ground for Jewish comics. It was there that he met Sid Caesar, who brought him to television as a writer, first for the short-lived *Admiral Broadway Review* variety show, then, and most famously, on *Your Show of Shows*. There, alongside Larry Gelbart and Neil Simon, Brooks wrote for television's first truly great comedy. Imagine a 90-minute comedy show composed of sketches, recurring bits, and parodies, aired live on NBC on Saturday nights. Only funny. The winning formula proved to be easy enough to imitate but tough to duplicate.

After *Shows*' four-year run, Brooks wrote for *Caesar's Hour*, along with newcomer Woody Allen. His work with Carl Reiner led to a series of comedy recordings of a bit they'd worked up together, called the "2,000 Year-old Man." Following his fifties heyday, Brooks looked for work that would lead to films. He married actress Anne Bancroft in 1964, and the following year he developed *Get Smart* for TV with writer Buck Henry. Its success gave him the wherewithal to script his first film, *The Producers* (1968). This story of a Broadway producer who hits upon the idea of staging a musical so awful (*Springtime for Hitler*) that he can turn a profit by declaring losses actually became a highly successful Broadway show decades later. Although barely noticed at the time, it led to a series of genre spoofs that established Brooks in Hollywood throughout the seventies, *Blazing Saddles* (1974), *Young Frankenstein* (1975), and *Silent Movie* (1976) among them. Love it or hate it, the Brooks style was characterized by manic energy and unabashed vulgarity. As Brooks tells it, he's the only Jew ever to make money off of Hitler.

4. DR. TIMOTHY LEARY, PROFESSOR, FUTURE POP ICON

The only Harvard professor to be turned into a Moody Blues song, Leary was regarded by the youth of the sixties and seventies as a wise elder who had "crossed over." Unlike so many other "adults" who warned of the dangers of dabbling in hallucinogenics, Leary knew where of he spoke; he first tried LSD in 1962, when it was still largely unknown (and legal). His experiments led him to espouse a regimen of expanding one's consciousness, summed up by: "Turn on, tune in, drop out." This naturally made him anathema to a generation of parents in general and to Art Linkletter in particular. On the surface, nothing in the man's straight-arrow background suggested anything counterculture: he'd been educated at a Jesuit college, then at West Point. His military stint was followed by a career in psychology.

While teaching at Berkeley in the early fifties, Leary studied the less-than-effective treatment of depression sufferers with psychotherapy. This subject hit home chillingly when his wife took her life on Leary's 35th birthday in 1955. He went to Europe to clear his head, meanwhile churning out a widely respected stream of articles on personality disorders. It was while he was overseas that a colleague awakened him to the effects of so-called magic mushrooms on psychological transformation. Leary sampled them in 1960 while he was in Mexico; to say he returned a changed man is understatement. By now teaching at Harvard, he persuaded the university to let him conduct research on psilocybin. When word got around, he found himself teaching the most popular class on campus. Experiments done on prisoners using the drugs showed a 90 percent rehabilitation rate upon their release. Likewise, divinity students given psychedelics reported true spiritual experiences, while those who'd been given placebos did not. Leary was convinced he was onto something before the university ended the experiments in the face of community, religious, and institutional resistance to his work. In 1963, he was fired. But for Leary, his work was just beginning.

5. REDD FOXX, NIGHTCLUB COMEDIAN, FUTURE TV ACTOR

The man who became a TV star in the seventies was something of an underground pleasure in the fifties, issuing a steady stream of "party records" consisting of blue material from his nightclub act. Born John Elroy Sanford in Saint Louis, he left home in his teens and headed for Chicago, working as a musician. "Red" had been a nickname early on (he was part Seminole Indian), to which he eventually added an extra 'D' to match the last name he chose in honor of baseball player Jimmy Foxx. After his band folded, Foxx sought opportunity in New York City, finding employment as a dishwasher alongside a fellow from Michigan, also nicknamed Red. To keep them straight, Foxx was known as "Chicago Red"; his friend, Malcolm Little, became "Detroit Red." Years later, "Detroit Red" wrote in his autobiography about his experiences working with "the funniest dishwasher on this earth"—by then, he'd dropped Little and replaced it with X.

In 1951, the 29-year-old comic teamed up with Slappy White, and for the next five years, the two made a name for themselves on the "Chitlin' Circuit," performing their act in black-owned theaters and clubs. After their split, Foxx established a residency at Los Angeles's Club Oasis. By now his act was getting a reputation for raunchiness—a tell-it-like-it-is polemic on race, sex, and any other taboo he could think of. It was also sidesplittingly funny. Never known for his financial acumen, Foxx was offered a contract by tiny Dooto Records to release his act on vinyl. For $25, he agreed. Exact sales are not known, but beyond question *Laff of the Party* was an underground monster. The first of some 50 releases, it was readily available in black-owned record stores, but was banned from white ones. Eventually, word-of-mouth demand compelled the latter to sell it, but only under the counter. At a time when Foxx was feted as a scatological genius, Lenny Bruce was pilloried for covering much of the same ground. Though the nature of his material precluded any mainstream television exposure, Foxx did manage to score a bit part in 1960's *All the Fine Young Cannibals*, as an unbilled piano player in a club scene. Eventually, with the help of some high-profile fans like Frank Sinatra (who signed Foxx to his record label in the sixties), he started to achieve the kind of visibility that ultimately landed him the role he's best known for, on TV's *Sanford and Son* in 1972. (The character was named for Foxx's deceased brother.)

6. CHARLES MANSON, SMALL-TIME CRIMINAL, FUTURE MASS MURDERER

In 1947, a troubled 13-year-old was admitted to Father Edward Flanagan's world-famous Boys Town in Nebraska. Four days later, the youth and another resident stole a car and fled, never to return. Flanagan died not long after, living just long enough to rethink his credo, "There's no such thing as a bad boy."

Manson was born to 16-year-old Kathleen Maddox in 1934; his father ran off upon learning of the pregnancy. A brief marriage to one William Manson gave the boy a name. Charlie grew up being shuffled from one relative to another as his drink-addled mother regularly appeared in and disappeared from his life. Her habit of supporting her binges with robberies taught her son how to obtain what one needs. His first crimes, which included burglary and bicycle theft, led him to Boys Town, which in error believed him to be Catholic. A pair of armed robberies followed the car theft and landed him in the Indiana School for Boys, where he was beaten and raped regularly, leading him to 18 escape attempts. The last time, at 16, he and a pair of inmates set out for California, stealing cars and robbing gas stations along the way. Arrested in Utah and charged with federal crimes (for crossing state lines), on March 9, 1951, Manson was ordered incarcerated in a Washington Juvenile Deliquency facility until he reached legal adulthood. Any chance of early parole was shattered by his sexual assault on another boy in January 1952. This attack and subsequent offenses caused him to be transferred to federal reformatories in Virginia and Ohio. Though his files recorded patterns of hostility, aggression, and criminal sophistication, by 1954 he changed into a model inmate, learning car repair and how to read. He even received a Meritorious Service Award before his May 8 parole.

During his newfound freedom Manson met and married a teenaged waitress in early 1955. To support himself, he worked as a carhop, relieving the boredom of routine with auto theft. That autumn, he was arrested in California with his now-pregnant wife. In short order, he received probation, violated it, and ended up sentenced to three years at Terminal Island. While Manson was in stir, Charles Jr. was born. Before his September 1958 parole, his wife divorced him, taking their son. Manson finished the decade facing charges of pimping and check forgery. (He *ate* the evidence for the second charge but was jailed anyway.) In jail, he studied Scientology and learned guitar, until he was eventually paroled on March 21, 1967.

7. ROSE MARIE, FORMER CHILD STAR, FUTURE TELEVISION ACTRESS

It is doubtful that any of the millions of viewers of *Dick Van Dyke Show* reruns ever for a moment suspected that Rose Marie, the actress who played raspy-voiced Sally Rogers, had been a gifted child star who predated Shirley Temple. Born Rose Marie Mazzetta in 1923, she began performing at the age of three, wowing people with her imitations of the vaudeville performers she'd seen. Winning a talent show contest led to an extensive radio and stage career, where she was billed as Baby Rose Marie. Her father, a performer himself, was well-connected with many mobsters, including Al Capone. The latter is said to have doted on the precocious girl, who stood out among the cutesy child stars of the day by performing adult blues and torch songs, made up as a miniature Louise Brooks. She starred in several musical shorts of the early Vitaphone "talkie" era (one of which, *The Child Wonder*, is occasionally seen as a "One-Reel Wonder" on Turner Classic Movies) before making her big screen debut opposite W. C. Fields in *International House* (1933).

Though Rose Maria's performing career advanced quite successfully throughout the thirties, her father managed to gamble away her earnings, while simultaneously beating her and banning any contact with would-be suitors. By the forties, she managed to break away, heading west and enjoying a successful run as a nightclub singer/comic, aided by some well-known Mob personas, including Bugsy Seigel, who booked her for his Flamingo Hotel in Las Vegas. Though typed years later on the *Van Dyke Show* as a man-hungry spinster, she in fact married trumpeter Bobby Guy in 1946; the union produced a daughter and lasted until his death in the sixties. In 1954, she reactivated her film career in *Top Banana*, opposite Phil Silvers. Her renewed visibility led to numerous guest roles on TV, some of which paired her with her good friend Morey Amsterdam. When tapped for the role of female writer on the show Carl Reiner was developing for Dick Van Dyke in 1961, she recommended Morey as the perfect Buddy Sorrell, and the rest is sitcom history. Though often speculated about, she still refuses to explain her trademark black hair-bow, seemingly a permanent fixture.

8. YOKO ONO, ARTIST, FUTURE POP ICON

To most, musicianship is not something usually associated with Yoko Ono's work. Her fame (or infamy) usually rests on two beliefs: that she cannot sing to save her life, but only screeches, and that she "broke up the Beatles." To the second charge, a more accurate observation may be that she was around to witness the inevitable—it wasn't as though any of the Fab Four were enjoying the warmest of relations after 1968. As to the first, understanding where she was coming from as a *classically trained* musician and conceptual artist, while not guaranteed to make her any easier on the ears, may at least make her work comprehensible. She was born in Tokyo to a wealthy banker whose ambitions as a concert pianist went unfulfilled. Business kept him in America, and he only first met his daughter when she was two. Her earliest memories were of his examining her fingers to divine whether she had the makings of a pianist. For the Onos, that was the only acceptable form of artistic expression. As a child of privilege, she gained entry to Japan's top institute for composers and, at age four, gave her first public performance. The war hit the Ono family hard, and by 1951, they had relocated to Scarsdale, New York. Yoko continued her music studies, secretly longing to be a composer, something her father told her was out of the question.

At the prestigious Sarah Lawrence College, she was inspired by the songs of birds to write her first composition, which she called "Secret Piece" (1955). She was in New York at the time and hung out with a loose aggregate of outcast musicians inspired by Schönberg and John Cage. They fired her imagination to apply musical disciplines to art and artistic conceits to music. Her resulting work has been termed avant garde, which translates to most as "avant garde a clue," but it did get her noticed. She eloped with Toshi Ichiyanagi, a Juilliard student and one of the leading lights of the experimental movement in 1956. (To this day, he is highly regarded as one of Japan's top composers.) Their loft on Chambers Street on New York's Lower West Side became a staging ground for "happenings." Yoko's work became less traditionally musical, more poetic, and, to the uninitiated, bizarre. It was groundbreaking in its demand for audience participation, requiring viewers not merely to judge but to recognize the limitations of their perceptions and see the world anew—in a word, "imagine." Yoko returned to Japan in 1962 with Toshi, but they divorced shortly after she suffered a nervous breakdown and attempted suicide. Feeling lost in the shadow of a famous husband became an issue she struggled to master.

9. JOHN GLENN, NAVAL AVIATOR, LATER ASTRONAUT AND U.S. SENATOR

Nowadays, a younger generation knows Glenn, if at all, as that old guy who flew in the space shuttle (and left the turn signal on for thousands of miles). But back in the day, he was cutting edge: a man whose bravery and daring made him—to use an overused term—an American hero. After Pearl Harbor, Glenn left college to volunteer for duty with the Navy, which transferred him to the Marines once he'd earned his wings. Beginning in 1944, Glenn flew 59 bomber missions in the Pacific, mostly near the Marshall Islands. He changed his plans to become a commercial pilot after the war and stayed with the Corps, volunteering a second time when fighting in Korea broke out. There he became known for his low-level strafing missions, 63 in all; he also shot down three MIGs. (Wing man for his flights was Ted Williams, who interrupted his baseball career to serve.) The much-decorated pilot's honors included six Distinguished Flying Cross medals.

Following the Korean conflict, Glenn signed up for the Navy's test pilot school in Maryland. He first entered national consciousness on July 16, 1957, when he set a speed record for flying an F-8U Crusader fighter jet from Los Angeles to New York in three hours and 23 minutes. He followed up his feat with appearances on the game shows *I've Got a Secret* and *Name That Tune* (Winning $12,500 on the latter). In 1958, President Eisenhower laid the groundwork for what was to become the National Aeronautics and Space Administration, deciding that only military test pilots need apply. Glenn volunteered immediately. (Much of this period was covered, with great historic license, in the 1984 film *The Right Stuff*, which Glenn derided as "Laurel and Hardy Go to Space.") Despite reservations about Glenn's age (he was 37), his hard lobbying paid off when he was selected as one of seven original Mercury astronauts in April 1959. Though disappointed at being passed over for the first flight, he achieved glory when his *Friendship 7* spaceship completed three Earth orbits in February 1962. His acclaim as a brave soul and all-around good guy led President Kennedy to quietly ground Glenn, lest the country lose its national treasure. As consolation, Kennedy and his brother mentored Glenn into politics; his first attempt at a Senate run in 1964 ended prematurely when Glenn grounded himself with a fall in his bathtub.

10. MARTHA STEWART, MODEL, FUTURE DOMESTIC GODDESS

It is not surprising to learn that the future head of an empire was often described as "driven" while she was still a teen, engaged in as many extracurricular activities as humanly possible. Though Stewart was naturally competitive, her socially ambitious father never stopped pushing her, reminding her that she *would* go to college, despite his inability to pay for it. The former Martha Kostyra was born in 1941 to first-generation Polish immigrants living in Jersey City. Named after her mother, Martha was the second of six children and mostly took after her father with her gift for self-promotion, her need to be the leader, and a fiery temper. For years, most of what was known about her childhood in Nutley, New Jersey, was filtered through her carefully spun reminiscences in her books and magazines. Years later, the image of the Kostyras as a warm, loving family, living in warm, cozy surroundings was revealed to be completely at odds with reality. Peers recall their home as the scene of much fighting and her father as a strict, unpredictable man, who was often held up as a negative example: "You don't want me to be like Mr. Kostyra, do you?"

By high school, the tall, thin, and pretty "Marty," as she was called, began getting noticed for her looks, something her father encouraged. Though he all but forbade her to date, his real interest was in the money she could make modeling. To that end, he posed her himself in the basement, clicking away until he came up with a rudimentary "portfolio." The 17-year-old was then sent to make the rounds at the agencies in Manhattan, before settling on Foster-Ferguson. They steered her into some high-fashion modeling at Bonwit Teller, which led to an audition for a television commercial. Lifebuoy deodorant soap signed her up to appear fully lathered in a 30 second spot to air during the hugely popular *Have Gun, Will Travel* on Saturday nights. Not above a certain amount of boasting, the excited teen called everyone in her circle of acquaintances, reminding them to tune in for the broadcast. Though shooting a TV ad ranked as an impressive achievement for any unknown, the ensuing glow was tempered. To the astonishment of the viewers who knew her, and to Martha herself, the ad company had decided that her thick Jersey accent was unsuitable for public consumption and dubbed in a more acceptable tones from a voice-over artist. It took years and some effort by the mortified Martha to cultivate the Wasp-ish articulation so familiar to the public now, recognizing her native speech as an impediment to future ambitions. And that's a good thing.

It Doesn't Matter Anymore

H ere we examine the familiar things of the day that came to an end. Changing tastes, times, and trends dictated paving over the old order. Technological progress, stymied by the war, now began to explode. While certain industries looked forward to resuming business as usual, they often found that the playing field had changed, to their detriment. Economic and demographic shifts remade the face of major league baseball as well. Similarly, the public's appetite for certain time-honored pleasures began to wane, as people discovered new ways to entertain themselves. Here are 10 items of interest that failed to survive the decade.

1. THE LAST GREAT AMERICAN LINER, SS *UNITED STATES*, IS LAUNCHED, 1952

The grotesque floating hotels that trawl the Caribbean today have nothing on the sleek ocean liners that regularly crossed the Atlantic during their 20th-century heyday. Sea travel before and between the wars was the rare arena where Europeans relegated America to also-ran status. Luxury liners like the *Queen Mary*, *Normandie,* and *Ile de France* were the shining stars of traffic between America and the continent, representing a lock on luxury and glamour this country could only envy. Only after World War II did American shipping interests begin to compete seriously with the masters, but their victory was short-lived. While most people are familiar with the legend of the *Titanic*, few know the story of the SS *United States* can be read as a reverse tragedy. Rather than the crew and passengers who were doomed, it was the ship—not by any disaster or mishap, but by coming into the world far too late. A vast amount of effort, money, and energy went into building a vessel that never experienced the seagoing career its builders intended. By the time she set sail, the *United States* was obsolete.

Shipbuilder William Francis Gibbs's vision called for a passenger liner that could outperform the best on the seas. He believed he could access the finest shipbuilding technology as well as government funding by selling his conception as a *troop* ship that merely slid into passenger mode during peacetime. His instincts proved to be correct, and in February 1950, work began. While the ship still in dry dock, the Navy announced its intent to commandeer it immediately for use in Korea, giving her builders a coronary. But by November the powers that be had changed their minds. The $79 million, 17-story, 990-foot vessel was launched in June 1951, with First Lady Bess Truman offered christening duties. (She declined, owing perhaps to difficulties in breaking the bottle during a previous launching).

Upon her maiden crossing a year later, the "Big U" set the new Atlantic crossing record, reaching port in just under three and a half days. Business was good those first few years, with a steady stream of attention and goodwill generated by the ship's contingent of celebrity passengers. But her timing was just beyond salvage. In 1957, for the first time, more people crossed the Atlantic by air than by sea. Jet traffic soon followed, making her end inevitable. The enormous running costs of the SS *United States* put her deeply in debt, compelling her owners to sell her in 1964. She limped along for several troubled years before her days at sea ended in 1969.

Newly christened SS *United States*, bound for oblivion.

2. THE LAST ORIGINAL INDIAN MOTORCYCLE, AUGUST 1953

The only real competition Harley-Davidson ever had in the United States came from this Springfield, Massachusetts, manufacturer. Founded in 1902, the company came about when amateur tinkerer Oscar Hedstrom and entrepreneur George Hendee joined forces. They quickly gained a reputation as innovators and in 1913 made the first motorcycle equipped with an electric starter. By World War I, they were the largest manufacturer of motorcycles in the world. At the same time, they were the biggest name in racing, overshadowing all other competition. Hendee and Hedstrom retired from the company by 1920, setting Indian on the road to its eventual demise. Still, for the time being, the company thrived, continuing to churn out high-quality machines even through the depths of the Depression, which claimed all of the other motorcycle manufactures except them—and Harley. Though both companies supplied the military with bikes during World War II, Indian got the short end of the deal, and ended the forties cash-poor. The company's death knell stemmed from its decision in 1953 to drop the Chief, a V-twin model that might have been its salvation in favor of the vertical singles and twins modeled after English bikes, which were badly designed. Financial reorganization resulted in the company's breakup just as the Blackhawk Chief, an 80-cubic-inch, chrome-laden beauty that represented a return to form, hit the market. Latter-day Indians came along decades later, attempting to cash in on the company's once-good name, but they were mostly poorly engineered.

3. THE LAST OF THE MARTIN AND LEWIS COMEDY TEAM, JULY 24, 1956

Perhaps the only thing less likely than the comedic partnership between the smooth pop crooner and the loud, boisterous comic was their breakup at the height of their success. Ten years to the day after they first teamed up at Atlantic City's *Club 500*, they found themselves at the end of their creative rope, after 16 films, a successful radio and TV career, and countless nightclub dates. With much the same reaction that followed the Beatles' announced disbanding in 1970, the public was stunned to learn that the duo was no more. As in most dissolved partnerships, the real wonder was less that it ended than that it lasted as long as it did. The collaboration began in 1946 upon the serendipitous absence of a scheduled act on the bill, with Martin being called in as a substitute. Lewis remembered the singer from a booking they had shared months before, when each had informally "sat in" on the other's set. By the third night, it was evident that something special was unfolding before the patrons of the club. Their polar opposite personas—Martin, cool, suave, and adult, and Lewis, disruptive, noisy, and infantile—made for an unbeatable comedic blend, providing a context that truly enhanced each other's act.

My Friend Irma (1949) catapulted them into the big time. Soon they were headlining the most prestigious theaters in the country when they weren't busy appearing on radio or in movies. In July 1950, they became television stars on *The Colgate Comedy Hour*, establishing their primacy as *the* comedy duo of the decade. On the small screen, their balance between script and spontaneity showed them at their best. Meanwhile, Martin enjoyed a successful recording career with hits like "Memories Are Made of This" and "That's Amore." The grind of so much activity took its toll, however. Lewis entertained grander notions of "maturing" his art like his idol, Charlie Chaplin, while Martin grew ever more resentful at being the overlooked organ grinder to Lewis's monkey act. Tensions between them had reached the point of no return by July of 1956, and it soon became common knowledge in show business that their string had been played out. Following their final contracted obligation, an appearance at the *Copacabana* in New York, the two shook hands and never again shared a stage (except for a brief "reunion" in 1978 prompted by Frank Sinatra during a Labor Day telethon). They did, however, engage in much sniping in the press. Lewis's Buddy Love persona in 1963's *The Nutty Professor* was widely presumed to be his take on Martin as an oily, womanizing lounge act, though he has repeatedly denied this.

4. THE LAST DUMONT NETWORK BROADCAST, AUGUST 6, 1956

Mention the *fourth* network to anyone today and the person will think you mean Fox. But to anyone growing up in the fifties, one network stood apart from the alphabet broadcasters: DuMont, named for owner Dr. Allen DuMont, a pioneer in the development of television technology going back to the thirties. A true visionary in most areas, DuMont lacked business acumen, which paved the way for the network's ultimate failure. He was granted a broadcast license in New York for station WABD (now WNYW) in 1944; two years later, a lineup largely comprised of sporting events, game shows, and at least one soap opera (*Faraway Hill)* marked the network's entry into TV. Coupling its manufacturing of high-quality TV sets with financial backing from Paramount film studios, the fledgling outfit seemed poised to be a player if not a leader. But it soon became apparent that some critical handicaps would doom the network to also-ran status. For one, unlike rivals CBS and NBC, DuMont did not have an existing stable of radio talent from which to draw. Much of early TV's programming was created simply by adapting popular radio shows already owned (and sponsored) to the new medium. Another fatal issue was the lack of affiliates. Once again, the radio networks had a leg up because of Federal Communications Commission approval for TV outlets, while DuMont was hamstrung by the Byzantine regulations that denied it access to certain markets, forcing it to accept time-share deals with networks owned by others. (In Chicago, for example, DuMont programs aired on WGN, owned by the *Tribune.*) The one powerhouse market DuMont could claim as its own was Pittsburgh, where it was the only game in town. Still, the network soldiered on, creating imaginative programming within tiny budgets. Several bona fide hits aired, including *Captain Video and his Video Rangers*; *Cavalcade of Stars,* which gave Jackie Gleason his start; and Bishop Fulton Sheen's *Life Is Worth Living*. The problem became holding onto the talent when rival networks lured them away by offering big bucks DuMont could not possibly match. The lack of funding was chronic; DuMont was finally forced to sell its one big asset, the Pittsburgh outlet, but the sale only delayed the inevitable. One last shot at survival was an attempted merger with the equally foundering ABC network, but the deal fell through. Paramount seized control from Dr. DuMont and set about breaking up the network. The celebrity panel show *What's the Story?*, the last regularly scheduled program, ended on September 23, 1955. The last gasp came nearly a year later with *Boxing from St. Nicholas Arena.*

5. THE LAST OF RKO STUDIOS, 1957

Film buffs have this studio's famous logo emblazoned in their memory: a rotating globe with a radio tower upon it, beeping out a Morse code message. RKO Radio Pictures was an industry mainstay throughout the glory years of Hollywood studios in the thirties and forties. It was responsible for its share of cinematic classics, including *King Kong* (1933), *Bringing Up Baby* (1938), and *Citizen Kane* (1941), among many others. It was also where stock players Fred Astaire and Ginger Rogers were first paired (in 1933's *Flying Down to Rio*), elevating them to superstardom. With so much success under its belt, the studio was a real loss, having surviving so many hard times. What few people know is that RKO's roots predated motion pictures: the "K" in its moniker stood for B. F. Keith, who started a string of vaudeville houses in the 1880s. In the early days of film, the major studios saw the wisdom of owning their own nationwide chains of theaters from which to market their wares. Many a film studio, through mergers and buyouts, maintained this practice well into the 1960s. In the twenties, mogul Joseph Kennedy began to build a Hollywood empire by buying up what he needed, acquiring Keith's theaters as well as Pathé Studios. RKO was formed when Kennedy merged his holdings with David Sarnoff's RCA; the latter had hoped to capitalize on a system for motion picture sound he'd developed. Kennedy bailed out, but the studio carried on, scoring a coup with distributorship of Walt Disney's films that lasted until 1954. By the forties, management changes led to uneven output, with "art" films by Hitchcock and Welles balanced by lowbrow series efforts (*Lum and Abner, Tarzan, The Mexican Spitfire*).

The sale of RKO in 1948 to the unstable and eccentric Howard Hughes doomed the studio. Managing by personal whim rather than by established business practices meant shutdowns, layoffs, and selling off of assets. The final decade saw some film noir gems (*Out of the Past*, *They Live by Night*, and *The Hitch-Hiker*, to name a few) overshadowed by Hughes's obsession with Jane Russell (*His Kind of Woman*, *Double Dynamite*, *Underwater!*). At least his work with Russell had cheap titillation going for it, which is more than can be said for *The Conqueror* and *Test Pilot*. His interest spent, Hughes broke up RKO's holdings, selling the film catalog to a division of General Tire. The extensive soundstages and studio lots were sold in toto to ex-employee-made-good Lucille Ball and husband/producer Desi Arnaz. The property became home to Desilu's numerous TV projects, and RKO's days as a movie factory were over.

6. THE LAST DODGERS GAME AT EBBETS FIELD, SEPTEMBER 24, 1957

The only major league baseball team based in a *borough* rather than a city proper, the team formerly known as the Bridegrooms acquired its better-known name for good in 1932. (The team had flirted with its name, beginning in 1911 as the Trolley Dodgers, before reverting to the more conventional Robins from 1914 to 1931.) In 1913, Ebbets Field was built. Cramped but cozy, it was the kind of park described charitably as having "personality." The right field featured a billboard from local menswear retailer Abe Stark that read, "Hit Sign, Win Suit." (As insurance against a batter taking him up on his offer, Stark quietly offered a suit to right fielder Carl Furillo to make sure no ball hit his sign.) With a tradition of Yankee hating, generations of fans longed for the day their team would come out on top, originating the plaintive cry, "wait till next year." While boasting of some stellar talent through the years (pitcher Dazzy Vance, shortstop Pee Wee Reese, catcher Roy Campanella, among others), one particular signing made history. Jackie Robinson was plucked from the Negro Leagues and offered up as sacrificial lamb in the 1947 season, paving the way for racial barriers to be lifted on his way to being voted rookie of the year. (He was voted MVP in 1949.)

The Dodgers had at last come into their own by the forties, winning the pennant three times but in the end losing to the Yankees in the World Series. In 1951 they lost a National League play-off against the Giants, but they rebounded to secure pennant wins in 1952 and 1953. (The latter was the team's best year ever.) However, "subway series" defeats by the Yankees again vexed the fans. Finally, in 1955, the law of averages caught up with them—after five attempts, the Dodgers beat the Yankees four games to three to take the championship. The year 1956 saw a return to form, with the Yankees snatching the title back, but 1957 saw heartbreak without recovery. After several years of unanswered begging for a new stadium, Dodgers president Walter O'Malley accepted an offer from Los Angeles to build the team a park of its own. Brooklynites were shattered, for their team was as much a part of their identity as the Brooklyn Bridge. The final game of a mediocre season saw 6,673 fans show up to see their team shut out the Pirates 2-0. At last there would be no next year as the Brooklyn Dodgers were baseball history. Ebbets Field remained shuttered until its February 1960 date with a wrecking ball.

7. THE LAST GIANTS GAME AT THE POLO GROUNDS, SEPTEMBER 29, 1957

Beginning in the 1880s, another New York-area National League franchise came into being (named "Giants" for its abundance of six-footers). For the first quarter of the 20th century, they were the most successful team in baseball, winning the pennant 10 times and the World Series three times under the legendary John McGraw. In the 1930s, he was succeeded by Bill Terry, who racked up three more pennants and one World Series win before the end of the decade. The forties saw the team's fortunes slump, until a resurgence led by manager Leo Durocher and center fielder Willie Mays saw the Giants add a pennant in 1951 and a World Series victory in 1954 to their record. Nonetheless, the franchise was plagued by falling attendance and hard economic times. The once state-of-the-art park (built from steel and concrete in 1911 to replace the earlier wooden one, which had mysteriously burned) was in disrepair, its irreversible slide into decay mirroring that of the neighborhood. (During a July 4th double-header in 1950, a fan was killed by a stray bullet fired outside the stadium.)

The Giants proved no luckier than the Dodgers in securing a deal for a new stadium, so they, too, looked west. Though tempted by an offer from Minneapolis, the home of their farm team, they opted instead to relocate to San Francisco, breaking the hearts of thousands of fans. For the team's final game, manager Bill Rigney stacked the lineup with players from their last great years, 1951 and 1954. The Pittsburgh Pirates, unmoved, proceeded to pound the old-timers, winning 9-1 before a crowd of 11,606, startlingly small considering the history being witnessed. Barely had the last out been made when the fans swept onto the field, making off with anything they could physically remove. Little did they know, but unlike Ebbets Field the Polo Grounds was not yet through with baseball. The upstart Mets played their first two seasons there before Shea Stadium was completed. The Polo Grounds finally came down in 1964, making way for a public housing development.

8. THE LAST PACKARD BUILT, JULY 13, 1958

It was a sad passing when the final Packard car drove off the assembly line in the summer of 1958. For nearly 60 years, the marquee had epitomized engineering excellence, style, and luxury, with a modicum of snob appeal thrown in for good measure. "Ask the man who owns one" had been Packard's slogan, asserting its primacy as a driving experience available only to a select few. Indeed, the company's production output had been quite low for years, as the Packard brothers insisted on hand-building each car. The low numbers meant that while Henry Ford could get away with selling a Model T for $440, prices for a Packard *started* at $2,600. For the money, you got a lot of car—Packard was the first to offer a 12-cylinder engine as well as backup lights, air conditioning, and padded dashboards, to name just a few features. The Depression hit car manufacturers hard, and by the end of the thirties, hundreds of automakers had bitten the dust. Battling for survival, Packard finally succumbed to mass production; its last handmade product was built in 1939. The power and elegance of its name made it a favorite with Hollywood as well as political royalty. (Joseph Kennedy, by then U.S. ambassador to Britain, was riding in his Packard limousine when he learned that Germany had invaded Poland.)

Following the wartime conversion to military production, Packard found a changing fifties market inhospitable to its product. As Detroit's "Big Three" consolidated their position as sales leaders, the independents foundered. Packard spurned an offer from Nash Motors to merge in the early fifties; instead, Nash and Hudson partnered to form American Motors. But the writing was on the wall, and in October 1954, Packard and the struggling Studebaker Company were united. They attempted in vain to compete in the market as a second-string, mid-priced car like a Plymouth or a Mercury, trading on the Packard star quality. But with the production of the Hawk in 1957, Packard at last reached the end of the road.

9. THE LAST GASP OF 78 RECORDS, 1958

The twin nails in the coffin of decades' worth of recorded sound came in 1948 and 1949, with the introduction of the $33\frac{1}{3}$ long-playing record and the seven-inch 45 single. Both took some time to truly catch on and usurp the 78's place (even now, with 45s so strongly identified with fifties rock and roll, it's a little disorienting to see, for example, early Elvis singles in the 78 format), but by 1958, the common currency had seen its day. By the end of the decade, and at last bested by the 45 in sales, most manufacturers dropped the format. Still, turntables continued to be made with the 78 rpm option throughout the sixties, delighting children who wished to turn every song into a rendition by the Alvin and the Chipmunks.

10. THE LAST MARX BROTHERS JOINT PERFORMANCE, MARCH 8, 1959

Having wound down their film career with the anemic *Love Happy* in 1949, the brothers went their separate show business ways. Apart from a couple of small solo film roles, Groucho stayed busy first on radio, then TV, hosting *You Bet Your Life*. Chico found work on the short-lived TV show *College Bowl*, with periodic live dates, performing his unique brand of piano heresy, while Harpo did numerous guest shots on television, most memorably in May 1955 on *I Love Lucy*. In that episode, he encored his famous "mirror" scene from *Duck Soup*, with Lucille Ball identically garbed in Harpo attire.

Several producers had been trying to arrange a Marx Brothers reunion for a while. Groucho later claimed that Irwin Allen duped him into signing on for 1957's *The Story of Mankind* so that he and his brothers could have one last cinematic send-off, but Allen ended up casting them in separate scenes. Then, in early 1959, *GE Theater* signed them for what would be their last filmed project. A cops and robbers farce titled "The Incredible Jewel Robbery" saw Harpo as a thief and Chico as a policeman. Alas, their entire time together would be fleeting: Groucho only turns up at the end for essentially a cameo as part of a police lineup. More might have been made of the occasion had CBS been allowed to promote the show for what it was, but with Groucho under contract at NBC with *You Bet Your Life*, CBS was forbidden to mention his involvement. As disappointing as the finished product was to their fans, it may not have been intended as their last project. Later that year, plans were put into motion for a new series to star Chico and Harpo at least (with Groucho guesting) as a pair of bumbling angels, called *The*

Deputy Seraph. They got as far as starting to shoot a pilot when the deal was scratched, owing to no insurer's willingness to cover Chico. He died in October 1961, followed by Harpo less than three years later. "The Incredible Jewel Robbery" marked a weak ending to a half-century-long career.

Selected Bibliography

To list each and every publication consulted in researching this work represents an exercise in futility that I won't even attempt. Not that you care, do you? The following is a list of sources consulted time and again, essential to the content of *The 1950s' Most Wanted*.

Ambrose, Stephen E. *Nixon: The Education of a Politician 1913–1962*. New York: Simon and Schuster, 1987.

Blair, Joan, and Clay Blair. *The Search for JFK*. New York: Berkeley, 1976.

Bonsall, Thomas E. *Disaster in Dearborn: The Story of the Edsel*. Stanford: Stanford University Press, 2002.

Brode, Douglas. *The Films of the Fifties*. New York: Citadel, 1976.

———. *The Lost Films of the Fifties*. New York: Citadel, 1988.

Brooks, Tim. *Complete Directory to Prime Time TV Stars: 1946–Present*. New York: Ballantine, 1987.

Brooks, Tim, and Earle F. Marsh. *The Complete Directory to Prime Time Network and Cable TV Shows: 1946–Present*. New York: Ballantine, 1999.

Bugliosi, Vincent, and Curt Gentry. *Helter Skelter: The True Story of the Manson Murders*. New York: Norton, 1975.

Capote, Truman. *In Cold Blood: A True Account of a Multiple*

Murder and Its Consequences. New York: Random House, 1965.

Cowan, David, and John Kuenster. *To Sleep with the Angels: The Story of a Fire.* Chicago: Ivan R. Dee, 1996.

Crimes of the 20th Century. Lincolnwood, IL: Publications International, 1991.

Dallek, Robert. *An Unfinished Life: John F. Kennedy.* Boston: Little, Brown, 2003.

Davis, Stephen. *Say Kids! What Time Is It? Notes from the Peanut Gallery.* Boston: Little, Brown, 1987.

DeJonge, Alex. *Stalin and the Shaping of the Soviet Union.* New York: Morrow, 1986.

Fischer, Stuart. *Kids' TV: The First 25 Years.* New York: Facts on File, 1983.

Forrester, Jeffrey. *The Three Stooges: The Triumphs and Tragedies of the Most Popular Comedy Team of All Time.* Los Angeles: Donaldson, 2002.

Fried, Richard M. *Nightmare in Red: The McCarthy Era in Perspective.* New York: Oxford, 1991.

Glenn, John. *John Glenn: A Memoir.* New York: Bantam, 1999.

Goldberg, Lee. *Unsold Television Pilots: 1955–1989.* Jefferson, MO: McFarland, 1990.

Goldrosen, John. *Remembering Buddy: The Definitive Biography of Buddy Holly.* New York: Da Capo, 1996.

Gribin, Dr. Anthony J., and Dr. Matthew M. Schiff. *Doo Wop: The Forgotten Third of Rock and Roll.* Iola, WI: Krause, 1992.

Gunnell, John A., and Mary L. Sieber. *The Fabulous Fifties: The Cars, The Culture.* Iola, WI: Krause, 1992.

Guralnick, Peter. *Last Train to Memphis: The Rise of Elvis Presley.* New York: Back Bay Books, 1995.

Halberstam, David. *The Fifties.* New York: Villard, 1993.

Heyman, C. David. *Liz: An Intimate Biography of Elizabeth Taylor.* New York: Birch Lane, 1995.

Higham, Charles, and Roy Moseley. *Elizabeth and Philip.* New York: Doubleday, 1991.

Ingram, Billy. *TVparty! Television's Untold Tales*. Chicago: Bonus, 2002.

Jacobs, Frank. *The Mad World of William M. Gaines*. Secaucus, NJ: Lyle Stuart, 1972.

Kelley, Kitty. *Nancy Reagan: An Unauthorized Biography*. New York: Simon and Schuster, 1991.

Kohn, George C. *Encyclopedia of American Scandals*. New York: Facts on File, 1989.

Lewis, Albert L., and Walter A. Musciano. *Automobiles of the World*. New York: Simon and Schuster, 1977.

Liv, Peter. *The Fifties: Transforming the Screen*. New York: Scribners, 2003.

Long, Mark A. *Bad Fads*. Chicago: Independent Publishers Group, 2002.

Maurer, Joan Howard. *Curly: An Illustrated Biography of the Superstooge*. Secaucus, NJ: Citadel. 1985.

McCullough, David. *Truman*. New York: Simon and Schuster, 1992.

Nash, Jay Robert. *Bloodletters and Bad Men*. New York: M. Heinz, 1973.

———. *Darkest Hours*. New York: Burnham, 1976.

Oppenheimer, Jerry. *Martha Stewart—Just Desserts: An Unauthorized Biography*. New York: Morrow, 1997.

Pike, Jeff. *The Death of Rock 'N' Roll*. Boston: Faber and Faber, 1993.

Shannon, Bob. *Behind The Hits*. New York: Warner, 1986.

Sheridan, Liz. *Dizzy and Jimmy: My Life with James Dean*. New York: HarperCollins, 2000.

Spoto, Donald. *Marilyn Monroe: The Biography*. New York: HarperCollins, 1993.

———. *Rebel: The Life and Legend of James Dean*. New York: HarperCollins, 1996.

Stallings, Penny. *Rock 'N' Roll Confidential*. Boston: Little, Brown, 1984.

Tosches, Nick. *Hellfire: The Jerry Lee Lewis Story*. New York: Delacorte, 1982.

———. *Unsung Heroes of Rock and Roll.* New York: Scribners, 1984.

Wallace, Irving, et al. *Significa.* New York: Dutton, 1983.

Weiner, Ed. *The TV Guide Book.* New York: HarperCollins, 1992.

West, J. B. *Upstairs at the White House.* New York: Coward, McCann & Geoghegan, 1973.

Whitburn, Joel. *Billboard Top Ten Singles Charts.* Menomonee Falls, WI: Record Research, 2001.

Zhisui, Dr. Li. *The Private Life of Chairman Mao.* New York: Random House, 1994.

www.findadeath.com

www.lbdb.com

www.lmdb.com

Index

(Illustrations in italics)

About the Author

Robert Rodriguez lives with his wife and son in Elmhurst, Illinois. A graduate of Shimer College, he contributed to *The Sixties Chronicle*. *The 1950s' Most Wanted* is his first book. He cannot promise that it will be his last.